UNIVERSITY DEVELOPMENT IN AFRICA

University Development in Africa

Africa

The Nigerian Experience

by

VINCENT CHUKWUEMEKA IKE

IBADAN · OXFORD UNIVERSITY PRESS, 1976

OXFORD UNIVERSITY PRESS

OXFORD LONDON GLASGOW NEW YORK
TORONTO MELBOURNE WELLINGTON CAPE TOWN
DELHI BOMBAY CALCUTTA MADRAS KARACHI LAHORE DACCA
KUALA LUMPUR SINGAPORE JAKARTA HONG KONG TOKYO
NAIROBI DAR ES SALAAM LUSAKA ADDIS ABABA
IBADAN ZARIA ACCRA BEIRUT

ISBN 0 19 575324 0

Filmset and Printed by Academy Press Ltd., Lagos
Published by Oxford University Press Nigeria
Oxford House, Iddo Gate, P.M.B. 5095, Ibadan, Nigeria

FOR
MY OLD SCHOOL
GOVERNMENT COLLEGE, UMUAHIA

ACKNOWLEDGEMENT

It all began in 1962, when I spent six months (May–November) on a study tour of several universities and other educational establishments in the United States of America and the United Kingdom, sponsored by the University of Nigeria, Nsukka and the U.S. Agency for International Development. That study tour removed some of the blinkers from my eyes, enabling me to view university development in Nigeria and Africa much more critically. It was from that time that my appetite for the study of the problems of university development in Nigeria became whetted.

I paid short visits again to the U.S.A. and Europe in 1964, but the opportunity to devote several months to the study of higher education did not come until late in 1965 when I received a grant from the Ford Foundation to enable me to study higher education for one year. I spent January to December 1966 at Stanford University in California, U.S.A., taking courses in the School of Education and the Stanford International Development Education Centre (SIDEC), while at the same time gathering material for this book.

The book is a record of my own thinking, and hopefully a contribution to the collective thinking which is so essential if the Nigerian university is to emerge. My primary purpose in publishing it is to stimulate discussion on the problems of university development in Nigeria and Africa, and consequently to trigger off further thinking by many more people.

I have already referred in passing to the generosity of the U.S. Agency for International Development, and the Ford Foundation. Without the far-sightedness and the magnanimity of the Council of the University of Nigeria (then my employers), I would not have taken advantage of the two awards. The University of Nigeria also contributed financially to both visits. I humbly acknowledge my indebtedness to these benefactors.

The professors at Stanford with whom I came in contact were surprisingly accommodating, recognizing that my major concern was Nigerian (rather than American) higher education. Professor Lewis B. Mayhew was particularly helpful. So were Professor Paul B. Hanna and his colleagues of the Stanford International Development Education Centre who provided a congenial atmosphere for me and facilitated a useful cross-pollination of ideas.

I owe to Professor W.H. Cowley, then David Jacks Professor of Higher Education, the system of bibliographical references adopted in this book. I am grateful to all at Stanford who helped me in many ways.

When I left for the 1962 study tour, I had to abandon my wife, Adebimpe, at the time she needed me most—shortly before the arrival of our son, Osita, who was four and a half months old before I saw him. The three of us made the Stanford trip together, my wife ignoring her serious allergy to cold and interrupting her professional career in order to minister to my needs at Stanford. I owe her more than I could acknowledge.

Finally, I acknowledge my gratitude to Mrs. Ellen E. Nylander and Mr. J. B. Ayim-Nyarko who kindly typed the manuscript.

Bibliographical References

The system adopted eliminates the use of footnotes. The bibliographical references appear at the end of each chapter, for the reader who is interested in them. Each quotation or bibliographical reference appearing in the text carries a number and is enclosed by brackets, e.g. (5.1). The number normally consists of a whole number (5 in the example) and a decimal (·1 in the example). In the example (5.1), 5 refers to the fifth book listed in the reference at the end of that chapter, while ·1 refers to the first reference made to that particular book in that chapter. The exact page from which the reference comes follows the decimal in the references at the end of the chapter.

Vincent Chukwuemeka Ike
West African Examinations Council
Head Office
P. O. Box 125
Accra
Ghana

December, 1974

TABLE OF CONTENTS

ix

CHAPTER 1

INTRODUCTION

THE AFRICAN UNIVERSITY: FACT OR FICTION?

The continent of Africa had some fifty or more universities at the beginning of the 1970s. Although most of these universities were founded in the decades when most black African countries attained political sovereignty, a few (including Fourah Bay College in West Africa) had been in existence for over a century. In the circumstances, one might ask why it was necessary for the Association of African Universities (which came into legal existence in Rabat, Morocco in November 1967, and which already had a membership of more than forty universities) to organize, in July 1972, a workshop on the theme: 'Creating the African University'. If the African University was only being created in 1972, how would one categorize the universities which had been in existence in Africa before then, some for well over a hundred years?

In the early years of University College, Ibadan (now the University of Ibadan), the students proudly referred to their institution as 'the University of London situated at Ibadan for purposes of convenience'. Was the theme of the workshop suggesting that the universities in Africa at the time were no more than American, British or French universities located in Africa for purposes of convenience, and that the *African* University was yet to be created?

Some distinguished educationists have propounded the theory that universities everywhere belong to a supranational or world community, and that there can be and should be no creature known as the African University, as distinct from an English University or an American University. Universities in Africa, yes; but *not* African universities. In an unpublished paper entitled 'The African University and the further and post-graduate education of experienced teachers' presented at the September 1964 Lake Mohonk (U.S.A.) Conference on 'The African University and National Educational Development', Eric Lucas, then Director of the Institute of Education at Makerere University College, Uganda declared:

> I am sure I shall not be the first to point out that 'the African University'—like the African Personality—is a fiction.

The underlying assumption in this book is that what African countries require are indigenous *African universities*, designed and equipped to serve the needs of specific African societies. They do not require American, Russian, English or French universities located in Africa. In so far as the needs of an African society differ from the needs of an English or French society, so should the African University, established to serve African needs, differ from the American, English or French University. It is not necessary to be apologetic about this. In fact in so far as the needs of society may vary from one part of the vast continent of Africa to another, so would the character of the African University vary from one part of Africa to another.

The following statement quoted by James Perkin in *The University in Transition* and credited to the University of Witwatersrand is relevant:

> Every civilized society tends to develop institutions which will enable it to acquire, digest, and advance knowledge relevant to the tasks which, it is thought, will confront it in future. Of these institutions, the university is the most important. (2.1)

The report of the UNESCO sponsored seminar on the development of higher education in Africa, held at Tananarive from September 3–12, 1962, also contains a pertinent statement:

> ... no single type of foreign university can, in itself, meet the aspirations of the African people for social and economic development. Each country has its own genius and its special characteristics. Its institutions must bear the stamp of those special characteristics. Consequently, in addition to the traditional role of giving a broad liberal education, African universities must reflect the needs of the African world by providing African society with men and women equipped with the skills that will enable them to participate fully and usefully in the economic and social development of the continent. (3.1)

Has the African University emerged, or is it still in the creator's mould? How serious are the claims of the leaders of the universities in Africa that they have established universities geared to the needs of the African society? An attempt is made in the chapters that follow to answer these questions by drawing primarily on the Nigerian experience. In the African context, Nigeria is comparatively rich in universities, with six autonomous universities offering a wide variety of courses. There are also a dozen or so other institutions of higher learning going under a variety of names, most of them no doubt waiting for the opportune moment to proclaim themselves universities. Nigerian universities are more diversified than one is likely to find in many other African countries. Some are owned and controlled by the Federal Government, while the ownership of the others was until August 1975, vested in individual States or groups of States within the country. Nigeria's political and ethnic problems have left their mark on its universities. Also of significance is the fact that Nigerian universities have provided a battleground for foreign (notably American and British) university traditions. These and other considerations make the study of university development in Nigeria an interesting case study for the problems of university development in Africa.

REFERENCES

1 Yesufu, T.M. (ed.), *Creating the African University: Emerging Issues of the 1970s*, Ibadan, published for the Association of African Universities by Oxford University Press, 1973.

2 Perkins, James A., *The University in Transition*, Princeton, New Jersey, Princeton University Press, 1966, 2.1 : pp 3–4.

3 UNESCO, *The Development of Higher Education in Africa*, Paris, UNESCO, 1963. 3.1 : p. 12.

CHAPTER 2

HISTORICAL SURVEY

As can be seen from the paragraphs which follow, the history of university development in Nigeria has been reasonably well documented. No attempt will therefore be made in this chapter to produce another 'history' of university education.

UNIVERSITY DEVELOPMENT IN NIGERIA PRIOR TO JANUARY 1948

Nduka Okafor gives an interesting account of the unsuccessful efforts made by eminent intellectuals of African descent to establish university education in West Africa in *The Development of Universities in Nigeria*. He devotes a chapter to the abortive attempt by Nigerians resident in Lagos to establish the Lagos Training College and Industrial Institute in 1896, an attempt which might have resulted in the first vocational university in Nigeria. He also traces the history of Yaba Higher College, the nearest approach to a university in Nigeria before the birth of Nigeria's university institution in January 1948. The Higher College served as Nigeria's local source of teachers, medical assistants, assistant agricultural officers, forest supervisors, surveyors and administrators during its life span (1930–1947).

Chapters II and III of A. Babs Fafunwa's *A History of Nigerian Higher Education* also provide useful data on the beginnings of higher education for Nigerians and on the Higher College, Yaba. The Government Survey School opened in Lagos in 1908 is considered the British colonial government's first attempt to provide some kind of higher education for Nigerians. Some reference is also made to the various departmental training courses established by government to train Nigerians for the lower echelons of the civil service only.

The failure of Yaba Higher College was perhaps, the first casualty of the attempt to establish an African institution of higher learning in Nigeria. The courses at the College were said to be designed specifically for the Nigerian environment. The local diploma awarded to the few students who battled through the programme with flying colours was not recognized outside Nigeria. The students were not officially allowed to sit the external degree examinations of the University of

4

London. It is doubtful whether any tears were shed when the students still enrolled at the College transferred to Ibadan to join the pioneer students of University College, Ibadan in January 1948.

UNIVERSITY DEVELOPMENT IN NIGERIA, JANUARY 1948–OCTOBER 1960
The story of the events leading to January 1948 when University College, Ibadan admitted its first batch of students has been adequately covered by Kenneth Mellanby, first principal of the college, in *The Birth of Nigeria's University* (London, Methuen & Co. Ltd., 1958). Sir Alexander M. Carr-Saunders, in his *New Universities Overseas*, (London, George Allen & Unwin, Ltd., 1961) gave adequate coverage to the work of the Asquith Commission (of which he was a member) and its impact upon the development of higher education in the overseas territories which then formed part of the British Empire. Fafunwa's *A History of Nigerian Higher Education* referred to earlier has a chapter (Chapter IV) on the commissions on Higher Education in West Africa and the colonies. It is therefore unnecessary to go over the same ground here. The relevant point in the events culminating in the opening of University College, Ibadan in January 1948 is that Ibadan was established when Nigeria was a British colonial territory, as part of the British policy of extending higher education to its colonies. A crucial part of this policy was that each of these overseas university colleges should be affiliated to the University of London, under what became known later as the 'scheme of special relation'. An Inter-Universities Council for Higher Education Overseas was established to help the young colleges with such responsibilities as the recruitment of teaching and senior administrative staff, and to give them general guidance.

J.T. Saunders, in his book *University College, Ibadan* (Ibadan, Cambridge University Press, 1960) gave a detailed account of the development of the college from the year he succeeded Mellanby as the principal of the college in 1953 until 1960. His book and Mellanby's give a fairly exhaustive account of the history of Ibadan from January 1948 to October 1960, during which period Ibadan remained the only university institution in Nigeria. No attempt will be made to go over the same ground in this book. Attention will be focussed only on those events, issues or problems in the history of Ibadan during this period which have influenced subsequent development in Nigerian universities.

The history of the University of Ibadan commissioned by the University Council to commemorate the institution's Silver Jubilee, attempts to assess the growth and impact of Ibadan in its first 25 years (1948–1973). Edited by J.F. Ade Ajayi and T.N. Tamuno, *The University of Ibadan* 1948–73 is a very valuable resource book.

THE UNIVERSITY COLLEGE IDEA

At the time Ibadan was established, it was the general practice within the British Empire for a new university institution to begin as a university college. The university college was generally affiliated to the University of London which had the power to grant its degrees to external students. This pattern of development was not limited only to the 'overseas' colleges: a number of present day English universities (e.g. Exeter and Hull) began as university colleges preparing students for degrees of the University of London.

Although students in these colleges received the 'external' degrees of London (as distinguished from the 'internal' degrees given to the regular students enrolled in any of the constituent colleges of London University), the scheme of special relation made it possible for some changes to be made in their curricula, generally to provide for the study of local history, geography, fauna, etc. Outside such provisions, the curriculum patterns were essentially those of London. No changes could be made to them without the prior approval of London. Although London did not have to approve or to be consulted on the appointment of the teaching staff of the colleges, it had to give prior approval before any member of the academic staff could serve as an examiner in any of the examinations leading to the conferment of degrees.

Questions for the examinations leading to London degrees were initiated by the academic staff in the colleges and then sent to the appropriate London examiners for approval. The answer scripts were marked first at the college and then airmailed to London to be marked afresh by the London examiners. During an agreed period, the college examiners travelled to London for joint meetings with their corresponding London examiners. The success or failure of each student was agreed upon at these meetings. In cases of disagreement, the London examiner had the last word. The writer's experience at the meetings he attended in July 1959 was that such disagreements were infrequent.

As is evident in Mellanby's *Birth of Nigeria's University,* Ibadan was not immediately accepted by the Nigerian public. Part of the criticism stemmed from the high academic standards set by the college from the beginning. When in 1949 the college expelled some students for low performance there was public outcry. Nigeria being then a colonial territory, it was not difficult for many Nigerians to regard Ibadan as a tool in the hands of the British 'imperialists' for stifling the aspirations and honest endeavours of brilliant Nigerians, in the way its predecessor the Higher College, Yaba had been used.

Part of the reason for the slow acceptance of Ibadan stemmed from what was normally referred to as 'colonial mentality'. As a result of years of contact with his colonial masters, the average Nigerian had developed an uncritical attitude towards anything coming from the 'white man's land' and a derogatory attitude to anything produced locally. A degree obtained from England had prestige value. Very few could aspire to it since, because of the limited number of government scholarships, only persons from wealthy families or men who had accumulated enough savings after many years of work could find the funds to go abroad for study. To go overseas in quest of a degree was likened to the quest for the legendary golden fleece. It was unusual to proceed from the secondary school to the university. The opening of Ibadan meant that the 'golden fleece' could be acquired locally. The relatively low fees at Ibadan meant that many could go straight from school to the university. This was unprecedented in Nigeria, and consequently many Nigerians could not accept that the fleece at Ibadan was just as golden. Many Nigerians asked the early Ibadan graduates when they would go overseas (to England) to finish up! Doubts were expressed as to whether a graduate of Ibadan should be accorded the same perquisites and status in the civil service as a graduate of British universities. A Nigerian newspaper columnist created tremendous fun some years later when he wrote on the possibility of conferring local degrees such as M.A. (Nsukka) and Ph.D. (Awo-Omamma): such an idea sounded crazy.

In the light of this, it was natural for the authorities, staff and students of Ibadan to play up the special relationship with London. It was a matter of great pride to the successful student that he had been adjudged successful by the impersonal examiner in London, and that he would receive a London degree as if he had studied in London. The lecturer who was approved as an examiner by London saw in this a recognition of his qualifications: the frequency with which these lecturers mentioned this 'appointment' when applying for teaching positions in other universities shows how much value they attached to it. The Nigerian appointed to a senior lectureship or a professorship did not want the impression to be created that he received the appointment because of a deliberate policy to Nigerianize some senior positions. He wanted it to be known that he received the offer in open competition and after the field had been thoroughly ploughed by the Inter-Universities Council located in London, a body whose judgements were never open to question. Some non-Nigerian writers on Nigerian Higher Education refer to this attitude of local staff and students towards high standards and the attachment to London without understanding the underlying contributing factors.

Part of the opposition to Ibadan was political. It was inconceivable to some that a nation would abrogate to an educational institution in another country the responsibility to determine who among its youth should be granted university degrees. The affiliation to London was viewed as a subtle avenue to enable Britain to control the number of graduates produced by Nigeria's only university institution and the nature of the education they received, so that it could always make the case that Nigeria did not have enough qualified Nigerians to shoulder the responsibilities of self-government.

THE IBADAN IMPACT

In spite of all the criticism and opposition, Ibadan finally became accepted by the Nigerian public. Its affiliation to London, the performance of its students 'by London standards', and the performance of its graduates in overseas graduate schools had won the college world-wide recognition. The impact of this acceptance on subsequent university development in Nigeria has been tremendous.

(i) The fact of its acceptance has virtually prevented Ibadan from being innovative, even after its umbilical cord with London had been cut in 1962. Of the three Nigerian universities whose curricula will be analysed in this book, Ibadan is the least original and the most British-oriented in curriculum structure. The decision of its authorities to retain the colours of London University hoods on the new Ibadan hoods as a momento of fourteen years of association with

London could be interpreted as a reluctance to break completely away from the security of the London umbrella.

(ii) The Nigerian public came to regard the university college pattern of development as the only pattern for establishing new universities, even after the pattern had died a natural death in the United Kingdom where it was first conceived. This accounts for the scepticism with which the country greeted the establishment of the University of Nigeria in 1960. Even top officials of the Federal Ministry of Education were anxious to know the overseas university to which the new university was affiliated, and many prospective students unconsciously addressed letters to the University *College* of Nigeria instead of the shorter University of Nigeria.

Dr. Nnamdi Azikiwe, who founded Nsukka almost as an antidote to Ibadan, appears also to have been influenced by the Ibadan pattern of development. In the proposals for the establishment of the University of Nigeria, provision is made for London University to co-operate by granting their degrees and qualifications in certain areas, to make the professional qualifications in those areas acceptable. (1.1) London did not accept the proposal, if it was ever forwarded to London, but accepted an invitation to join in guiding the young university in its early years. Some of the pioneer Nsukka students sought permission to register concurrently for external London degrees, fearing that the degrees they obtained from their new and unaffiliated university might not be readily accepted within Nigeria, much less outside the country.

(iii) Ibadan came to be regarded as the symbol of what a Nigerian university should be, especially in view of the fact that it took fourteen years of tough apprenticeship under London to be proclaimed of age. This enabled Ibadan, after its attainment of full university status, to introduce degree programmes in such unusual fields as Nursing, Physiotherapy, and Medical Laboratory Technology without invoking any adverse comment within the country. Bedlam would have been let loose had such programmes been introduced first at Nsukka rather than at Ibadan. The Home Economics degree programme introduced at Nsukka in 1961 has not yet won full recognition. Critics of the admission standards at the University of Nigeria muzzle their criticisms when they are informed that Ibadan has been applying the same standards since its inception. It is all right if Ibadan also does it!

Thus, although the report of the Commission on Post-School Certificate and Higher Education in Nigeria recommended that 'it would not be in the national interest if one single pattern were to be imposed on all Nigerian higher education', and affirmed that 'The hope for Nigerian higher education lies in its diversity', (2.1) the prevailing wind is blowing towards complete similarity to Ibadan. It is significant that those areas in which the National Universities Commission was highly critical of Nsukka in its 1963 report (3) were the areas in which the latter differed significantly from Ibadan. These areas included the general studies programme (which Ibadan did not consider necessary), the decision not to use external examiners at Nsukka, and the differences in the constitutional structure of the two institutions. Nsukka had to make radical modifications to its initial degree curricula in order to reduce the dissimilarity to Ibadan. Its general studies requirements for the advanced level students had to be reduced by a half in order to allow the students to graduate in three years, as at Ibadan. It has also had to institute final degree examinations to be more in line with Ibadan.

It is also significant that the effect of the few changes made in the University of Nigeria Law 1961 by the Military Government of Eastern Nigeria in February 1966 was to bring Nsukka in line with the constitutional structure of Ibadan. This trend has been continued as far as practicable by the first post-civil war Nsukka Vice-Chancellor.

Partly as a legacy from the former colonial government and partly because of the pattern of development at Ibadan, the average Nigerian has come to associate British university education with high academic standards, while associating American university education with inferior standards. Consequently there is a tendency to accept uncritically any curriculum pattern or practice if it is known to be copied from Britain, whereas any innovation in higher education known to have American origins is initially held suspect no matter what its merits. The initial antagonism to the general studies programme at Nsukka cannot be dissociated from the fact that it symbolized to many people the introduction of American-style education into Nigerian universities, particularly that part of it which had been described derisively many years ago as 'horizontal education'.

The overall effect of the dominance of the Ibadan pattern has been to reduce the enthusiasm for originality among the new Nigerian universities.

UNIVERSITY DEVELOPMENT SINCE OCTOBER 1960

The University of Nigeria was ceremonially opened on October 7, 1960, as part of the week-long celebrations marking the attainment of political independence by Nigeria on October 1, 1960. The university was fully autonomous, with the power to grant its own degrees. Technically speaking, therefore, it became the first fully-fledged university in Nigeria, since Ibadan was still at that time a university college granting London degrees. It also became the first university established by a Nigerian Regional government.

In the same year the Report of the Commission on Post-School Certificate and Higher Education in Nigeria (popularly known as the Ashby report) was released. The commission recommended, *inter alia*, the establishment of three universities in addition to Ibadan—one in Lagos, one at Zaria in Northern Nigeria (on the site of the Northern branch of the Nigerian College of Arts, Science and Technology) and the third the University of Nigeria which had already been planned by the Eastern Nigeria Government. Each of the three existing Regions would thus have located in it one centre of higher education, with a fourth university in Lagos.

The commission also recommended that each of the new universities should be autonomous and have the power to grant its own degrees. The years immediately following saw the birth of three new universities in the country. The Report of the Inter-University Council Delegation on a Proposed University of Northern Nigeria was submitted in April 1961. Resulting from the report and the recommendations of the Ashby Commission, Ahmadu Bello University was officially opened in October 1962. The Western Nigeria Government pressed ahead with its plans to build its own regional university, even though such a university was not among those proposed by the Ashby Commission. The Federal Government yielded to the pressure and made available to the Western Nigeria Government the site and assets of the Ibadan branch of the Nigerian College (which were to have been turned over to University College, Ibadan). The University of Ife began to offer classes in October 1962, though the political misfortunes which beset Western Nigeria in the same year prevented the university from making any significant impact until a change of leadership in 1966 provided rays of hope.

Following the Report of the Unesco Advisory Commission for the Establishment of the University of Lagos (Paris, Unesco, 1961), the University of Lagos came into being in 1962 as the second Federal university institution, Ahmadu Bello and Ife being, like Nsukka, regional universities receiving part of their support from the Federal Government. The Enugu branch of the Nigerian College was turned over to Nsukka as a second campus instead of being converted into a full-scale university.

Thus within a space of two years from the date the country attained independence, four brand new universities were established, each empowered to grant degrees. Ibadan, the oldest university institution, cut its umbilical cord with London in October 1962, becoming the University of Ibadan. In July 1965, it turned out the first graduates holding Ibadan (rather than London) degrees, by which time Nsukka had produced two crops of graduates and taken all the publicity for turning out the first graduates of an autonomous Nigerian university.

NSUKKA MARKS NEW ERA

The period beginning with the opening of Nsukka in October 1960 is a crucial period in the history of university development in Nigeria. Prior to that date, Ibadan was monarch of all it surveyed. University education in Nigeria was synonymous with Ibadan: there was nothing else to compare with Ibadan, especially when it was widely acknowledged that standards at Ibadan were similar to (and most Ibadan students believed they were higher than) standards in British universities. Under the leadership of Dr. Nnamdi Azikiwe, the Eastern Nigerian Government had talked about building a University of Nigeria as far back as 1955. Most people, however, regarded this as a political stunt which, in the words of Shakespeare, was 'full of sound and fury, signifying nothing', particularly as little was heard about the proposal in between election years. The choice of Nsukka as the site of the university added to the disregard with which the proposal was treated: it sounded ridiculous that a university could be located in such an arid, backward part of the country, sixty-four kilometres (forty miles) away from the nearest city.

Many people doubted the wisdom in establishing a regional university; some, like the authors of *The Emergent University*, were definite that Nigeria did not as yet need a second university because Ibadan could not fill every available place with fully qualified students. To some, the university idea was sure to be as short-lived and ill-conceived as the many corporations established by the Eastern Nigeria Government at the same period.

In April 1960, work began on the site at Nsukka. On October 7 the university was formally opened by H.R.H. Princess Alexandra of Kent (who represented Her Majesty the Queen of England in the Nigerian Independence celebrations), and on October 10, about 220 students arrived—the pioneer lions and lionesses of Nsukka, as they were later designated. *Nigerian Education* [O. Ikejiani (ed.), Ikeja, Longmans of Nigeria Ltd., 1964] has given details of the establishment of Nsukka and it is not necessary to duplicate them here.

Nsukka has been the most controversial university in Nigeria. Many within and outside Ibadan were infuriated by its immodest choice of the name: University of Nigeria, a name which Mellanby claimed in his *Birth of Nigeria's University* he had tried unsuccessfully to give Ibadan in its early years. A former bursar at Ibadan once proposed in jest at the senior staff club that Nsukka should be designated the University of the World! It was the first university to challenge the monopoly which Ibadan had claimed over university education in Nigeria for twelve years, and little love was lost between the two institutions in the early years: the intense rivalry was later taken over by the undergraduates and led to the split of the National Union of Nigerian Students into Ibadan and Nsukka factions. The general feeling at Ibadan was that Nsukka was prostituting higher education; Nsukka tried hard to show that it was more sensitive than Ibadan to the needs of Nigeria and that it was certain to do a better job for Nigeria than Ibadan.

Nsukka had a tough time winning its way into the hearts of Nigerians, even in Eastern Nigeria. Up till at least January 1966, there were still many Nigerians, including some top people in the Government of Eastern Nigeria which then owned the university, who were sceptical about Nsukka. Interviews with many of these sceptics revealed the following reasons for their scepticism:

(a) Nsukka did not begin as a university college, like Ibadan, and it is difficult to convince many people that without such an initial period of tutelage a young university is qualified to grant its own degrees.

(b) The excess publicity given to American participation in the running of the university made many people regard Nsukka as an American university, and consequently a university with inferior standards. The general studies programme, which was undoubtedly the major contribution Nsukka made to university education in Nigeria, was discredited as one evidence of American education. The adoption by the university of the system of credit hours with the confusion it brought to employers and sponsors who were not used to credit hours and cumulative grade point averages; the fact that its first two Vice-Chancellors were Americans and at one time both the Vice-Chancellor and the Registrar were Americans; the fact that the brain behind the university was American trained and a known critic of Ibadan; and the idea that the university was based on the American land-grant philosophy, all fortified the image of Nsukka as an American university even though the official publications of the university emphasized that Nsukka was neither British nor American but Nigerian.

(c) It was widely known that Nsukka was biting off more than it could chew. The rate of expansion in student numbers was simply unprecedented: Ibadan, the model for most Nigerians, had expanded very slowly (and many had come to regard the Ibadan rate as the only rate that would not compromise high academic standards). Student numbers rose at Nsukka from about 220 in October 1960 to about 900 in October 1961, about 1200 in October 1962, and about 1800 in October 1963. In the 1965/66 academic year (Nsukka's sixth year of existence) the enrolment was nearly 2,600.

Even more crucial than the expansion in student numbers was the expansion in the number of academic disciplines offered. In the 1965/66 academic year the university had 39 different degree programmes, most of them established within its first three years of existence: this did not include non-degree diplomas. There were instances in which the University Council decided to establish new degree programmes, and students were registered for them only to discover that no curriculum had been drawn up because it had not been possible to find qualified lecturers for the programme. The pioneer students in engineering arrived before their lecturers and before the foundations were dug for the engineering laboratories: the first bursar of the University appeased them by coaching them in engineering drawing. Students were also admitted in business administration and accountancy before the arrival of qualified lecturers. The first curriculum for the students in accountancy was put together by someone in the Registrar's office!

Much of the hasty expansion might have been motivated by the urge to be the first Nigerian university to span all possible disciplines, to beat Ibadan in as many fields as possible. Its effects were hard on many students. Some programmes such as the two diploma programmes in Education, begun in January 1961 were abandoned because of inadequate preliminary planning, and the students transferred to other programmes. In some others, such as the degree programme in Secretarial Studies, the curriculum underwent several radical changes within the career of the same group of students as leadership within the department changed hands or as the department developed clearer ideas about the kind of programme it should be offering. (A decision was taken by the end of the 1965/66 academic year to abolish the programmes in Secretarial Studies entirely.)

(d) The excessive powers of its first Chancellor did not help the Nsukka image. The University of Nigeria Law 1961 made him a unique Chancellor, compared with Chancellors in other Nigerian and British Commonwealth universities. (Equivalent positions do not exist in American universities.) Chancellors of the other Nigerian universities were appointed generally for 5–10 year periods, and were normally ceremonial heads of the universities whose main functions were to confer degrees on the incepting graduates at degree convocations. The first Nsukka Chancellor was appointed for life (unless he chose to resign or became insane). He was also, by virtue of his office, Chairman of the university governing body (Council) and its executive committee (Finance and General Purposes Committee) for life. The University Council could delegate all its powers to him except the power to amend the statutes. Anxious to ensure that the university which owed its origin to his dreams developed the way he wanted it, he made full use of the powers vested in him by the University Law.

When trouble broke out in the University of Lagos in March 1965 over the replacement of its Vice-Chancellor, there were rumours of a proposal by the Eastern Nigeria Government to build a university in Port Harcourt to absorb Eastern Nigerian staff and students who withdrew from Lagos as a result of the crisis there. When asked why it was considered necessary to build a second university in Eastern Nigeria, the reply was that Nsukka was being run as the private property of one man hence the government was losing interest in it. (It is interesting to observe, in passing, that the government of the short-lived 'Republic of Biafra' did proceed to establish a University of Science and Technology in Port-Harcourt. The university lived as long as 'Biafra', i.e. from 1967 until January 1970.)

THE NSUKKA IMPACT

Nsukka has been given this much space because of its significance in the history of university development in Nigeria. It marked a sharp break from the Ibadan tradition of university development to which the country had been accustomed. It was the first of the 'independence era' universities, conceived as a result of Nigerian initiative rather than as part of British colonial policy for her overseas territories. These 'independence era' universities carried the imprints of independence. In keeping with the national foreign policy of non-alignment, these new universities were free to shop for ideas and support from any corner of the globe, not only from the United Kingdom. American ideas, which had hitherto been discredited in the country, penetrated nearly every facet of Nigerian education. A Nigerian-British-American combination replaced the former British predominance: the Ashby Commission led the way in that direction, followed by Nsukka with its London/Michigan State/Nsukka Joint University Advisory Committee. The advisory committee for the establishment of the University of Lagos was a UNESCO international panel. Nsukka received technical assistance from America, the Netherlands, the U.K. and Western Germany, and obtained on loan the temporary services of a professor of history from Karl Marx University in Leipzig, East Germany. The other Nigerian universities have generally followed the same pattern of international co-operation, although the countries involved may have varied. Even Ahmadu Bello University which was founded on the recommendations of an Inter-University Council delegation (a U.K. body) now receives technical assistance from other countries, including the U.S.A.

The implications of these expanded horizons on university development are considerable. They introduced new ideas and approaches to Nigerian higher education. The major influences were American and British. Even though other countries also rendered invaluable assistance, the rivalry was between the American and the British influences. Some Americans felt their opportunity had come to sweep off any traces of the British educational system, and lost no time in denouncing any facets of that system (like sixth forms, external examiners, intensive specialization) which were alien to the American system. The British emphasized high academic standards and the fine distinctions between university and non-university disciplines. Nsukka provided the first melting pot for what appeared irreconcilable approaches to higher education. The Nsukka curriculum pattern which will be reviewed later is the offspring of a tete-a-tete between two hardly compatible bed-fellows. A victory here, a concession there, a pronouncement here about the needs of Nigeria, and a compromise solution that would meet each opposing side half-way— these characterized many of the faculty meetings for the development of academic regulations. The result was the throwing away of an excellent opportunity to develop fresh curriculum patterns for the Nigerian situation.

In some other universities, the different technical assistance groups were assigned to separate faculties to minimize clashes. At Lagos, before the 1965 crisis, for example, the faculty of law came under British control, while the faculty of business and social studies came under the control of New York University. Thus pockets of technical assistance groups might be dotted all over the university, each an empire unto itself. There were two such pockets within the Public Administration department at Ahmadu Bello. Where the university did not have clearly known goals to guide its development, the consequences were obvious.

As the first 'revolutionary-type' university, Nsukka received more than its fair share of mud-slinging. However, it saved Ife, Ahmadu Bello, Lagos and Benin similar experiences. Nobody appeared shocked at the fact that they began as autonomous universities: the university college idea appears to have been dead, buried and forgotten after the establishment of Nsukka.

The introduction of the general studies programme at Nsukka was in keeping with the growing trend in England towards broadening the undergraduate curriculum. The significant change made in the Ibadan curriculum after the university became autonomous in 1962 was aimed at breadth. It is difficult to determine whether Ibadan was influenced by developments at Nsukka or by the trend in England, particularly as the resulting curriculum pattern has been English. However, the recent introduction of the 'course' system (complete with course numbering) and the radical change in the methods of determining a student's eligibility for a degree are unmistakable signs of the impact Nsukka has made even on Ibadan!

Nsukka received considerable criticism when it introduced degree programmes in subjects like vocational education, physical education, fine arts, journalism and home economics which hitherto had not been traditional degree granting disciplines in British universities, the fact that the Ashby Report recommended the introduction of some commercial and technical subjects notwithstanding. It would not be surprising if Ibadan developed the courage to introduce degree programmes in fields such as nursing and medical laboratory technology because Nsukka had absorbed the initial tremours attendant upon such 'revolutionary' changes.

THE POST-NSUKKA UNIVERSITIES

As stated earlier, the Commission on Post-School Certificate and Higher Education in Nigeria (the Ashby Commission) was set up by the Nigerian Federal Government to advise on Nigeria's needs in post-secondary and higher education for the twenty-year period following the attainment of political independence in 1960. It recommended the establishment of two new universities in addition to Ibadan and Nsukka. One was to be situated in Lagos, and to be non-residential offering day and evening classes in commercial subjects and the social sciences. The University of Lagos was also expected to offer correspondence courses. At the request of the Federal Government, a UNESCO Advisory Committee for the Establishment of the University of Lagos was set up in June 1961. The Committee submitted its report in September 1961, and in April 1962, a law establishing the University of Lagos was passed. The university admitted students in October 1962 in the faculties of Medicine, Business and Social Studies, and Law. Lagos steered a course which lay between Ibadan and Nsukka in its academic programmes as will be discussed later. Unfortunately, barely three years after its opening, Lagos was plunged into a major crisis following the decision of its provisional council not to re-appoint its first vice-chancellor. More on that later.

The second new university recommended by the Ashby Commission was to be situated at Zaria in Northern Nigeria, on the site of the headquarters of the Nigerian College of Arts, Science and Technology which the Commission recommended should be abolished. A group appointed by the Inter-University Council for Higher Education Overseas advised the then Northern Nigerian Government on the establishment of the university. Unlike the UNESCO Commission on the University of Lagos, the IUC group was all British with Sir Alexander Carr-Saunders as Chairman. In June 1962 the Northern Nigeria Government passed the law establishing Ahmadu Bello University named after the Premier of Northern Nigeria at the time. Like Lagos, Ahmadu Bello admitted students in October 1962. Considering the composition of the IUC delegation which recommended its establishment and that it was, at least until 1966, run predominantly by British nationals, it is not surprising that it swung heavily towards Ibadan in its orientation and academic programmes.

Although the Ashby Commission did not recommend the establishment of a second university in the Western Region of Nigeria, the Western Nigeria Government announced in 1960 its intention to establish a university of the highest standard. It established a 59-member University Planning Committee comprising persons of Western Nigeria origin to advise on the planning of the university and to do the preliminary work for its establishment, as well as a University Parliamentary Committee to advise the Western Nigeria Minister of Education on the establishment of the university. Ife thus became the first Nigerian university to be established on the recommendations of an all-Nigerian committee. A law establishing the University of Ife was passed in June 1961. In October 1962 the university admitted its first students, using the facilities at the Ibadan Branch of the former Nigerian College of Arts, Science and Technology which the Federal Government had made available to the university. In January 1967 the first batch of students were transferred to the permanent site of the university at Ile-Ife.

Ife began with great promise. Its top management was in Western Nigerian hands, and it had quite a core of Nigerian academic staff. Unfortunately the severe set-back suffered by the Action Group in Western Nigeria between 1962 and the overthrow of the political regime in January 1966 had its toll on the university which had been established by an Action Group government. The unfortunate events will be considered in greater detail in the section on academic freedom. Ife has enjoyed stability and taken giant strides forward since 1966 when it came under new leadership and became liberated from political tangles.

The University of Benin is the most recently established university. It was established by the government of the Mid-West State of Nigeria in 1970 as the Mid-West Institute of Technology, 'located in Benin, capital of the State. It was to have begun as a campus of Ibadan but the negotiations fell through. It changed its name in 1972 to the University of Benin, after it had been accorded full university status by the Federal Military Government. Until October 1974, the University did not have a stable Vice-Chancellor. With the large number of suitable Nigerian intellectuals and administrators in the academic market-place, it was surprising that the authorities of the institution did not think it fit to appoint a long-term vice-chancellor from among them instead of chasing after short-term expatriate vice-chancellors.

REFERENCES

1 Eastern Region of Nigeria: *University of Nigeria Progress Report,* Eastern Regional Official Document No. 7 of 1960, Enugu, Government Printer, 1960. 1.1: p. 5

2 *Investment in Education:* Report of the Commission on Post-School Certificate and Higher Education in Nigeria, Lagos, Federal Ministry of Education, Nigeria, 1960. 2.1: p. 25

3 Federal Republic of Nigeria: *University Development in Nigeria:* Report of the National Universities Commission, Lagos, Federal Ministry of Information, 1963.

Other Sources

Mellanby, Kenneth., *The Birth of Nigeria's University,* London, Methuen & Co. Ltd., 1958.

Carr-Saunders, Alexander M., *New Universities Overseas,* London, George Allen & Unwin, Ltd., 1961.

Saunders, J.T., *University College, Ibadan,* Cambridge University Press, 1960.

Olubummo A. & Ferguson, J., *The Emergent University,* London, Longmans Green and Co. Ltd., 1960

Ikejiani, Okechukwu (ed.), *Nigerian Education,* Ikeja, Longmans of Nigeria Ltd., 1964.

Okafor, Nduka., *The Development of Universities in Nigeria,* A study of the influence of political and other factors on university development in Nigeria, 1868–1967, London, Longman, 1971.

Hanson, John W., *Education Nsukka* (a study in institution building among the modern Ibo), East Lansing, Michigan State University, 1968.

Zerby, Lewis & Margaret, *If I should Die Before I Wake: The Nsukka Dream* (A History of the University of Nigeria), East Lansing, Michigan State University, 1971.

Fafunwa, A. Babs., *A History of Nigerian Higher Education,* Lagos, Macmillan & Co. (Nigeria) Ltd., 1971

Ajayi, J.F. Ade and Tamuno, T.N. (eds.), *The University of Ibadan* 1948–73, A history of the first twenty-five years, Ibadan, Ibadan University Press, 1973. Akintoye, S.A., *Ten Years of the University of Ife* 1962–1972, Ile-Ife, University of Ife Press, 1973.

CHAPTER 3

OBJECTIVES OF UNIVERSITY EDUCATION

Serious indictments on the African university have been handed down from time to time by non-African educators (*e.g.* Sir Eric Ashby and Thomas Balogh). Nigerian universities qualify for these indictments as much as universities in other parts of Africa, and one reason for this is that very few have any clearly defined and meaningful statement of institutional objectives upon which their curricula are based. Surprisingly, the University of Ibadan which is the most widely acclaimed Nigerian university is the most arid in this regard, as will be seen later in this chapter.

One's initial reaction is to ask on what basis Ibadan is adjudged successful when the university itself has not made known what it sets out to accomplish. The answer, of course, lies in the fact that Ibadan began as direct transplantation of the University of London, from London to Ibadan. The objective was clearly to establish as close a version of London as possible at Ibadan, hence it was unnecessary for the new university to have any other objectives. Its success lay in how closely it approximated to London.

This was part of Britain's policy for extending higher education to its colonies and territories overseas. Universities comparable to Ibadan were also established in other parts of the former British Empire, for example the Universities of Ghana, Makerere, and the West Indies. However, by the time Nigeria attained independence in 1960, it was no longer expedient, for political and other reasons to transplant university models from England to Nigeria. Political freedom also conferred on Nigeria the freedom to develop the Nigerian university rather than the English university located in Nigeria. The decision by the Nigerian governments to break free from the special relationship pattern of development was a deliberate attempt to create room for 'the experiment, the innovation and the adaptation to local needs which Nigerian universities must have'. (1.1) Unfortunately it turned out to be merely a change of tune from transplantation to *adaptation* alone. The policy of adaptation was achieved in different ways. In some cases adaptation was limited to the content of the undergraduate curriculum, leaving the structure to betray the university system from which it was imported. In some cases it was a matter of grafting or welding something from one university tradition onto another, sometimes resulting in an amalgam which each of the contributing systems would not hesitate to disclaim.

The Commission on Post-School Certificate and Higher Education in Nigeria propounded another approach to university development. While urging the discontinuation of a policy of direct transplantation (*i.e.* the university college, special relationship approach), it strongly recommended its replacement with a system of sponsorship. Each Nigerian university was advised to choose one of 'the great universities of the world' to act as its sponsor, if the new university was to attract foreign staff, establish currency for its degrees, and gain admission to the 'supranational community' of world universities.

> We are sure that some of the great universities of the world would be willing to sponsor new Nigerian universities. The sponsorship need not be onerous either for the new university or its sponsor; but if a well-established overseas university is to underwrite with its prestige a new Nigerian university, we would expect the sponsoring university to have a place on the [University] Council, to be consulted about the general pattern of courses, to appoint some of the examiners and to be assured that the university has a sound constitution and reliable sources of finance. (1.2)

This system of sponsorship does not appear significantly different from the special relationship pattern which the Commission recommended should be scrapped, except that the name of the university written in brackets after the degree would be that of the Nigerian university. The 'great' university may be more concerned with propagating its own philosophy of education (no matter how irrelevant to Nigeria), if it must protect its image, than in helping the new Nigerian university to develop something new and relevant to the Nigerian environment.

It is surprising that Sir Eric Ashby, who served as Chairman of this Commission, should turn round a few years later to castigate Nigerian (or African) universities for lack of originality. The emphasis of the Commission appeared to have been more on the benefits to be derived from apprenticeship to an overseas university of prestige than in the definition of the objectives of a Nigerian university and the development of appropriate curricula.

Direct transplantation, adaptation, and sponsorship appear to derive their support from a number of assumptions which are worth challenging. The assumptions are:

(a)   that the trodden path is the safe way;

(b)   that ideal universities have been developed outside Nigeria and Africa;

(c)   that the new university must as a rule turn to the old university for guidance in its years of infancy if it is to develop into a respectable member of the university club.

I shall consider these assumptions, one at a time, rejecting all three as the basis for developing the Nigerian university.

(a)   The trodden path assumption. 'The safe ways are the trodden paths'. W.H. Cowley, in an unpublished address at the Presidents' Institute of the Institute for College and University Administrators of Harvard University on June 22, 1960, attributed those words to President Josiah Quincy of Harvard as the latter blasted the efforts of those urging reform at Harvard in 1840. Two quotations illustrate how a similar philosophy influenced university development in Africa and Nigeria a little over a century later.

The Commission on Higher Education for Africans in Central Africa gave the following reasons for rejecting the representations made to it that the undergraduate curriculum in the proposed university college intended to serve the needs of Africans in the short-lived Central African Federation should include a programme of general education:

> A number of those with whom we discussed educational problems in Central Africa laid emphasis on the importance of general education: they believe that students are poorly informed about matters of general interest and of relevance to the life of a member of a modern community. They were interested in certain experiments which are being made in universities in Europe and the United States of America .... We believe that these experiments are concerned with a real problem; moreover we do not doubt that the problem of general education is more pressing in Central Africa than in a country where students can learn much from their homes and from the society in which they mingle outside the university. But unsatisfactory as things may be in this respect in

universities, wherever they are situated, we are not convinced that an innovation in university practice is the best
way to make them better . . . . We are therefore proposing
a scheme of study of a normal kind. We recommend that
application be made by the College to be received into
'special relations' with the University of London. (2.1)

The quotation hardly needs further comment. The Commission
considered the plea for the inclusion of general education reasonable
in view of the background of the prospective African students. It
rejected the plea because it was easier to do so than to evolve a
pattern of university education that would come to grips with the
peculiar problems of the Central African students. The trodden
paths were considered the safe ways; consequently the Commission
proceeded to recommend the safe way—special relationship with
the University of London, which would enable the students to take
London degrees. Again, London was to be transplanted in Africa.
    The authors of *The Emergent University,* in justifying the establish-
ment of the University of Ibadan initially as a university college in
special relationship with the University of London, argued as
follows:

> Those who founded University College, Ibadan, were in
> no doubt. They applied the university system which had been
> evolved in Great Britain to Nigeria, and this has been the
> normal practice in founding new universities. . . . The
> establishment of UCI was no doubt pragmatic rather than
> critical: it arose from the acceptance of a system which was
> there and worked, rather than from an examination of first
> principles. (3.1)

Here again, the trodden paths were considered the safe way.
A trodden path could indeed be the safe way, but it would appear
an oversimplification to transfer the analogy to university development. When the authors of *The Emergent University* argued that it
was pragmatic to plant a system which was there and worked,
they ignored the possibility that a system which exists and works
in one culture may not work in a different culture. Moreover, it
might have been relatively easy to determine which trodden paths
to follow when Nigeria was a protectorate within the British Empire.
With the attainment of sovereign status and the subsequent adoption

of a foreign policy of non-alignment, the number of trodden paths grew overnight—trodden paths in America, in Russia, in the United Kingdom, in Europe—each different in many important respects from the other and thereby making it difficult to determine which trodden path was the safe way. One outcome of this has been to play safe by putting a limb on each trodden path, or at least on American and British trodden paths, instead of examining first principles, formulating the objectives of university education in Nigeria and building a university to achieve those objectives.

In the course of this book, the curriculum patterns in three Nigerian universities will be analysed. This analysis will show that the three universities have relied on curriculum patterns developed by universities in Britain or America, countries which are attempting to solve problems often not identical with problems facing a developing African country like Nigeria. Even the controversy over sixth form education in Nigeria reveals how much Nigerian educators have depended on developments in other parts of the world, no matter how inappropriate, to pre-determine the pattern of university development in Nigeria.

Recent developments in many of the highly developed countries to which Nigerian and other African universities turn for curriculum patterns which have stood the test of time, show that these countries are dissatisfied with many of these patterns being copied by Nigeria, and are seeking more effective approaches to the problems of higher education.

(b) Ideal universities have been developed outside Nigeria and Africa. In the United Kingdom, the newest universities with their 'schools' and their integrated curricula suggest that what held good in higher education in the past may not be applicable in the same country today. The appointment by the British Prime Minister in February 1961 of the Committee on Higher Education under the chairmanship of Professor Lord Robbins was indicative of a dissatisfaction with the status quo. The terms of reference of the Committee testify to this:

> .... to review the pattern of full-time higher education in Great Britain and in the light of national needs and resources advise Her Majesty's Government on what principles its longterm development should be based. In particular, to advise, in the light of these principles, whether there should be any changes in that pattern, whether any new types of

institution are desirable and whether any modifications should be made in the present arrangements for planning and co-ordinating the development of the various types of institution. (4.1)

The so called Robbins Report, prepared at an estimated cost of £128,770 and consisting of the report itself, six volumes of five appendices and volumes of evidence, has already had a tremendous influence on the development of higher education in Great Britain since its submission to Parliament in October 1963. Even the Oxford University has had to re-examine its constitutional structure following the recommendations of the report. (4.2)

The Soviet Union re-examined its educational trodden paths in the late fifties. On November 12, 1958 the Plenum of the Central Committee of the Communist Party of the Soviet Union adopted resolutions based on draft theses from the speech of Comrade N.S. Khrushchev to be delivered at the XXI Congress of the Communist Party of the Soviet Union entitled 'Control figures for the development of the public economy in the U.S.S.R. during the years 1959–65'. The theses were 'On strengthening the Relationship of the School with Life and on the Further Development of the System of Public Education in the Country'. George S. Counts commented on the theses:

> Here we see an all-powerful state . . . . assessing the experience of the past forty-one years, taking into account the present domestic and world situation, and guided by its apocalyptic goals, engaged in a bold, comprehensive, and imaginative effort to reconstruct radically the entire system of schools. (5.1)

The question, 'What are we trying to teach?' which Huston Smith asked in *The Purposes of Higher Education* shows that the United States of America has not yet arrived at the ideal answers. He continued:

> This is the most important question any educator can ask. It is also the one which is today being fumbled more than any other. What is the basic purpose of education? To transmit the past or to control the present? To nurture an elite or to make all men equal? To impart information or to elicit criticism? To cultivate minds alone or men as well?

> Should it take as its object man universal, stripped of all irrelevancies of time, fortune, and motivational intent, or man particular, shaped by crucial variables of culture and idiosyncracy? (6.1).

One would wonder what America had been doing all these centuries if such basic questions had not been resolved by 1955. The convocation on 'The University in America' organized on May 8–10, 1966 under the auspices of the Centre for the Study of Democratic Institutions, Santa Barbara, California is strong evidence that Smith's fundamental questions were still a live issue in the America of 1966 which has had a history of higher education dating back to the opening of Harvard College in 1638.

When Huston Smith's question is considered alongside a question raised by Aristotle years before the birth of Jesus Christ, the striking similarity tempts one to conclude that the fundamental problems of education are as controversial today as they were in Aristotle's day and have been ever since, and that each age and each culture grapples with them to the best of its ability, providing answers and solutions which may serve the peculiar circumstances of that age and culture but which may not necessarily continue to meet the needs of succeeding ages and cultures. Aristotle stated in *Politics* VIII 2:

> It is clear that there should be legislation about education . . . . But consideration must be given to the question, what constitutes education and what is the proper way to be educated. At present there are differences of opinion to the proper tasks to be set; for all peoples do not agree as to the things that the young ought to learn, either with a view to virtue or with a view to the best life, nor is it clear whether their studies should be regulated more with regard to intellect or with regard to character. And confusing questions arise out of the education that actually prevails, and it is not at all clear whether the pupils should practice pursuits that are practically useful, or morally edifying, or higher accomplishments—for all these views have won the support of some judges; and nothing is agreed as regards the exercise conducive to virtue, for to start with, all men do not honour the same virtue, so that they naturally hold different opinions in regard to training in virtue.

It is obvious from these references to movements for educational reform in some of the more developed countries that none of these countries has so far developed the ideal system of education to satisfy the demands of every age. Each generation in every culture, no matter its level of development or sophistication, faces the same fundamental questions posed by Aristotle and Smith. Its answers to those questions are inevitably and inextricably interwoven with the social, political, cultural, and economic conditions of that generation and society.

(c) *The young university must always turn to the old university for guidance.* This assumption has successfully been challenged by developments elsewhere. Recent experience shows that even within the same culture the older universities can no longer claim the monopoly for dictating the pace of development in higher education. Generally the older and more firmly rooted universities, heavily weighed down by centuries of tradition, are much slower than the newer universities in their receptivity to new ideas. The current revolution in higher education in the United Kingdom has been initiated largely by the newest universities in that country. It was the University of Keele (founded around the same time as Ibadan) for instance, which pioneered the movement which killed special relationship with London and also led to the broadening of the undergraduate curriculum among English universities. Its efforts were initially scorned, but the story is now different. Bruce Williams described the initial years in *Keele After Ten Years*:

> . . . . the decision to found Keele met with a great deal of hostility and scorn in the academic world . . . . I well remember how my academic friends pleaded with me not to end a promising career by going to Keele Part of this hostility was due to the nature of the Keele curriculum; part to the power to give degrees without a tedious apprenticeship to the University of London. It is a great and deserved tribute to Keele that new approaches to university education are now respectable and that the old system of apprenticeship is not. (7.1)

Thanks to Keele, it is now fashionable to advocate core, integrated, or common curricula among English universities.

In his assessment of the Franks Report (the report of the Oxford Commission, headed by Lord Franks), Halsy recognized the University of Sussex, opened in 1961, among the influences that have made it necessary for Oxford established in the 12th century to go over its centuries old trodden paths, with a view to restructuring them in twentieth century or even twenty-first century terms. (8.1) The fact that at the time of writing only one Nigerian university has been in existence for up to two full decades need not therefore be a handicap; on the contrary it could constitute a tower of strength.

I take the stand that Nigerian universities should accept the challenge of their age and seek their own answers to the problems of Nigerian higher education. They are more likely to succeed in doing this through 'an examination of first principles' than through the so-called pragmatic approach of attempting to transplant, graft, or adapt university models from the more developed countries. They are better placed to develop the Nigerian University than the foreign universities for which they seem to play the role of extension agencies.

Now to the objectives of university education, which is the take-off point. First, the national objectives of university education, followed by the institutional objectives of each university.

NATIONAL OBJECTIVES OF HIGHER EDUCATION

The Robbins report, considering the needs of the United Kingdom for national goals for higher education, recommended as follows:

> . . . .higher education is so obviously and rightly of great public conern, and so large a proportion of its finance is provided in one way or another from the public purpose, that it is difficult to defend the continued absence of co-ordinating principles and of a general conception of objectives. (9.1)

The report felt that "the largely unco-ordinated activities and initiatives of the past" were "not good enough" and recommended that there should be a system of higher education. Such a system would allow individual initiative to the universities, but within the framework of some co-ordinating principles. The report then went on to attempt a definition of the general aims and objectives of higher education—instruction in skills, promotion of the general powers of the mind, advancement of learning, and the transmission of a common culture and common standards of citizenship. It argued that every institution of higher learning must provide for these four essentials. The degree of emphasis on each may vary from one university to the other; but there must be "at least a speck of each in all". (9.2)

At the time I began collecting the material for this book, it was impossible to find any single document carrying a clear statement of Nigeria's national objectives for university education. Although all the universities were government-owned and financed, no serious effort appeared to have been made to provide them with statements of objectives, to enable them to know what was expected of them so that they could plan their curricula accordingly. One had to fish these objectives out in bits and pieces, from pronouncements made by the Prime Minister, Regional Premiers and other government functionaries on different occasions.

The National Curriculum Conference held in the midst of the civil war on 8–12 September, 1969 under the auspices of the Nigerian Educational Research Council attempted to define the purposes of university education in Nigeria as follows:

1. take part in the process of national development through the basic faculties of the university;
2. develop and transmit the national cultural heritage and blend this with our larger world heritage;
3. provide intellectual life sustained by an intellectual community;
4. develop national consciousness and loyalty to truth and academic honesty;
5. provoke and promote an enlightened and informed public opinion;
6. re-establish old and new values worthy of sustaining the nation;
7. co-ordinate national research under its umbrella;
8. become a catalyst for change;
9. engender a spirit of national and community service;
10. develop and encourage Nigerian human resource talents to the full;
11. encourage and develop critical and analytical attitudes;
12. create an atmosphere for love of learning and the use of knowledge;
13. foster international relations through scholarship;
14. pursue the goal of free enquiry after truth;
15. disseminate the knowledge for the use of humanity. (10.1)

A Seminar on National Policy on Education held in Lagos on 4–8 June, 1973 and which received the report of the 1969 conference,

proposed four objectives for higher education in Nigeria, namely:
(a) the acquisition, development and inculcation of the proper
value—orientation for the survival of the individual and society;
(b) the development of the intellectual capacities of individuals
to understand and appreciate their environments;
(c) the acquisition of both physical and intellectual skills which
will enable individuals to develop into useful members of the
community;
(d) the acquisition of a detached view of the local and external
environments. (11.1)

One clearly established national objective of university education
in Nigeria is the development of high-level manpower. No matter
whether it is referred to as the development and encouragement of
Nigerian human resource talents to the full, or as the acquisition of
both physical and intellectual skills to enable the individual to
develop into a useful member of the community, this is undoubtedly
one of the most frequently articulated objectives of university education in Nigeria. No society could exist without providing training
in those skills which are considered essential for its survival and
growth. The Ashby report emphasized that its recommendations
for a seven-fold increase in the capacity of universities within a ten-
year period were based on the estimates of national manpower needs
during that period:

> The foundation for our proposals about university education
> is Harbison's estimate of the need for high-level manpower.
> He believes that there must be an output of at least 2,000
> graduates a year from Nigerian universities.... We accept
> Harbison's estimate as the first objective of Nigeria's univer-
> sities. (1.3)

The second national objective of great importance is citizenship
training. The fifteen objectives listed by the 1969 National
Curriculum Conference included the development of 'national
consciousness' and 'a spirit of national and community service'.
They also included the objectives of developing and transmitting
'the national cultural heritage' and blending this with the larger
world heritage, as well as re-establishing 'old and new values worthy
of sustaining the nation'. The 1973 Seminar on National Policy on
Education listed as the first objective of higher education 'the acqui-

sition, development and inculcation of proper value—orientation for the survival of the individual and society'.

Citizenship training featured prominently in the address by the late Prime Minister of Nigeria, Alhaji Sir Abubakar Tafawa Balewa, on the occasion of his installation as the first Chancellor of Ibadan. One of the greatest tasks which he identified as confronting the governments of newly independent countries, and which the university was expected to help in solving, was the task of promoting social and political cohesion. Any person who has followed political developments in Nigeria since the attainment of independence, and particularly since 1966, will appreciate the gravity of that statement. Balewa himself was among the first casualties of the turbulent waves of political unrest in Nigeria. The declaration of the 'Republic of Biafra' on May 30, 1967 and the civil war which raged from July 1967 until mid-January 1970 were further tragic manifestations of the lack of political and social cohesion. Had 'Biafra' survived, Nigeria would have broken up not through a lack of men and women with the education in skills to keep her going, but because the education received by these men and women did not equip them to grapple with and surmount the forces of political and ethnic divisions.

The launching in 1973 of the National Youth Service Corps is evidence of the priority the Nigerian Federal Military Government now attaches to the promotion of national consciousness. The emphasis is on citizenship and leadership training. The requirement that each participant must serve for a year in a State other than his own is regarded as an effective method of promoting cohesion and national consciousness. The fact that every university graduate was required to participate, and that the programme was begun with university graduates only is undoubtedly an admission that the universities are still deficient in the provision of effective citizenship training.

The third national objective so far identified is the training of the mind. The late Balewa also mentioned this in his address:

> We therefore need the kind of education which will enable us to produce men and women who know how to think; and knowing how, to do it.... The universities' unique function is to stimulate the clash in thinking between orthodox and dissentient views. (1.2)

Balewa's address also recognised the need for an understanding of and cooperation with other national communities in Africa. The 1973 Seminar appeared silent on this objective; it could not be what they referred to as the "acquisition of a detached view of the local and external environments".

A start has been made, regardless of its belatedness, to formulate national objectives of university education. It is yet to be seen what steps are to be taken to ensure that these objectives influence the work of the universities.

INSTITUTIONAL OBJECTIVES

First, an examination of the objectives of three Nigerian universities, as contained in their official publications. The three chosen are considered representative of Nigerian universities; they are Ibadan, Lagos and Nigeria (Nsukka).

University of Ibadan

The only statement on the goals, objectives or functions of Ibadan available in the 1972–73 Ibadan Calendar appears as part of The University of Ibadan Act 1962. It reads:

> It shall be the general function of the university to encourage the advancement of learning throughout Nigeria and to hold out to all persons the opportunity of acquiring a liberal education; . . . . to provide such facilities for the pursuit of learning and the acquisition of a liberal education as are appropriate for a university of the highest standing.

None of the faculties published any statement in the Calendar on the kinds of graduates they hoped to produce. The university has not published its philosophy; there is no evidence that it has any philosophy of education. Like most of the older British universities, its charter of incorporation is the only source of information on its objectives, contrary to the practice among American universities which often devote many pages of their official catalogues or bulletins to their philosophy or goals. The newest English universities have found it necessary to publish statements defining their objectives.

The fact that Ibadan has no detailed statement of objectives makes it difficult to evaluate its academic programmes. It is difficult to express opinions on the effectiveness of any curriculum without knowing what the authors of the curriculum hope to accomplish through it. Lack of a clear statement of goals leaves room for doubt as to whether the authorities of the institution themselves have clear ideas as to what they wish to achieve. Robert M. Hutchins, in *The University of Utopia*, maintains that it is impossible to conceive of an effective educational system without first having a philosophy of education.

> Education is the deliberate attempt to form men in terms of an ideal. It is the attempt of a society to produce the type of man that it wants. . . . If it does not know the type of man that it wants, how does it judge the educational efforts it makes? 'Education without a philosophy of education' that is, a coherent statement of the aims and possibilities of education, is impossible'. (13.1)

One kind of education which Hutchins considers possible in a situation without a lucid philosophy of education is the 'custodial system' whereby a society 'decides to leave the matter to chance, providing harmless accommodation and occupation for the young until they reach maturity'. (13.2)

In the absence of objectives, the Ibadan curriculum structure could be viewed in relation to the 'general function' published in the university act. The main function appears to be to provide a liberal education for persons equipped to benefit from it. So much has been written about the two worlds 'liberal education' that it would have been of tremendous help if the Ibadan authorities had provided an interpretation of their meaning or chosen a less elastic term. As will be seen later, the same term is used in the University of Nigeria Law and yet the degree structures at Ibadan and Nsukka are miles apart.

'Liberal education' immediately calls to mind the American liberal arts college which differs from the multi-purpose university in that it restricts its offerings to the arts and sciences, leaving out the professional or vocational schools. John Henry Cardinal Newman considered 'liberal education' the main business of a university and stated that it could be achieved by training the mind rather than by preparing students for vocations. The term has been used by many other educationists to exclude professional education or training leading to any vocation which some of them argue should be carried out by institutions other than the university. The charter of one

British university made this distinction when it empowered that university to provide for 'a Liberal and Professional education'. The provision by Ibadan of degree programmes in veterinary medicine and agriculture, and the more recent addition of programmes leading to degrees in physiotherapy, medical laboratory technology, forestry, nursing and radiography would suggest that Ibadan uses the term 'liberal education' in a different sense. One possible interpretation may lie in the method rather than the content of the education it offers.

Hutchins points out that it is:

> possible to learn something from anything. . . . If the teacher is a genius, he can draw the most significant lessons from the most trivial occasions. . . . The educational program for school janitors at Teachers College, Columbia. . . . or for circus performers at Florida State University, or for teachers of driving in the University of California might be truly educational if Socrates were the teacher; for he, beginning with incidents in the life of a janitor, ... clown, or chauffeur, would undoubtedly end with the deepest philosophical conclusions about the organization of society and the destiny of man. (13.3)

Unfortunately the calendar is also silent on the methods of teaching adopted.

University of Lagos

The passage of a detailed constitution for the University of Lagos was deliberately delayed until the university had functioned for a year or two, to enable the provisional council of the university to draft a suitable constitution for presentation to the Nigerian Parliament through the Prime Minister. It had been hoped that this would be accomplished within two years of the commencement of the university. Unfortunately by January 1966 when the army took control of the country the new constitution had not passed through parliament largely as the result of the crisis in the university in 1965 over the change in vice-chancellorship. It was not until March 1967, five years after the university had been in existence, that the Federal Military Government issued Decree No. 3, The University of Lagos Decree 1967.

The University of Lagos Act, 1962 (which had been enacted to enable the university to open and operate, pending the enactment of the detailed constitution) empowered the university to 'provide courses of instruction and learning in the faculties of arts, law, medicine, science education, commerce and business administration, engineering and any other faculties which may from time to time be approved under this Act'. The objects of the university, as embodied in the 1967 Decree, closely resemble the provisions in the University of Ibadan Act, the major difference being in the use of the term 'higher education' by Lagos in place of 'liberal education' in the Ibadan Act. Also 'political conviction' is added by Lagos among the qualifications which must not be used to withhold higher education at the university from any person otherwise qualified to receive it.

In addition to the Act, Lagos has been more articulate than Ibadan in declaring its goals beyond the legal provisions of the Act. The information supplied on each faculty in its 1972–73 Calendar includes a statement on the kinds of graduates the faculty hopes to produce. What is lacking is a statement of the objectives of the institution, which would be reflected in the objectives of the various faculties and schools. The objectives of some of the faculties and schools are given below.

The objective of the School of African and Asian Studies as well as the School of Humanities are two-fold: to work closely with the College of Education in the training of graduate teachers, and secondly to develop specialist and post-graduate courses. The Schools of Administration and Social Studies declare as their objective the production of 'essential functional categories such as Administrators, Executives and Managers in Commerce, Industry and Government, as well as specialists for such staff functions as Accountants, Economists, Bankers and Marketers'. (15) The Faculty of Engineering describes the qualities of the kinds of engineers it hopes to produce— well qualified to initiate and implement engineering design, to engage in industrial management, and to accept responsibility at an early age. The engineering graduates should also be capable of engaging in research.

University of Nigeria (Nsukka)

If Ibadan has been inarticulate in making known its objectives, Nsukka has been most articulate, at least by Nigerian standards. It is the only Nigerian university which includes a chapter in its calendar on its philosophy of education.

It would appear from the documents on the establishment of the university that one of Nsukka's goals would be character develop-ment. Apart from the need to raise the population of university students in Nigeria from the ratio 1 : 70,000 of the population to an estimated 1 : 1,400 as soon as possible, the second reason given to justify the establishment of the university was character development. Reference was made to a statement by the founders of Achimota College (in Ghana) that:

> the immediate aim of African education should be to develop character, initiative, and ability of the youth of the country, so that they may be reliable, useful, and intelligent in the rapidly changing life and circumstances of their own people.

Reference was also made to the words of Sir Gordon Guggisberg that the British educational policy for Africa would fail:

> if the sole place in which the African can get his higher education and professional training is Europe. Much learning and of the best, he can get there: character-training, none.

Nsukka was meant to provide these facilities locally so that 'the foundation of Nigerian leadership shall be securely laid'. (16)

The theme of character and personality development emerges again in a document published two years later, in 1960. In an attempt to justify the establishment of the university (a proposal that received severe criticism and became an election issue), the document asserted that:

> such a Temple of Knowledge should be so organised as to give physical and spiritual poise to Nigerians and facilitate the development of their personalities as free men and free women in a free society. The University should impart knowledge to its students, teach them skills, and influence the development of their personalities constructively. It should challenge them to build a brave new world where man shall no longer be wolf to his fellow man. It should also imbue those who study within its portals with a sense of mission in the building of a new nation. (17.1)

The document hoped that the students would acquire the skills to enable them to expand the national economy and usher in an era of material prosperity, 'while at the same time developing their mental faculties that they would guard jealously the fundamental rights of man'. (17.2)

The document proceeded to stipulate a curriculum structure for the university which makes interesting reading. The degree programme would take four years for students with the West African School Certificate (or the equivalent of the General Certificate of Education at ordinary level). Such students would, however, be required to pass a matriculation examination at the end of their first year. The courses were assigned credit hours, a total of 192 being required for graduation. *1st year* 48 credit hours, leading to Parts I and II of the matriculation examinations of the university. The subjects to be studied were: Modern Language, Public Speaking, Geography of Nigeria, History of Nigeria, Ethics, Sociology, Economics, Political Science, and General Science—all in one year! Part I of the matriculation examination would consist of 7 papers, and Part II of the same number. It is not stated whether the two parts are to be taken at different times of the year: the fact that the student is required to pass the elementary stage of the foreign language in Part I and the intermediate stage in Part II suggests an interval between the two examinations. Although not mentioned among the matriculation subjects, World Literature, World Geography, and World History were to be included in the matriculation examinations. *2nd, 3rd, and 4th years:* 96 credit hours would be required in either one major subject or in two minor subjects. In addition, the student would be required to take courses totalling 48 credit hours in any subject or subjects of his choice. Students failing to qualify for degrees might receive diplomas from any Institute or College of the University.

There is no reference in the details of the curriculum or elsewhere in the document to character and personality development, suggesting that the writing of objectives and curriculum planning are two different things. It is hoped in the document that London University would grant its degrees in certain subjects, to give international currency to such professional qualifications. This would suggest a different curriculum structure for such London courses, as London University would not underwrite degrees that did not conform to its own specifications.

Apart from the 192 credit hour aggregate, the pioneer staff of Nsukka took little else from the prescribed curriculum. When the University of Nigeria Law, 1961 was enacted after the university had existed for one year, the legal objects of the university included no reference to character development:

The objects of the University are—

(i) to hold forth to all classes and communities without any distinction whatever an encouragement for pursuing a regular and liberal course of education;

(ii) to promote research and the advancement of science and learning;

(iii) to organise, improve and extend education of a University standard. (18)

The major objective in terms of undergraduate education is (i), and this hardly differs from the legal objective of Ibadan (which has already been quoted), except for the addition of the word 'regular', a word difficult to interpret in this context. In spite of this similarity, the curriculum structure in the two universities is vastly different. The 'philosophy' of Nsukka, as published in its calendar, provides clues for this difference:

> Our dedication is to breadth as well as depth in curriculum, distinguished scholarship and academic excellence, and significant contribution to the enlightenment of mankind. (19.1)
>
> . . . . the community of scholars . . . . who have gathered themselves on the plains of Nsukka have launched a venture in higher education that is somewhat different for this part of the world. They are attempting to sift out the most appropriate aspects of traditional universities, and by blending them into the Nigerian scene, to evolve a programme specifically suited to the needs and interests of the people of Nigeria, as they take their rightful place in the world community of nations. (19.2).

Even before Nsukka admitted any students, the principle of 'sifting' and 'blending' had been established. The first committee to advise on the feasibility of establishing the university comprised the Vice-Chancellor of the University of Exeter in Britain, the President and the Dean of International Programmes of Michigan State University in America, a university to which Dr. Nnamdi Azikiwe was attracted because of its land-grant philosophy. The

British and the American governments agreed to send personnel from their countries under their respective technical assistance schemes to help in getting the university firmly established. Michigan State University received the contract for selecting the American personnel: the British personnel came primarily though not exclusively from London University.

A Joint University Advisory Committee was established comprising representatives of the University of Nigeria, Michigan State University and the University of London. Although the Government of the Netherlands through the Netherlands Universities Foundation for International Cooperation (NUFFIC) also gave substantial support (to the faculty of Engineering) and some help came from the West German and Canadian Governments, the effort at Nsukka prior to the outbreak of the Nigerian civil war in 1967 was to sift what was considered appropriate to the Nigerian context, largely from American and British university traditions and blend them into the curriculum structure. As events would have it, the preponderance of American personnel in comparison with other nationals, coupled with American publicity and some of the characteristics of American foreign aid, tended to blur this picture and to convey the erroneous impression that Nsukka was an overseas campus of Michigan State University. The backlash came in 1971, with the appointment of a vice-chancellor for Nsukka who behaved as if he was allergic to American education and tried to swing Nsukka away from Michigan State University to Oxford University!

There does not appear to be any consensus among Nigerian universities on the objectives of university education. The vocational objective is generally accepted whether expressly stated in university publications or not. A major objective of Nigerian universities is to produce the nation's high-level manpower. The graduates of each university are likely to be called upon to shoulder important responsibilities much sooner after graduation than their counterparts in the developed countries.

Outside the vocational objective, there is little agreement. Is it, for instance, the function of a Nigerian university to develop character? Nsukka's *raison d'etre* would appear to agree with this, notwithstanding the fact that the university has done very little in that direction. Olubummo and Ferguson, writing from Ibadan, disagree; they argue that this is the function of the lower schools, while the function of the university is to train the mind. (3.2) With respect to enculturation, Lagos and Nsukka seem to agree with the Robbins Committee and the Nigerian Seminar on National Policy on Education that the role of the university includes "the transmission of a common culture and common standards of citizenship". (4.3) Ibadan does not agree that this can be done through formal courses.

A few quotations on the non-vocational objectives of university education may be pertinent here, especially as they tend to underscore some of the recommendations mentioned earlier when considering the national objectives of university education.

The UNESCO Tananarive Seminar on the Development of Higher Education in Africa made the following observations:

> . . . . it is felt to be of profound importance for the happiness and self-confidence of Africans as persons that their education should lead them to a greater understanding and appreciation of their own societies and cultures. The effect of education has too often been to remove them from that sense of oneness with their societies. (20.1)

The emphasis here is on cultural transmission. Hodgkin makes the same emphasis even more forcefully when he argues that the sole purpose of the African university is not to train specialists for posts of responsibility within the state. If it were, the predominance of European-centred studies might arouse no opposition, since one way of raising specialists could be by applying techniques of higher education which have been tried out in Europe and proved effective. He referred to Ortegay Gasset's thesis that the primary function of a university is the transmission of culture. If the thesis is accepted, argued Hodgkin, then African universities must regard as their function the formation of African men of culture. (21.1)

John Hanson directs his own plea to citizenship education:

> . . . . citizenship education must make its demand upon the curriculum of the higher education institutions in a particularly significant way. New nations will find they have ill-served their cause if they produce a set of experts who lack understanding of the basic problems which confront the citizen (and especially the intellectual leader) in communities confronted by both competing ideological claims and the vagaries of the economic future (22.1)

Busia, in the following comment, focuses the search light more directly on the student as an individual rather than as part of man-power statistics, the individual who emerges from the African university, the individual who is going to play a leadership role in his society. How crucial are the personal qualities of this potential leader, and what role should and can the university play in developing those qualities?

> It seems to me that there is a tendency to lay greater emphasis on what students are going *to do* than on what they are going *to become* as persons. Of all Africa's resources, her young people are the most valuable. Educators have a responsibility to consider what sort of human beings come out of the educational institutions, particularly the universities. In the last resort, it is that which will determine the role Africa plays in the world. If our concept is that education should enhance human dignity and freedom, that fact will affect the kind of university that is advocated, what is taught, and how it is taught. (23.1)

Busia's remarks need to be borne in mind by Nigerian universities as they formulate their educational objectives. A very apt illustration of their pertinence is the judgement Socrates passed on the work of Pericles as a democratic statesman:

> The brilliant statesman had enriched and embellished the city; had erected protective walls around it; had built ports and dockyards; had launched navies; had eternalized the glory of the city by temples of undying grandeur and beauty; had multiplied in Attica the feasts of arts and reason; but he did not occupy himself with the problem of how to make the Athenians better men and women. As a result his work has remained incomplete and his creation caducous. (24.1)

Sir Richard Livingstone holds a similar view when he asserts that:

> .... the influence of universities on the world is disappointingly limited; .... this is due to their being too little concerned with ends, with human values, with a philosophy of life. Yet the world at any time is good or bad according to the values which rule it and which it embodies. (25.1)

Writing earlier than Livingstone but making a similar point, Kotsching calls on the universities to define their ideal of man:

> We are bound indeed to question seriously the universities' ability to train the leaders we need. . . . We cannot conceive the quest of a New University without asking not only what ideal of learning it should advance, but also what kind of an elite it should endeavour to form. And this goes deep... . The university, having clarified its idea of truth and learning, must define its ideal of man. (26.1)

Nevitt Sanford of Stanford University regards individual development as the foremost goal of higher education and the nerve centre for the other major goals:

> I put individual development first because in my view it is the most important goal in its own right. . . . it is favourable to the achievement of all other legitimate goals. Is it our aim to preserve culture? This can best be done by individuals who have been developed to a point where they can appreciate it. . . . Preparation for a high-level profession? Good performance in any profession depends heavily on qualities found only in highly developed individuals. Ask professors of engineering to characterize a good engineer, and they will list such qualities as leadership, capacity to make wise decisions, flexibility of thinking and so on. They ask how such characteristics are to be produced, and, receiving no answer, they go back to teaching mechanics and thermodynamics. (27.1)

Olubummo and Ferguson, as already mentioned, would not agree with this if it included character training, which they do not regard as part of the function of the university. They feel the lower schools should train the whole person—the body, the mind, and character—while the function of the university should be limited to the training of the mind. Character training at university level should, according to them, be incidental; the university is a community, and community life is incidental to character training. (3.3)

The Ibadan 'formula of inception', that is the statement read at the time incepting graduates are presented for the conferment of degrees, shows a concern on the part of the authorities of Ibadan for character development. The incepting graduate is considered qualified 'in character and learning' to receive the particular degree. An incident at another Nigerian university during the 1965/66 academic year indicates similar concern. The faculty of education was unwilling to grant a degree in education to one of their students who could readily satisfy all prescribed academic requirements but who, in the view of the faculty, was not the kind of person who should be placed in charge of young pupils.

RECOMMENDATIONS

It is not my intention in this book to formulate either the broad national objectives of Nigerian higher education or to formulate specific objectives for each university. The intention is to emphasize the absolute necessity for such objectives to be formulated, and to present a few important objectives as illustrations of possible objectives. So much hinges or should hinge on these objectives, that it is difficult to imagine how the universities will develop meaningful curricula without such guide-posts. The curriculum content and structure, the extra-curricular activities, the appropriation of the university budget, the methods of teaching, student participation in university government, admission requirements—all these are linked to the objectives of the university.

(i) Reference has already been made to the recommendation of the Robbins report for national objectives in the U.K. A 1963 statement by the Nigerian National Universities Commission supports the view that Nigerian universities also require national guidelines which need not infringe upon the autonomy of each university:

> We recognize the importance of the universities being free to decide how best to meet the educational needs of the country . . . . We believe, however that this independence need not be prejudiced by a national machinery for the consideration of the needs of the country. The universities are among the most potent instruments by which our national aspirations, whether these be social, economic or cultural, can be fulfilled. We, therefore, hold that all the governments of the Federation have a special responsibility to concern themselves not only with providing the funds necessary to maintain the universities, but with the positive task of planning and developing a national and coherent system of higher education to meet the needs and aspirations of the nation. We hold, further, that investment in education is more than a social overhead. It is the very bedrock upon which all economic and social development must rest. (28.1)

(ii) Each Nigerian university needs, in addition to the national objectives of higher education, its own objectives. As Tyler rightly points out:

> . . . . if an educational program is to be planned and if efforts for continued improvement are to be made, it is very necessary to have some conception of the goals that are being aimed at. These educational objectives become the criteria by which materials are selected, content is outlined, instructional procedures are developed and tests and examinations are prepared. All aspects of the educational program are really means to accomplish basic educational purposes. Hence, if we are to study an educational program systematically and intelligently we must first be sure as to the educational objectives aimed at. (29.1)

The academic staff of each university should be involved in the formulation of these objectives and in their periodic review. This way they will not regard the institutional objectives as the utopian expressions of day dreamers on the university council or the university administration. To be effective, the objectives should not be too many. They should be clearly stated, not couched in cliches, or in such slogans as producing 'a new breed of Nigerians' or 'the watch-dogs of our nation'. Such slogans may be appropriate for soap box orations, but they hardly influence curriculum planning because of their vagueness or sometimes meaninglessness. The objectives should be contained in the calendar or other official publication of the university. They should be made known to the students so that they may know what their institution expects of them.

How to Determine Objectives

Formulation of meaningful objectives is not an easy task, but a university with its sociologists, philosophers of education, psychologists, political scientists, and subject-matter specialists should find it a truly integrating experience. This book does not propose a single method; however it puts forward a few factors that should be taken into consideration in attempting to formulate objectives.

The objectives of the university must be considered in the context of the Nigerian situation. The university is at the apex of the educational pyramid and its objectives cannot be formulated without taking into account the goals and accomplishments of the other components of the pyramid. Both the 1969 National Curriculum Conference and the 1973 Seminar on a National Policy on Education have attempted a comprehensive review of the educational system as a whole. Their reports should serve as guidelines to the universities.

A study of the student clientele is an important source of guidelines for formulating objectives. It will also enable the university to know something of the behaviour patterns of students, which is necessary if it is accepted that one of the functions of education is to change the behaviour patterns of people. If every student enters the university with a high sense of national identity, for example, it would be unnecessary for a university to focus all its energies on trying to inculcate a sense of national identity into its students.

A study of contemporary life outside the university should provide valuable suggestions for formulating objectives. Among the slogans one hears ever so often on every Nigerian university campus is that undergraduates are future leaders of the country. Leadership in what? Is it political leadership, or leadership in skills or leadership in individual integrity? A study of life outside the university, including the problems of university graduates employed in many positions and professions in Nigeria, should provide some guidelines.

For the final selection of objectives, the following quotation is pertinent:

> An educational program is not effective if so much is attempted that little is accomplished. It is essential therefore to select the number of objectives that can actually be attained in significant degree in the time available, and that these be really important ones. Furthermore. this group of objectives should be highly consistent so that the student is not torn by contradictory patterns of human behaviour. (29.1)

It is also absolutely important to recognize that the university does not exist merely to carry out the bidding of the society or community. The role of the university goes beyond being the mirror of society; it includes educating the society and providing it with the leadership which it may not always immediately appreciate for one reason or the other. In its choice of educational objectives, the Nigerian university must therefore look beyond the immediate and more obvious needs of its society; it must recognise that it has a responsibility to assist society in determining its present and future needs.

An attempt worthy of emulation was made at Nsukka in the months immediately following the end of the civil war in 1970. I call the attempt worthy of emulation, not because I was the chairman of the University's Planning and Management Committee which initiated it, but because it represents the only known attempt by any Nigerian university at a comprehensive self-study. The Planning and Management Committee which was responsible for reopening the University after the end of the war and which managed its affairs from January to November 1970, recognized the existence of conflicting schools of thought among its academic and senior administrative staff on the philosophy of Nsukka and the nature of its degree programmes. The political events of 1966 and early 1967 had resulted in Eastern Nigerian academicians and senior administrative staff as well as students from Ibadan, Lagos, Ahmadu Bello and Ife seeking refuge at Nsukka, including persons who had had little respect for the university. Some of them had resigned from Nsukka to join the staff of the University of Science & Technology which the 'Biafran' Government had decided to establish in Port Harcourt, but had again returned to Nsukka at the end of the war in January 1970 when the idea of the Port Harcourt University died a natural death. My Committee saw in the self-study an opportunity to draw the different factions together in the search for ideas to help to transform the war ravaged University into a university of which every one would be proud. We took the occasion for educational reconstruction as well.

Fourteen Committees were set up, comprising academic and administrative staff, alumni and students of the University, to study different facets of university life and submit recommendations. The following areas were to be reviewed:

> Objectives or Goals of the University, Undergraduate Education, Post-graduate Studies, Continuing (or Extra-Mural Education), Admission Policies and Procedures, the Extra-Curriculum, Residential Requirements, Campus Environment, Library Services, Administrative Structure, Academic Calendar, Continuing Self-Study, Staff Matters, and the Control and Financing of Higher Education.

The review exercise came up with the following as the objectives of the University:

(a) to advance learning;

(b) to teach modern skills relevant to national needs and the needs of the times;

(c) to provide education for good citizenship, with emphasis on Ethics, Self Reliance, Creativity, Constructive Productivity, Civic Responsibility, and the Development of Sound Body and Mind;

(d) to develop and promote indigenous culture.

Unfortunately the University of Nigeria never formally adopted these objectives because the Vice-Chancellor who took over from the Chairman of the Planning and Management Committee arrived on the campus with his blueprint for transforming Nsukka into an Oxford University located at Nsukka! Consequently he did not wish to see or hear about the comprehensive and highly educative reports of the fourteen committees.

REFERENCES

1 *Investment in Education.* Report of the Commission on Post-School Certificate and Higher Education in Nigeria, Lagos, Federal Ministry of Education, Nigeria, 1960. 1.1: p. 121; 1.2: p. 122; 1.3: p. 22

2 Central African Council. *Report of the Commission on Higher Education for Africans in Central Africa,* Salisbury, March 1953. 2.1: pp. 34–35

3 Olubummo, A. & Ferguson, J., *The Emergent University,* London, Longmans Green and Co. Ltd., 1960. 3.1: p. 21; 3.2: p. 25; 3.3: p. 25

4 Committee on Higher Education, *Higher Education* Report of the Committee appointed by the Prime Minister under the Chairmanship of Lord Robbins 1961–63, London, Her Majesty's Stationery Office, October 1963. 4.1: p. 1; 4.2: p. 224; 4.3: p. 7

5 Counts, George S., *Khrushchev and the Central Committee speak on Education,* University of Pittsburgh Press, 1959. 5.1 p. 23

6 Smith, Huston, *The Purposes of Higher Education,* New York, Harper & Brothers, 1955. 6.1: p. 1

7 *Keele After Ten Years.* Published under the auspices of the Students' Union at Keele and the Keele Society, 1961. 7.1: p. 29

8 Halsey, A.H., 'Oxford after Franks', *Universities Quarterly,* Vol. 20, No. 3 June 1966, 257–266. 8.1: p. 257

9 Committee on Higher Education, *Higher Education,* Report of the Committee.... under the Chairmanship of Lord Robbins 1961–63, London, Her Majesty's Stationery Office, October 1963. 9.1: p. 5; 9.2: p. 7

10 Nigerian Educational Research Council, *A Philosophy for Nigerian Education* (edited by Adeniji Adaralegbe), Ibadan, Heinemann Educational Books (Nigeria) Ltd., 1972. 10.1: p. 76

11 Federal Ministry of Education, *Report of the Seminar on A National Policy on Education* held in Lagos June 4th–8th 1973, Lagos, 1973 (mimeograph). 11.1: p. 22

12 'An Address by the Prime Minister of the Federal Republic of Nigeria on the occasion of his installation as the first Chancellor of the University of Ibadan', Sir Abubakar Tafawa Balewa. *West African Journal of Education*, Vol. VIII, No. 1 Feb. 1964 5–6.

13 Hutchins, Robert M., *The University of Utopia*, Chicago, The University of Chicago Press, 1st Phoenix edition 1964 (first published 1953). 13.1: p. 52; 13.2: pp. 52–53; 13.3: p. 32.

14 University of Lagos, *Calendar* 1965–66, University of Lagos, Nigeria, p. 90

15 University of Lagos, *Calendar* 1972–73, University of Lagos, Nigeria, p. 75.

16 Eastern Region, Nigeria, *University of Nigeria*, Eastern Region Official Document No. 2 of 1958, Enugu, 1958.

17 Eastern Region of Nigeria, *University of Nigeria Progress Report*, Eastern Regional Official Document No. 7 of 1960, Enugu, Government Printer, 1960. 17.1: pp. 2–3; 17.2: p. 3.

18 *University of Nigeria Law*, 1961, E.N. Law No. 21 of 1961, Supplement to Eastern Nigeria Gazette No. 75, Vol. 10, dated 21st December, 1961 — Part A. p. 4.

19 University of Nigeria, 1970—1973 *Calendar* 19.1: p. 26; 19.2: p. 24

20 UNESCO, *The Development of Higher Education in Africa*, Paris, UNESCO, 1963. 20.1: p. 48.

21 Hodgkin, Thomas, 'The Idea of an African University', *Universities Quarterly*, Vol. 12, No. 4, August 1958, 375–384. 21.1: p. 382

22 Hanson, J.W., 'The Land Grant Philosophy and African Higher Education', *West African Journal of Education*, Vol. V, No. 2, June 1962, 80–84. 22.1: pp. 83–84

23 Saunders, J.T. & Dowuona, M. (eds.), *The West African Intellectual Community*, Papers and Discussions of an International Seminar on Inter-University Co-operation in West Africa., held in Freetown, Sierra Leone, 11–16 December 1961, Ibadan, Ibadan University Press, 1962. 23.1: pp. 84–85; 23.2: p. 57.

24 Demiashkevich, M., *An Introduction to the Philosophy of Education*, New York, American Book Company, 1935. 24.1: p. 295 (quoting from Georgias, 516 ff.)

25 Livingstone, Sir Richard, *Some Thoughts on University Education*, London, Cambridge University Press, 1948. 25.1: p. 27

26 Kotschning, Walter M., 'Introduction' in *The University in a Changing World*, Walter M. Kotschning & Elined Prys (eds.), London, Oxford University Press, 1932. 26.1: pp. 8–9.

27 Sanford, Nevitt, 'Conclusions and Proposals for Change' in *College and Character*, Nevitt Sanford (ed.), New York, John Wiley & Sons, Inc., 1964. 27.1: pp. 288–289

28 Federal Republic of Nigeria. *University Development in Nigeria*, Report of the National Universities Commission, Lagos Federal Ministry of Information, 1963. 28.1: p. 20

29 University of Chicago, *Basic Principles of Curriculum and Instruction* (prepared by Ralph W. Tyler), Chicago, The University of Chicago Press, 24th impression 1966 (first published 1950). 29.1: p. 3; 29.2: p. 22.

CHAPTER 4

THE UNDERGRADUATE CURRICULUM

To provide an insight into the undergraduate curriculum in Nigerian universities, the first degree programmes of three Nigerian universities will be analysed in this chapter. Where these universities have declared their objectives, the analysis will show whether any relationships exist between such objectives and the curricula designed to achieve them.

The universities chosen for the analysis are, again, Ibadan, Lagos and Nsukka which were discussed in the chapter on objectives. These three institutions are a representative sample of Nigerian universities. Ibadan exemplifies the university college pattern of development. Nsukka occupies a unique place in the history of Nigerian education. It was the first Nigerian university to be established entirely on the initiative of Nigerians, and the first to be established by a Regional Government. It was Nigeria's first autonomous university, having granted its own degrees while Ibadan was still conferring London degrees. From all indications, it was built to teach Ibadan what a Nigerian university should be; Dr. Nnamdi Azikiwe, the brain behind its establishment, had been a severe critic of Ibadan and used his privileged position as Premier of Eastern Nigeria to establish a university tailored to his specifications. Nsukka provided the first platform for American influence on Nigerian higher education, as well as the first platform for large scale international cooperation in Nigerian higher education. Lagos lies between Ibadan and Nsukka in its approach to university education. It is the only university the Federal Government has so far established *ab initio* since the country became independent in 1960. Although the detailed analysis of the University of Ife is not included because the Ife degree structure is in many ways similar to that at Lagos, reference is made to the Ife approach to general education.

The analysis of the three curriculum patterns was based on the information contained in the official calendar of each of these universities. The limitations in the use of university calendars or catalogues for curriculum studies were recognized. In a rapidly evolving university, the calendar could be out of date in some respects before it is ready for distribution. Moreover different universities may have different views on what matters should appear and what matters should not appear in the calendar.

Dressel's statement on the use of the calendar (or catalogue) is considered an appropriate defence:

> Personal and extensive experience as a consultant on curricula matters provides at least a subjective basis for the view that a concept not reflected somewhere in the catalogue is unlikely to be a potent factor in curricular planning. . . . In any case, the catalogue is the institution's official statement on curricular matters, and it should both direct and depict actual practices and views. Otherwise, the institution has inadequately interpreted its programme to students, to parents, and to other institutions. (1.1)

I have supplemented the calendar information with personal knowledge of two of the three universities and consulted some members of the senior staff of the third university.

ANALYSIS OF CURRENT CURRICULA

University of Ibadan

The University of Ibadan offers three-year B.A. and B.Sc. degree programmes for students who enter the university with the General Certificate of Education at advanced level, the Higher School Certificate, or comparable qualifications. Students admitted with ordinary level qualifications are required to spend a preliminary year during which they study three subjects up to advanced level. Thereafter they proceed to the 3-year degree programme. The degree programmes described below are for the advanced level (or direct entry) students.

Bachelor of Arts Degree. At the time this chapter was written (1973), Ibadan had two sets of regulations for the B.A. degree—the Old Regulations and the New Regulations, as they are designated.

OLD REGULATIONS

1*st Year:* The student studies three subjects (chosen from a long list including Arabic, Islamic Culture, English, French, Hausa, History, Greek and Roman Culture, Geology, Political Science, different branches of Mathematics, Religious Studies, Sociology), leading to the Part I Examination at the end of the year.

2nd & 3rd Years: In the second year he studies either a single subject or two subjects selected from a more restricted list than for Part I (excluding the non-traditional arts subjects such as Political Science and Sociology) for the Part II examination which is taken at the end of the year. In his third and final year, he may take either one subject chosen from the same list as for Part II (save that Arabic and Islamic Studies are now combined in one subject) or he may choose from a list of possible two-subject combinations (e.g. Archaeology and Pre-History, Biblical and English Literature, English and French, Greek and Religious Studies, History and Sociology.) He sits the Part III *(i.e.* the finals) of the B.A. degree at the end of his 3rd year. The single subject students are normally required to take one or two supporting or subsidiary subjects.

It is not indicated whether the results of the Parts I and II examinations affect the final degree classification, nor whether the subject(s) for Parts II and III must have been studied for Parts I and II respectively.

New Regulations

The main difference between the old and the new regulations is the introduction of the course system. The student registers for courses rather than for subjects as such. Of the minimum of 90 course units required for graduation, at least 60 must be 2nd and 3rd year courses. Students are required to choose either 60 of the 90 units from one subject or at least 40 units each from a combination of two subjects. The subjects for the single subject or the combined subject degree are to be selected from a list of 13 subjects including Arabic & Islamic Studies, Linguistics, German, Yoruba, Mathematics, Drama, French, History.

Eligibility for a degree is determined by the student's performance in all the courses he takes, plus his performance in a final general evaluation.

Bachelor of Science Degree. Prior to October 1969, the following regulations were operative:

1st Year: Three subjects selected from a much shorter list than for Part I of the B.A. and comprising only science and marginal science subjects (e.g. Geography, Geology, Mathematics). The Part I examination was taken at the end of the year.

2nd Year: Two subjects selected from a longer list than for Part I, on the advice of a dean of faculty or department head, depending on what the student proposed to take in Part III. They led to Part II examination.

3rd Year: Either a continuation of the two subjects taken in Part II or a single subject (from a given list) which must also have been taken in Part II. The course led to Part III examination.

Eligibility for a degree and classification of the degree depended on performance in Parts II and III. The student was also required to demonstrate proficiency in French, German or Russian.

The New Regulations which came into force in October 1969 are similar to the New Regulations for the B.A. degree, except that no list of subjects is published in the 1972/73 Calendar of the University.

Professional degrees: In professional subjects like Agriculture, Veterinary and Human Medicine, the entire curriculum is devoted to the professional studies and any other subjects considered relevant to the professional programme. In Agriculture, for example, the student includes such subjects as Chemistry and Economics in the Part I examination. Here again there are no statements to indicate the objectives of the various programmes.

OBSERVATIONS

The Old and the New Regulations described above illustrate some of the major curriculum changes which have taken place in Ibadan since the institution attained full university status in 1962. The Old Regulations came as a major departure from the pre-1962 structure. Prior to its introduction, a student registered for an honours degree spent his three years at the college specializing in one subject only. Whatever he studied outside this subject (subsidiary or ancillary subjects) were calculated to facilitate his mastery of his special subject. The students registered for 'general' degrees in arts or science were required to study three subjects for the three years: the general degree which they obtained at the end of it was normally considered inferior to the single subject honours degree, no matter what the student's level of performance. Holders of the general degree were not often accepted for graduate studies at Ibadan or in British universities, and employers of labour in Nigeria also discriminated against them. The isolated voices which emphasized the advantages of the general degree received little hearing and made little impact.

The Ibadan pattern of honours and general degrees was imported from Britain, being the pattern in vogue in London University and most other English universities at the time. In view of the mounting dissatisfaction in Britain with the excessive and narrow specialization of the honours degree, the new English universities struck out in a new direction with degree programmes designed to remedy the ills of narrow specialization.

The University of Keele pioneered the idea of a compulsory general education in English universities. Every first year student at Keele was required to take 'foundation year' courses in the humanities, social sciences and natural sciences. Following the foundation year, the student registered for an honours course in two principal subjects, and was also required to take two subsidiary subjects. In the choice of these subjects, he was usually allowed a free hand (subject to the limitations of the time table) provided he put 'at least a toe across to the other side of that great divide between the arts and the sciences'. In this way the idea of integration which featured in the discussions that preceeded the founding of Keele was achieved. In view of the foundation year requirement, the undergraduate course at Keele takes four years (for students with the General Certificate of Education at advanced level) instead of three years as in other English universities.

Although the English universities established in the 1960s have not replicated the Keele foundation year programme nor lengthened their degree programmes to four years, they definitely accepted the idea of cutting down on narrow specialization and emphasizing as much as possible the unity of learning. The idea, as Lord James of Rusholme, Vice-Chancellor of the University of York put it, is 'to organize the curriculum so that the student has interests wider than those of a narrow specialist field'. (2) The University of Sussex which admitted its pioneer students in October 1961 led the way by abolishing the traditional department and faculty and replacing them with multi-subject schools.

The purpose of the Sussex experiment was to provide for its students the combined effects of 'specialized' and 'general' education. Sussex discarded the idea of requiring the student to study 'a multitude of unrelated subjects side by side or one after the other'; rather it required each student 'continuously to relate his specialized study to impinging and overlapping studies'. In this way, it expected to produce 'not only an educated person but potentially, at least, a better specialist' who would 'know about the bearings of a subject as well as about its content'. (3.1) The degree structure for all undergraduates was essentially the same; its objective was to ensure that each Sussex graduate had been trained 'to compare, to relate and to judge'.

Keele and Sussex symbolize the major post-World War II 'revolution' in English higher education, a revolution from the excessive specialization characteristic of English higher education but not total conversion to the American-type undergraduate curriculum with hardly any recognizable specialization. Their efforts have been described in some detail not because they are perfect, but to illustrate the progressive trend in British higher education for purposes of comparison with the Ibadan curriculum pattern which also came from the United Kingdom. Ferguson's 'Ibadan Arts and Classics' claims that the post-1962 Ibadan degree structure has also been designed to give breadth as well as depth. This may be so: what is surprising is that Ibadan should decide to copy British curriculum patterns which were being overtaken by developments within the same country. Perhaps it was in quest of 'a system which was there and worked,' in preference to new ideas that had not yet stood the test of time. Sir Eric Ashby had some pertinent comments on this decision by Ibadan:

> While the Asquith colleges were in special relationship with the University of London. . . . they had no option but to adopt the London degree pattern. . . . But when they acquired their independence they had an opportunity, rare in the life of any university, to plan anew and to make considered adaptations to African needs. . . . The University of Ibadan made enlightened changes in the structure of its courses in economics and social studies and introduced a B.Ed. degree in the Faculty of Education. But it seemed to me that the Faculty of Arts at Ibadan, however enlightened the *content* of its courses might be, had kept a structure which seemed to have disregarded recent trends in Britain and to have given insufficient weight to the kind of education which most Nigerian arts graduates are likely to need. (4.1)

The disregard by a Nigerian university of trends in Britain need not of itself necessarily merit criticism unless the trends are relevant to the Nigerian situation. Ibadan invoked the criticism on itself because its fourteen years of apprenticeship appeared to have provided it with experience in adapting the *content* of degree syllabuses (to give it what the early Ibadan undergraduates termed 'African bias') rather than in developing basic principles for curriculum development. While celebrating its independence from London, it could not attain independence from British-type curriculum patterns which every British university established since 1960 had gladly discarded. Ashby went on to ask:

> Was it wise for an arts faculty, able to plan *ab initio* and to rethink its whole structure in 1962, to omit from its pattern of courses (which must be distinguished from their *content*) any of the fruits of the re-thinking of its contemporaries also planning arts curricula, in England? (4.2)

It is not clear how much the Ibadan student registering under the post-1962 Old Regulations gains by being subjected to three subjects (which need not be related) in his first year. Each of these subjects is planned independently by the department which teaches it, and possibly consists of first year courses leading to advanced courses for students majoring in those subjects rather than terminal courses designed to provide a context for students majoring in other areas.

Considering that the three subjects are taken in the first year and do not count towards degree classification, it is not clear in what recognizable respect the post-1962 single subject honours graduate would be any different from his pre-1962 counterpart: each of them would qualify for graduation on his performance in one subject. And statistics show that most arts students enroll for the single subject honours programmes. Of the students admitted to first degrees in the Faculty of Arts in 1972, 199 were for single subject degrees while only 24 were admitted to degrees in combined (*i.e.* two) subjects.

It is clear from the arts and science curricula that the Ibadan concept of breadth consists of requiring the student to add more subjects to his programme rather than providing all students with a common core of knowledge. It is also clear that Ibadan does not accept the view that the university should enculturate its students through formal courses. Ferguson stated in his 'Ibadan Arts and Classics' that an Ibadan Board of Studies rejected the idea of a compulsory course in African Studies for its students. Here again Ashby posed a question:

> Since many arts graduates are likely to enter the government service or teaching, and are therefore likely to be dealing either with indigenous social problems or with children in rural backgrounds, would it be desirable for all arts students to have (as the De La Warr commission proposed a generation ago, and as students do in the universities of the West Indies, Lagos, Nigeria, and Ghana) some acquaintanceship with the study of indigenous societies, law, custom, and administration? (4.2)

It is probable that the Ibadan answer would have been in the affirmative had this been the prevailing practice in the United Kingdom. It happens not to be, so the Ibadan response has been negative. The reasons advanced by Ferguson for this negative response will be considered in the next section along with the General African Studies course at the University of Lagos.

If one may digress a little, the 3. 2. 2., 3. 2. 1., or 3. 1. 1. degree structure which Ibadan adopted in 1962 and appears to be modifying slightly with its introduction of the course system has only recently been introduced at the University of Ghana, Legon. The Vice-Chancellor proudly announced the introduction of the 'new' degree structure at the 1972 degree convocation, as one of the innovations the University was about to launch!

The new Ibadan regulations resemble the old in one essential respect—a student can graduate with honours by studying one subject only, plus subsidiaries if prescribed. There is no evidence that a common core of courses is required of students in any faculty, nor of all students irrespective of faculty.

It is possible that the gradual introduction of the course system in the United Kingdom has propelled Ibadan into introducing courses in the 1970s.

University of Lagos

Bachelor of Arts. The goal of the School of African and Asian Studies and the School of Humanities is to work closely with the College of Education in the training of graduate teachers; in addition, the two schools are expected to develop specialist and post-graduate courses. Students intending to teach on graduation are permitted (as at the University of Keele) to take concurrently with their normal requirements for the B.A. (or B.Sc.) degree a course in the theory and practice of education, to undertake practical teaching during the vacations as prescribed by the faculty of education and to pass the prescribed examinations for the Diploma in Education which they will receive along with their B.A. (or B.Sc.). Alternatively they may be allowed to register for the one year Diploma in Education course after completing the requirements for the B.A. (or B.Sc.).

As at Ibadan, the three-year degree programme is designed for students entering the university with the General Certificate of Education at advanced level (or similar advanced qualifications). The B.A. degree is taken in three parts like other first degrees, although performance in Part I does not affect the degree classification (which is based only on performance in Parts II and III).

1st Year: According to the Lagos 1972/73 Calendar, the student takes three subjects to be selected from a list comprising English, Geography, History, Mathematics (one subject), Mathematics (two subjects), Economics or Political Science, French, Hausa, Yoruba, Igbo, Philosophy, Edo. In addition to the three subjects, he must take a course entitled General African Studies. He must pass in all four subjects to proceed to the second year, though his grades would not affect his degree classification.

2nd Year: The student takes two of the Part I subjects (excluding Economics, Political Science, Edo and Igbo). It is not stated whether these subjects must have been taken in Part I. In addition it is stated that he must take Introduction to Science and Technology, though no examination will be set in that subject. (It is, however, understood that the Introduction to Science and Technology course is no longer offered). At the end of the year he takes the Part II examination in the three subjects and his performance counts towards his degree classification.

3rd Year: The student continues with the two subjects he studied for Part II or, exceptionally, with one of them for the Part III examination at the end of that year. (The list of students admitted to degrees of the University in June 1972, however, showed a higher number in the single subject category than in the combined subjects category).

Bachelor of Science. The degree structure is essentially the same as for the Bachelor of Arts degree.

1st Year: Three subjects to be chosen from a list comprising Biology, Botany, Chemistry, Geography, Mathematics (one subject), Mathematics (two subjects), Physics, Zoology, plus General African Studies, all four to be taken as Part I. Mathematics (one subject) cannot be taken along with Mathematics (two subjects). The student must pass in all four subjects, but his performance will not affect his degree classification.

2nd Year: Two subjects out of the three taken in Part I (excluding General African Studies and Biology). There was to be a compulsory course entitled Introduction to Modern Thought but it is understood that it has not been taught for some time. The two subjects lead to the Part II examination, performance in which counts towards the class of degree the student receives.

3rd Year: The two subjects of Part II (excluding Introduction to Modern Thought), or, exceptionally, one only, leading to Part III. (17 students received degrees in single subjects in 1972, while 24 qualified for degrees in combined subjects.) Students taking single subjects in Part III are required to attain some proficiency in French, German or Russian. Performance in Part III counts towards degree classification.

Professional Degrees. Courses leading to professional qualifications are offered in the Colleges of Education and Medicine, the Schools of Administration, Environmental Design, the Faculties of Engineering and Law, and the Institute of Mass Communication. As each of the other faculties have stated goals, it would be relevant to compare these with the respective curricula calculated to help in achieving them.

School of Administration. The School of Administration and the School of Social Studies aim at producing 'essential functional categories such as Administrators, Executives and Managers in Commerce, Industry and Government, as well as specialists for such staff functions as Accountants, Economists, Bankers and Marketers'. (5.1) The degree courses are designed specifically to meet the needs of Nigeria in a way similar programmes overseas cannot do. 'The curriculum anticipates specialization in business, political science, accounting and economics'. (5.1) The courses are intended to have 'a practical orientation' (5.1) and opportunities will be provided for part-time employment for the students and liaison maintained with commerce, industry, etc. The courses in the two Schools lead to honours degrees of B.Sc. in Accounting, Business Administration, Economics or Political Science. The Structure in the School of Administration is as follows:

1st Year: All students in the faculty take a common core of six compulsory subjects: Principles of Accounting and Elements of Costs (Accounting I), Principles of Economics, Elements of Business, Elements of Government, General African Studies, and Mathematics for Social Sciences. The Part I examination is taken at the end of the year.

2nd Year: The students separate into their special subjects, i.e. Accountancy or Business Administration, taking only courses related to these subjects or which facilitate an understanding of them. The courses lead to Part II examination.

3rd Year: The students prepare for Part III in their respective subjects.

Faculty of Engineering. The Faculty of Engineering aims at producing graduates who will be well qualified to operate and develop the public services, to initiate and carry out engineering design, to engage in industrial management and to pursue development and research. In a country developing at such a rapid rate as Nigeria, it is to be expected that university graduates in engineering will individually need and will utilize a wider range of general engineering knowledge than is customary in long established industrial communities. They will also be required to accept responsibility at an unusually early age. These facts will influence the structure of the engineering course which will be general in character. Adaptation in the approach to laboratory work and in teaching methods will also be made to meet local requirements. (5.2)

'While there should be relatively little specialization at the undergraduate level, it is thought that the development of a special interest in one branch will be a stimulus to study'. (5.2)

1*st Year:* All students in the faculty take General African Studies, Mathematics and seven other subjects related to engineering, all leading to Part I.

2*nd Year:* All students take Mathematics and a Language (French, German or Russian) in common. The bulk of each student's work is taken in his proposed branch of engineering, civil, electrical and mechanical, leading to Part II. The examination includes an assessment of laboratory and practical work throughout the year.

3*rd Year:* As in the 2nd year, all students take some Mathematics while the bulk of each student's work is taken in his proposed branch of engineering.

Observations. Like Ibadan, Lagos attempts to reduce specialization by increasing the number of subjects students are required to take. There is, however, one major difference between the Ibadan and the Lagos curriculum structures: all Lagos students are required to take General African Studies, irrespective of the faculty or school to which they belong.

In its earlier years, Lagos required its science students to take a course entitled Introduction to Modern Thought, while its non-science students were required to take a course entitled Introduction to Science and Technology. The introduction of non-science students to science and technology and the science students to modern thought was presumably an attempt at putting (to quote Keele again) 'at least a toe across to the other side of that great divide between the arts and the sciences'. It was part of an effort to foster co-operation between faculties. In a country where many students enter the university without any acquaintance of any kind with science and the scientific method, it is understandable why such introductory courses should be contemplated. It is significant that Lagos considered it essential to expose each student to something of another main body of learning, and that this exposure was considered important enough to affect the student's degree classification. The University, however, appears to have had a change of heart in

recent years. These requirements appear to have been dropped.
A professor at the University remarked that they just didn't work.

The idea of a General African Studies requirement for all students
had been rejected by Ibadan, according to Ferguson's 'Ibadan
Arts and Classics'. Ferguson stated that it had been rejected for
the following reasons:

> Firstly, such a course had been tried in Ghana under an
> exceptionally able director, and conversation with Ghanaian
> students suggested that it was unpopular and was tending
> to kill any real interest in African Studies.... Secondly,
> there is a major problem about any compulsory subject.
> If it is not examined, it is not taken seriously. If it is examined,
> you are confronted with a prospect of failing, say, a first-
> class chemist because he cannot write critical essays on
> African Studies. Ghanaian students feel that the need for a
> pass in African Studies is a millstone round their necks.
> Thirdly, the Nigerian members of the Board felt that the
> whole thing was too self-conscious; an English undergraduate
> does not have compulsory European studies; our culture
> surrounds us as the air we breathe. Fourthly, the general
> life of the university offers innumerable chances for African
> studies. Traditional art is displayed in public places. Dancing
> groups perform in the courts.... There is a Society for the
> Promotion of African Culture.... Fifthly, and most vitally,
> it was generally agreed that relevance is achieved, not by
> adding an extra subject to the curriculum, but by the way
> in which the subject is taught. (6.1)

It would not be fair to regard the view above as the official Ibadan
stand on the teaching of a compulsory course in African studies.
It is doubtful whether the university senate could reject a serious
proposal on the strength of an uncorroborated 'conversation with
Ghanaian students'. Also Ibadan could not have changed voluntarily
from the single subject honours to its post-1962 structure (Old
Regulations) in which a first-class historian may fail because of his
inability to pass a Part I examination in French, if it endorsed
Ferguson's second reason. Nor could it have increased the number
of first year subjects if it adopted his fifth reason. The reference to
Nigerian members of the Board of Studies implies a rejection of the
proposal by Nigerians. Significantly, the Vice-Chancellor of the
University of Lagos at the time Lagos introduced the General

African Studies course was a Nigerian who had served at Ibadan as professor, head of department and dean of faculty. The pertinent point in the passage, and which is a controversial issue in many academic circles, is the contention that cultural transmission need not be effected through formal courses. Also significant is the reference to 'an English undergraduate', regardless of the dissimilarity between conditions in Nigeria at the time and the situation in England.

The rationale for the Lagos requirement on General African Studies may be found in a speech by its first Vice-Chancellor at the formal opening of the University of Lagos Medical School:

> One of the oldest criticisms of universities is that if not properly organised they become merely degree producing factories and fail to bring about the development and enrichment of the individual which should foster in him a sense of social and civic responsibilities which it implies. In addition to this, our special circumstances in Africa lay upon us the duty of ensuring that our students develop an awareness of local problems and aspirations, cultivate the ability to analyse and seek solutions to those problems, and play their due role in the realization of national aspirations. (7.1)

He describes two main approaches to the problem of providing a general or liberal education as well as a more specialised or vocational education. One of these is by providing a diversity of disciplines and enabling the students to educate one another through contact with staff and other students with divergent interests. The second is through lengthening of the university course so as to devote the earlier years to formal general education. He considers both approaches unsuitable for Lagos. The first approach—leaving it to the student to educate himself—agrees with Ferguson's argument. The Vice-Chancellor ruled out the second because many students cannot afford the additional costs of an extra year in the university. 'We are left with only one line of action: To find a solution to the problem of broadening the students' education without increasing the years of study unduly'. (7.2)

One method of evaluating the General African Studies requirement would be through a detailed study of the students who have been exposed to the course, probably in comparison with Ibadan students who have not but whose degree programmes are comparable in other respects. The fact that the course is disposed of in the first year, and that performance in it does not affect degree classification, may tend to minimise its impact on the students, who could view it as a hurdle they must leap over before they can move on to the subjects that count. It is, however, significant that the course has remained a requirement for every student even after the Introduction to Modern Thought and the Introduction to Science and Technology courses had been given up.

The Lagos solution to the problems posed by its Vice-Chancellor reveals an interesting approach to curriculum planning. Convinced of the importance of the common 'general' courses, but unwilling to lengthen the duration of the programme, the university simply added these additional courses to the normal Ibadan curriculum. To cut down on the Ibadan subject requirements might have given the impression that the Lagos degree was cheaper. The result is more work for the Lagos students; the degree of thoroughness with which they will do the additional work remains to be seen.

In addition to the common requirements for all students already described, Lagos differs from Ibadan in the provisions of some core requirements for students within certain faculties or schools (see Faculty of Engineering and School of Administration) which make for greater integration within such faculties or schools.

It is claimed in the objectives of both the School of Administration, the School of Social Studies and the Faculty of Law that each school or faculty aims at producing administrators among other categories of executives and specialists. The Schools of Administration and Social Studies hope their programmes would produce 'Administrators, Executives and Managers in Commerce, Industry and Government'. (5.1) The Faculty of Law, in almost identical language, hopes to produce 'the administrators so urgently needed in Government service, industry and commerce'. (5.4) When the degree requirements in the three academic divisions are compared, the only course common to all three is the General African Studies course. The degree programmes in the Schools of Administration and Social Studies have some courses in common in the first year (e.g. Principles of Economics, Elements of Government and Elements of Social Relations), but most of the similarity disappears after the first year. Thus essentially different curricula are each claiming to inculcate identical qualities into the students taking them.

A further dimension to the issue is Ferguson's claim in 'Ibadan Arts and Classics' that Ibadan graduates in Classics have fitted admirably into administrative positions in the diplomatic service, business and industry, investment, building society and even economic planning. (6.2) This might suggest that practically any combination of courses or any discipline could produce administrators, and that the claims by the Lagos schools and faculty deserve no particular attention. It is doubtful whether the Deans of the Lagos Schools and Faculty under reference can pinpoint what in their curricula is responsible for producing these administrators (except, of course, in respect of the degree programme in administration).

After reading the claim by the Faculty of Law to produce 'a well-educated and well-rounded graduate who understands the economic and social environment in which the law operates', one is at a loss to see from the 1972–73 Calendar which courses within the Law degree programme are aimed at achieving this objective. Contrary to the claim on p. 76 of the Calendar that the 'subjects included in the curriculum are not exclusively legal ones', all the courses listed on pp. 112–114 *are* legal ones, with the lone exception of the General African Studies course. The introductory course in Economics appears to exist only as a declaration of intent— so the French language requirement.

With regard to the engineering curriculum, the faculty appears to be torn between two approaches to the training of engineers. One approach places the emphasis on general engineering training, equipping the students with the basic principles which would help them to fit into any branch of engineering on graduation, allowing settling-in time. The second is the traditional approach of training civil, electrical, mechanical, chemical and other types of engineers, each in his different compartment. The Lagos engineering curriculum aims at providing a course 'general in character' and with 'relatively little specialization at the undergraduate level'. This will give the graduates 'a wider range of general engineering knowledge than is customary in long established industrial communities'. The faculty, on the other hand, recognizes that the Nigerian engineer will 'be required to accept responsibility at an unusually early age', a responsibility that will include operating and developing public services, initiating and implementing engineering designs, and research. The result is a curriculum that appears too heavily loaded in the first year with eight courses in engineering (if you include what is described as General Engineering), and one in General African Studies, making nine in all. Although the introductory statement claims that the undergraduate curriculum would contain little specialization, after the first year the students divide into the traditional compartments of civil, electrical, and mechanical engineering, with very little common to all three except a common Mathematics course and another course called Engineering Technology. For the Part III examination there are no common courses except a Mathematics course. Since Part I does not affect degree classification, the first year core curriculum in effect prepares the students for launching into their special branches in engineering.

University of Nigeria (Nsukka)

The Nsukka curriculum is the outcome of the effort to sift out and blend, and it turned out to be in effect a median between the traditional excessive specialization of the British and the generous breadth of the American bachelor's degree. The curriculum structure is essentially the same for all degree programmes, professional or non-professional, with appropriate adjustments for engineering and other courses which last one year longer than most other degree programmes.

The typical 4-year programme (designed for students entering with ordinary level qualifications) comprises:

General studies: 27 credit hours (48 credit hours until 1971)

Major subject: credit hours vary: normally 96–120, but occasionally dropping as low as 78 for subjects such as Estate Management in the Faculty of Business Administration or soaring up to 140 for English.

Subsidiary subjects and electives: credit hours vary; usually well below 60, though occasionally going up to 100 or above in subjects such as Estate Management which require a knowledge of other related subjects.

Two of the three general studies courses are completed in the first year, and the remainder in the second year, except in a few faculties where the arrangements differ slightly. The total credit hour requirement for the 4-year programme is between 192 and 220.

For the benefit of readers unfamiliar with credit hours and electives, some definitions would be helpful. One credit hour is generally assigned per term for each time the class meets in one week, the usual duration of a meeting being one hour. A class which meets four times per week would therefore carry 4 credit hours per term or 12 credit hours per session (of three terms); a class meeting once a week would carry 1 credit hour per term, and so on. For practicals in laboratories, for art studio classes, or such classes which do not require prior preparation outside the class, two hours of class meeting per week usually carry 1 credit hour instead of 2.

Electives refer to courses offered within or outside the student's department from which the student is free to choose which to take. They differ from the major and subsidiary courses which are normally required courses for students within the department.

The typical 3–year programme for students admitted with advanced level qualifications differs from the 4–year programme in two respects. The general studies requirement is reduced to two courses totalling 18 credit hours, the use of English course being one of them and the second being a general studies course not related to the student's major field. The first year course in his major subject and a course in his subsidiary subject or an elective course are also waived depending on his qualifications, leaving him with a total credit hour requirement ranging between 144 and 180. He generally completes the general studies requirements in his first year, when they occupy less than 50% of his time.

EXAMPLES

	4–year programme Credit hours	3–year programme Credit hours
Bachelor of Arts in History		
General studies	27	18 (English & Natural Science)
Foreign language (2 years)	18	18
History (Including Archaeology)	141	114
Electives	18	18
	204	168

Bachelor of Science in Zoology

General studies	27	18 (English & Social Science or Humanities)
Zoology	62	62
Microbiology	4	4
Biology	39	27
Chemistry	12	—
Physiology	9	9
Plant-Soil Science	3	3
Statistics	12	12
Electives	30	15
	198	150

Law

General Studies	27	18 (English & Natural Science or Social Science)
French or Economics (one year)	9	—
Law	168	156
	204	174

Bachelor of Science in Electrical Engineering

	5–year programme Credit hours	4–year programme Credit hours
General studies	27	18 (English & Social Science)
Mathematics	33	21
Physics	12	—
Civil Engineering	13	13
Mechanical Engineering	39	39
Electrical Engineering	110	110
Electives, including Electrical Engineering electives	8 or 10	8 or 10
Introduction to Engineering	6	—
	240 or 242	209 or 211

B.A. or B.Sc. in combined subjects. The student chooses two subjects, (from the same Faculty in the Faculties of Arts and Science, or from combinations of two subjects drawn from the Faculties of Arts and Sciences). He takes 60–78 credit hours in each subject. Departments are encouraged to map out for these students what courses to take within their departments; in some cases these programmes include electives. The general studies requirement is unchanged.

Observations. Nsukka's major innovation in Nigerian higher education is its compulsory general studies programme, the function of which is 'to establish the broad basis of knowledge required for effective modern citizenship and to indicate the unity of existence by stressing the inter-relationship of all knowledge'. In conjunction with the student's major studies, the general studies programme 'prepares the graduate for useful service to Nigeria and mankind, in any place or in any capacity in which he finds himself'. (8.1) The programme is divided into four sections:

(a) The use of English, aimed at the improvement of writing as well as 'reading speed and comprehension'. (8.3) It carries 9 credit hours.

(b) Social Science, aimed at providing "an understanding of the scope and character of the disciplines of the social sciences and the relatedness of the knowledge represented by these disciplines". There is special emphasis on the application of this knowledge "to problems and issues of contemporary man and his social order", (8.3) with particular reference to Nigeria. This course carried 15 credits initially; the credit load was reduced to 9 following a review of the General Studies programme.

(c) Natural Science, aimed at tracing broadly 'the history and development of science' and considering 'the more important principles and concepts of the sciences, and the methods of acquiring scientific information'. The objective is 'to stimulate interest in science, establish the interrelationship between scientific disciplines, and create an awareness of the services of science to man and the effect of science on human society'. (8.3) The credit hours dropped from 12 to 9, in the bid to reduce the time given to General Studies in the degree programme.

(d) Humanities, which analyses 'the chief aspects of culture through exploring the creative action of man and the philosophy, religion, literature, arts and music of the three major cultural aggregates— African, Islamic and Western—in Nigeria, and seeks to set the whole

inter-relatedly in historical context'. (8.3) The credit hours dropped from 12 to 9 for the reason given above.

The general studies courses form a common core of learning for all students of the university, regardless of their special subjects. They provide a common topic for discussion between the engineering student and the music student. They also form a point of contact between lecturers from various disciplines who co-operate to draw up the curriculum and teach the courses. The programme represents the body of knowledge the university feels should constitute the common denominator for every Nsukka graduate. Until 1967, students on the 4–year degree programme were required to complete the four courses, while the student on the 3–year programme took two of the four. The review of the general studies programme referred to above resulted in a reduction in the requirements for the 4–year degree programme from four to three general studies courses.

Since the distinguishing feature in the Nsukka curriculum is the general studies requirement, it would seem fair to regard the programme as the panacea to many of the short-comings Nsukka was meant to rectify. If the programme is of such tremendous importance, it appears surprising that the bulk of it should be taken in the student's first year at the university and the programme completed two years before the student graduates. It is also surprising that the advanced student should be exempted from part of it in order not to lose anything in his special field, bearing in mind that his advanced level qualifications are not comparable with the general studies courses. Even more surprising is the outcome of the review of the programme already referred to, carried out during the 1966/67 academic year and implemented after the end of the Nigerian civil war, during the 1971/72 academic year. The review brought out the prejudice among staff to the programme. Not only were the overall credit hours for the four courses reduced, but also the credit hour requirements for the 4–year and the 3–year degree programmes were slashed down from 48 and 27 (or 24) to 27 and 18 respectively. The credit hours gained were in most cases piled on to the student's major subject(s).

The pioneer Nsukka graduates surprised even their lecturers by their remarkable performance in the 1963 competitive examination for entry to the administrative and certain other classes of the Western Nigeria public service. In view of the nature of that examination, it was believed that the high performance of the Nsukka graduates resulted from the foundation they received in the general studies programme. These pioneer graduates had the worst taste of general studies compared with succeeding students, having passed through Nsukka at the time few of their lecturers had clear conceptions of the general studies programme. In addition, the 1963 record of performance does not appear to have been maintained in the years immediately following. It is therefore doubtful whether the general studies programme was responsible for the 1963 achievement. It would be helpful to find out more about the competitors from Ibadan (the only other graduate-producing university in Nigeria at the time) and from overseas universities.

A study is also necessary to assess the impact of the general studies programme on the Nsukka students. Apart from some adaptation to local materials in the *content* of the courses, the general studies programme is roughly an abridged form of the general education programme at Michigan State University, which supplied the leadership for the Nsukka programme in its crucial formative period. Although the programme claims to prepare the Nsukka graduate for "useful service to Nigeria and mankind, in any place or in any capacity in which he finds himself", the emphasis appears to have been to adapt the Michigan State University type of programme to Nigerian conditions rather than to investigate the peculiar problems of citizenship in Nigeria and develop a programme to grapple with these problems. Many lecturers and students at Nsukka would be surprised to learn that there are other approaches to general education and citizenship training in American universities, and that some of them are considered more progressive than the pattern at Michigan State University. The following remarks by Professor Lewis B. Mayhew on the decline of the general education movement in America may also surprise them:

> General education, once regarded as a panacea for fragmentation of the curriculum, over-specialization and over-emphasis on science and practicality, is at present in an uneasy state. The action of Columbia College in suspending Contemporary Civilization B, of Chicago in restoring undergraduate responsibility to the divisions, of the seminar effort at Harvard as a fit substitute for general education courses for some students and of the University of Minnesota in abolishing the essential power of its division of general education, all suggest that the movement has expended its dynamic. (9.1)

Regardless of the fate of the general education movement in the United States, serious questions could be raised about the Nsukka general studies programme as it now stands. How possible is it to accomplish all the lofty aims of the programme in less than two terms' work? At Michigan State University and other American universities where such programmes exist, they occupy two years of the four-year curriculum. In spite of this, one of the criticisms of that approach to general education, as stated by Dressel (who was for many years Assistant Provost and Director of Institutional Research at Michigan State University) is that the major divisions of knowledge are many, and each would require several courses for a thorough understanding. To attempt to cover these divisions with a few courses only leads to no more than a quick tour which makes the student realise that knowledge exists but does not allow him to grasp its essence. (10.1) The position becomes much more serious when the period of study is reduced from two years to less than two terms. Nsukka, however, considered it necessary to limit the general studies programme initially to one year and later to less than two terms because of the fear that its graduates would suffer discrimination in the labour market or in gaining admission to graduate schools unless they covered roughly as much ground in their major fields as their counterparts in other Nigerian universities particularly at Ibadan. In fairness to them, the mere existence of a general studies programme decided many employers, secondary school principals and even members of the National Universities Commission early in the life of the University that the Nsukka degree was bound to be inferior to the Ibadan degree.

Dressel also went on to critize the use of English component of the general education programmes of American universities (the one requirement which Nsukka now makes compulsory for all its students):

> Despite widespread continuance of the requirement, there is no great satisfaction with it. Communication skills are broad objectives which should be of concern in all college courses. So long as the responsibility for writing or other communication skills is assigned to a single course at the freshman year, it may be expected that the dissatisfaction will continue. Typically, English departments have the responsibility for this course, but they are not always well prepared to fulfil it. The staff is generally trained in highly specialized aspects of literature. (10.2)

Leaving the general studies programme for the moment, there is nothing in the Nsukka calendar to suggest that anything special is being done to provide character training for the students. To spotlight this omission is not necessarily to assert that the university must train character. The omission is glaring because of the tremendous emphasis placed on character training in the documents leading to the establishment of the university. It is an omission likely to occur where there is little communication between the persons who formulate institutional objectives and the persons who develop the curricula and extra-curricular experiences for realising those objectives.

As with the Lagos Faculty of Law, the pre–1971 Nsukka law curriculum required one year of French. The Professor of French at Nsukka made it clear in 1965 that a year of French had little meaning. However the Faculty of Law was unwilling to reduce the number of required law courses so as to enable more time to be given to French. They did not want their law degree to be considered inferior to the law degrees given by Ahmadu Bello, Lagos and Ife. Their latest (1972/73) degree programme now exempts the direct entry student from the French course. It retains the course in the 4–year programme, but gives the student the option to take a course in Economics instead.

With regard to the major area component of the Nsukka curriculum, there is little difference between it and the curriculum pattern at Ibadan after the first year (for the three-year advanced level student), especially in the arts and science faculties. The two general studies courses he takes in his first year in addition to courses in his major subject take the place of the two extra subjects the Ibadan student takes in his first year. In his remaining two years both the Nsukka and the Ibadan student would take a single subject (with electives or subsidiaries, where required); in a few cases they would take two subjects leading to degrees in combined subjects. The obvious difference is that Nsukka has adopted the course system from its inception, with outlines and credit loads of the various courses making up the degree programme clearly set out in its Calendar. Ibadan has only recently decided to adopt the course system; Lagos is considering following suit, as Ife has already done.

GENERAL COMMENTS

In the preceding pages, an attempt has been made to describe and evaluate the curriculum structure in each of the three Nigerian universities. This exercise has given rise to the following general comments:

(a) The legal objectives, aims or functions of each university have not had any major influence on the curriculum structure within that university. This is because the responsibility for drawing up the curriculum rests with the department, and the paramount interest of the department is in the mastery of the departmental discipline by any student graduating from that department. The major concern is to produce a historian, or zoologist, or home economist who can stand his ground among his fellow graduates anywhere. No 'extraneous' requirements (such as General Studies) must be allowed to interfere with this. In this exercise, notice is seldom taken of any existing overall institutional goals.

(b) So far curricula models have been taken from abroad, notably from Great Britain and America. To give the curriculum Nigerian appearance (or African bias!) the department decides how much of it should be given local emphasis, and the nature of such emphasis. Each university has also accepted the traditional duration of a degree programme and the traditional academic year. One consequence of this is that theories of curriculum development have not been based on Nigerian experience, and no studies have been conducted on the effects of certain types of curricula on Nigerian university students.

(c) Each university has emphasized the need for academic excellence and high standards. Because of the relative paucity of universities, the country cannot afford a great disparity in standards between them. One outcome of this is that each department tends to load its curriculum to ensure that its students cover at least as much grounds as students from similar departments in other Nigerian universities. The super-imposition of General African Studies by Lagos has already been cited.

(d) The impression given by the calendars reviewed, particularly the Lagos calendar, is that the curriculum alone would produce the kinds of graduates desired. No reference is made to the role of extra-curricular activities, the halls of residence, the impact on the student of the university community to which he belongs. What happens to the student outside the classroom is not the concern of his academic department; the student; the Registrar's office, the Hall Warden can worry about such matters. The responsibilities of

the undergraduate do not extend to matters connected with planning or evaluating his curriculum.

(e) Occasional reference is made to methods of study other than the traditional lecture method. The history department at Nsukka gave credits for tutorials: All the universities mention practical work for the sciences. Nsukka requires a final year independent project for engineering students.

(f) Katz and Sanford state that 'Discrepancy between professed goals and actual achievement is a general phenomenon'. (11.1) The engineering curricula reveal discrepancies between professed goals and the curriculum structure designed for achieving those goals.

REFERENCES

1 Dressel, Paul L., 'Curricula Theory and Practice in Undergraduate Education', *The North Central Association Quarterly.* Vol. 40, No. 3, Winter 1966, 287–294. 1.1: p. 294.

2 Lord James of Rusholme, 'New Universities in England', *Insight,* Vol. 1, No. 2, October-December, 1962.

3 Daiches, David (ed.), *The Idea of a New University: An Experiment in Sussex,* London, Andre Deutsch Ltd., 1964. 3.1: p. 63.

4 Ashby, Eric, 'A contribution to the dialogue on African Universities', *Universities Quarterly,* Vol. 20, No. 1, December 1965, 70–89. 4.1: pp. 74–75.

5 University of Lagos, *Calendar* (1972–73) University of Lagos, Nigeria. 5.1: p. 75; 5.2: p. 77; 5.3: p. 78; 5.4: p. 76.

6 Ferguson, John, 'Ibadan Arts and Classics', *Universities Quarterly,* Vol. 19, No. 4, September 1965, 396–408. 6.1: pp. 400–401; 6.2: p. 403.

7 University of Lagos, *General Education in the University,* Speech delivered by the Vice-Chancellor of the University of Lagos, Professor Eni Njoku, at the formal opening of the University of Lagos Medical School on October 3, 1962. 7.1: p. 2; 7.2: p. 3.

8 University of Nigeria, 1970–1973 *Calendar,* 8.1: p. 26; 8.2: p. 24; 8.3: p. 132.

9 Mayhew, Lewis B., 'The Liberal Arts and the Changing Structure of Higher Education', *Liberal Education,* Vol. 51, No. 3, October 1965, 366–378. 9.1: p. 373.

10 Dressel, Paul L., *The Undergraduate Curriculum in Higher Education,* Washington D.C., The Centre for Applied Research in Education, Inc., 1963. 10·1: p. 34; 10.2: p. 45.

11   Katz, Joseph & Sanford, Nevitt, 'The Curriculum in the Perspective of the Theory of Personality Development' in *The American College*, Nevitt Sanford (ed.), New York, John Wiley & Sons, Inc., 1962 (4th edition, Sept. 1964). 11.1.

CHAPTER 5

PROPOSALS FOR CURRICULUM REFORM

SELECTION AND ORGANIZATION OF CURRICULUM CONTENT

The selection and organization of the content of the curriculum must be determined by the educational objectives of the institution which are presumed to take into account the national goals of higher education. A university, for example, which claims, as Michigan State University did, that the aim of its undergraduate education is not 'so much of graduating engineers or chemists or teachers or home economists or agriculturists or businessmen, as of graduating educated men and women, trained to be effective citizens of our democracy' would be expected to focus its curriculum emphasis more on training for effective citizenship in the American democracy than on intensive specialization in the various vocational or professional fields.

Several possible objectives for Nigerian higher education were listed in earlier chapters. In addition to the traditional research functions these included (*a*) education in skills, and (*b*) a group of other objectives which could be summarized as education in citizenship, or educating the prospective graduate for his role in Nigerian society. Passing reference was made to this role as one of leadership. It would be pertinent to give it further consideration before moving on to the selection or organization of the content of the curriculum which would assist in achieving the two major objectives.

When Ashby, in a paper entitled 'The Functions of West African Universities', referred to the products of West African universities as 'the men who will build nations in West Africa' (1.1), he was expressing an acknowledged fact. The status and responsibilities of the Nigerian (or African) graduate are tremendous when compared with those of his counterparts in the more developed countries. The concern of the American undergraduate that life in America offers few challenges to youth has not yet become a concern to the Nigerian undergraduate. Today many young Nigerians move literally from their degree examinations to positions of considerable responsibility, including headship of secondary schools and teacher training colleges, senior managerial and other administrative and technical responsibilities which their counterparts in the more developed countries would take many more years to attain. The Lagos faculty of engineering was not exaggerating when it claimed that its graduates would be required to accept responsibility at an unusually early age, and that such responsibility would be almost all-embracing.

Olubummo and Ferguson also emphasize this leadership role as they compare the role of the professor in an emergent university with the role of his counterpart in an established university in a developed country. In the latter situation, the students on graduation are absorbed:

> in a great mass of other people who have been trained else-where. In the emergent territories the impact of the University upon the nation's life is direct. We are . . . . training the future leaders, and we and they know it. Their prime interest may not always be in the subject of study, but they know why they are there and are anxious to succeed. (2.1)

Recognizing the situation in the new African countries, the UNESCO Tananarive Seminar recommended that primary consideration be given to the conditions under which the university products would work on graduation. In addition to the manpower surveys which estimate the *number* of qualified persons needed in the various skills categories, the Seminar felt it was necessary to find out the *nature* of the personnel needed in each of these categories so as to determine the qualifications such persons would need and the kinds of training needed to produce such qualifications.

The goodwill messages extended to the Nsukka graduating students in June 1966 by several officials of that university give some more precise information on the nature of the leadership which is expected of the Nigerian graduate. Professional leadership featured in many messages; the graduates' talents and training, the Vice-Chancellor commented, are 'surely needed and urgently required in the great task of national reconstruction'. (3.1) The faculty deans echoed this in different ways, assuring the graduates that their education had provided them with the necessary professional skills.

Practically every message, however, went beyond the question of professional leadership. The Vice-Chancellor claimed that the graduating students had been trained for service and, 'where necessary, for sacrifice in the national interest'. (3.1) The National President of the University of Nigeria Alumni Association charged the graduating students, among other things, to 'inculcate ethical principles as the basis of good character', to 'induce social consciousness as a means of community service', to 'resist social injustice in the universal cause of human freedom', and 'to develop a stable personality in the individual so as not to distort man's image as a creator and preserver of culture'. These qualities, plus two others, comprised the 'sacred mission of the University' which should determine the lives of the alumni. (3.2)

The Dean of the Faculty of Education devoted his message to the political situation in the country following the military overthrow of the First Republic in January 1966. After advocating an ethical and corruption-free Nigeria, he charged the graduates in these words:

> For some time to come University graduates will continue to form the bulk of Nigerian leadership. Much has been given to them by our economically poor society; but to whom much is given, much more is expected. As agents of change and enlightenment, the 1966 graduates should take up the challenge of *One Nigeria*. They must become the undisputed champions of *One Nigeria*. Anything short of this is a betrayal of the cause. . . . Armed with intellectual power, moral stamina and singleness of purpose, the 1966 graduates are sufficiently equipped to do battle with the Philistines of Nigerian unity. (3.3)

The conclusion from all the foregoing, including Balewa's address quoted earlier on, is that the Nigerian graduate is expected to give (a) professional leadership, depending on his field of specialization, and (b) leadership in civic responsibilities. It sounds logical that the university which catalogues these responsibilities for the student on the eve of his departure from the university should make conscious efforts to equip him for *both* responsibilities right from the start of his undergraduate career.

EDUCATION FOR CIVIC RESPONSIBILITIES
Education for civic responsibilities is taken first because it deserves first consideration in any attempt at selecting and organizing the content of the curriculum. It is one aspect of the undergraduate's

educational experience which unites him with every other under-graduate, regardless of his professional or vocational interests. This is because the civic roles expected of the Nigerian graduate know no disciplinary boundaries; the charge to the Nsukka graduates to do battle in the cause of Nigerian unity or to inculcate ethical principles was not aimed at graduates of any specific faculties. The analysis of the three university curricula reveals considerable uncertainty—and disagreement—among the three Nigerian univer-sities as to the role of the university in providing the student with this kind of education, and the methods for doing so.

Ibadan tends to adopt the attitude that it is unnecessary to take any formal action about it; the onus rests with the student to breathe in the air that surrounds him. Nsukka believes formal action is necessary, but adopts a diluted version of the Michigan State University pattern of general education. Lagos shares the Nsukka view that formal action is necessary: it therefore gives courses in African Studies. It would appear that the problem has not yet been adequately tackled by any of the three universities, nor by Ahmadu Bello, Ife, and Benin.

The Ibadan attitude presupposes that the air in which the under-graduates are enveloped is fresh and pure, wholesome and desirable. Anybody conversant with the Nigerian situation knows that this is not the situation. Devastating currents of ethnic hate had eroded Ibadan itself persistently from the 1950s when Nigeria was still a British territory, till the university reached a point where its future was in grave doubt following the resignation of its Vice-Chancellor, Dr. K.O. Dike, in 1966 to create room for a Yoruba successor. Undergraduates watched their professors, the best academic minds in the country, splitting into ethnic camps to elect a dean of faculty or chairman of the senior staff club. The city of Ibadan itself has seen more political weathercocks and manouvres since 1962 than any other Nigerian city in recent times. Even in the 1970s all cannot be said to be sweetness and light on the campus, notwithstanding the painful lessons of the civil war. To leave the student to breathe in such smog and do nothing else to help him to resolve the personal conflicts involved, would not appear to be the best preparation for the graduate who would be expected by his alma mater to 'do battle with the Philistines of Nigerian unity'. The university does not seem to be justified in expecting its graduates to promote social and political cohesion or integrity in public service when it declares itself unable to provide them as undergraduates with nothing more than a diet of chemistry or geography, plus any extra-curricular experiences the students care to arrange for themselves.

Ferguson's reference to the English undergraduate and the pattern of development at Ibadan suggest that the Ibadan attitude to formal education in civic responsibilities is derived from the attitude in the United Kingdom. There is mounting evidence of dissatisfaction in that country with their traditional first degree structure. Denbigh wrote about some of the dissatisfied British students:

> Such men recognize the usefulness to them of a qualification in science or technology. But they want something else as well. They wish to attain a wide-ranging understanding of the modern world, an imaginative grasp of its problems and the intellectual equipment needed to play an active part. (4.1)

A correspondent of the *Times Educational Supplement* quoted Dr. Geoffrey Templeman, Vice-Chancellor of the University of Kent (one of the new English universities) as criticizing the English university undergraduate curriculum for not equipping the prospective graduates for the role they were bound to play as leaders of opinion, whether they liked it or not. He declared that the graduates would find :

> that their training in universities has not fitted them to cope with a range of problems of this kind. They may discover that while they may very well have been *trained* in this, that or the other specialty, they are hardly educated at all. (5.1)

These and many other criticisms of the traditional British first degree structure, including the criticisms contained in the Robbins report, have led to a broadening of the curriculum and the integrated curricula of the newest universities. The breadth components however, must include courses or educational experiences specifically intended to prepare the student for his responsibilities as a potential leading member of the society whose views will carry tremendous weight and whose advice will be sought by many of his less educated countrymen on many problems outside his specialty. Mere breadth of curriculum will not provide the answer. The Ibadan or Lagos requirement of three academic subjects in the first year may equip the graduate to discuss or teach more academic subjects but would not necessarily give him citizenship education.

In his opening address at the 3rd General Conference of the Association of African Universities, on April 9, 1973, General Yakubu Gowon, the ousted Head of Nigeria's Federal Military Government charged African universities to ensure that their programmes are aimed not only at academic excellence but at producing the good citizen:

> I particularly wish to charge your Association to concern itself with social and moral issues. In the world of today, with moral development lagging far behind technological achievement, the possession by your students, and the production by your institutions, of academic excellence is no longer enough. Apart from the global task of imbuing in your students a humanistic outlook to counterbalance the modern threat of materialism and the worship of Mammon, you Heads of African Universities should consider it your duty to inspire in the youth of Africa respect for our traditions, concern for the masses and that love for the nation which is an essential ingredient of good citizenship and which no nation can afford to do without. Our institutions of higher learning should.... therefore, take care to ensure that their programmes are not aimed only at academic excellence but, more important, at producing the good citizen.

How can this be done? American and Soviet universities have made some attempts to provide what they consider the requisite citizenship education for their students, and it would be relevant to examine briefly the nature of these provisions, particularly in view of the Nsukka indebtedness to the American experience.

The term *general education* embraces the different kinds of formal programmes provided by American universities to prepare their students for effective citizenship in American society. Discussing the origins of general education, Daniel Bell claimed that Harvard University was steered to general education after World War II as:

> a response to the obligation, assumed in the name of democracy, of providing for all citizens 'some common and binding understanding of the society which they will possess in common'. (6.1)

Bell (6.2) summarizes the aims of general education (in the U.S.) as:

    (a)   to provide a common learning.

> *(b)* to give the student a comprehensive understanding of the Western tradition. (This has tended to be parochial in recent years).
>
> *(c)* to combat intellectual fragmentation with interdisciplinary courses.

He states that the third aim has suffered most and virtually disappeared from many general education programmes, with departments showing keener interest in disciplinary sequences than in developing truly interdisciplinary courses. As a result, distribution requirements are replacing the interdisciplinary approach; for example, a student in science is required to take at least two social science and two humanities courses, without stipulating which courses, and requiring no sequence in the courses. The assumption is that the simple act of taking courses outside the student's field broadens the student's education. Bell considers this return to distribution requirements a return to the disorder which led to the widespread adoption of general education in the mid-1940s and the 1950s, and 'an admission of intellectual defeat'.

Russell Thomas makes the point that the diversity in the general education programmes, requirements and procedures found in American universities indicates that nobody has yet discovered one single curriculum formula or one administrative or teaching procedure which can be said to define general education satisfactorily. The need for some general education is not, however, in doubt:

> All the colleges agree that some part of the student's program of studies lies outside any field of concentration and that the college is responsible for providing some kind of formal structure for this part of the student's work. (7.1)

Universities (or the higher schools) in the Soviet Union place tremendous emphasis on specialization. Elizabeth Moos quotes a British correspondent who wrote in the *Times Educational Supplement* of July 1954 that:

> a graduate of a Soviet university is required to present a thesis of a quality far higher than is customary in any British university . . . . the diploma granted at the successful completion of the five-year university course is equivalent to a Master's degree. (8.1)

In spite of this tremendous emphasis on specialization, Soviet higher education makes formal provision for citizenship training, as Prof. Yelyutin, Minister of Higher Education of the U.S.S.R. (in 1959) pointed out in *Higher Education in the U.S.S.R.*:

> Graduates of the Soviet higher schools must be able to understand the fundamental laws governing the development of nature and society and to apply them creatively in practice. This ability is due largely to the deep grounding in the socio-economic subjects. Regardless of the field chosen by students, they are all required to take courses in the History of the Communist Party of the Soviet Union, political economy and philosophy. The technical higher schools allocate about 8% of the time to these subjects; a greater number of hours is allocated to these subjects in the higher schools specializing in the humanities. (9.1)

Procedure for selection and organization. The following procedure is presented as one possible approach, not as a model.

The university would need to find answers to the following questions. Taking into consideration the national objectives for higher education, the institutional objectives, the role of the Nigerian university graduate as he takes his place in the Nigerian, African and world society, is there any common denominator that unites all students within the same university, regardless of their academic or professional interests? Are there any qualities or values which the institution regards or wishes to regard as the "trade mark" on each of its graduates, regardless of professional training? Are there any tools (e.g. knowledge of sociology, or ability to speak a second Nigerian language or French, or knowledge of ethics) which every graduate would require for effective living, regardless of his occupation on graduation?

If there are, these would form the core of university requirements for every student. These requirements would transcend all disciplinary barriers, and would remain a concern of the entire university. Each university would have to decide how much of these could be given through the formal curriculum and how much through properly coordinated extra-curricular activities.

Subject-matter specialists and psychologists should be of help in deciding what courses could facilitate the attainment of the different objectives. For example, Sanford suggests that natural science can teach students how to think, mathematics trains the intelligence, psychology and the social sciences can teach the student to think, while philosophy, religion, history of ideas can teach the student to challenge many of the ideas and values he held previously. He stresses, however, that all these are generalizations which depend on the manner in which the subject is taught or presented to the student. (10.1)

Each university would also need to decide how these core requirements are to be organized. Both the general studies programme at Nsukka and the Lagos African Studies course are disposed of at least two years before the student can qualify for graduation. Each university would have to decide whether this is the correct approach. Both Russell Thomas and Daniel Bell are opposed to the confinement of the general education programme of U.S. universities to the first two years. Thomas supports the colleges which have tried "through a controlled plan to engage students in their more mature years in problems and disciplines outside their fields of specialization". (7.2)

Among Bell's proposals for a reform of general education at Columbia University is a proposal whereby the integrative courses would come *not* at the beginning of the student's university career but later on, after he has acquired proficiency in a discipline. (6.3)

Mundelein College in Chicago is an example of an American College which took these criticisms into account. Its Basic Studies courses have been so planned that "they appear in the student's program at that point when they most logically relate to her area of special interest". (11.1) They are spread over the 4-year period. One of the final year courses is entitled Great Issues, and described as follows:

> An interdisciplinary course which explores in depth some current issue in the light of its philosophical, sociological, and religious implications, this course is planned to involve the graduating senior in the complexity of contemporary human problems. (11.2)

One could suggest many issues which could provide stimulating and profitable seminar experiences within the Nigerian setting. One example is Okoi Arikpo's Lugard Lecture entitled *Who are the Nigerians?* Here Arikpo gives the anthropologist's views on the often quoted view that Nigeria as a nation is a geographical expression, an arbitrary grouping of separate kingdoms which had no cultural or social ties before the advent of the white man. Such a theme would lead to a critical examination and sympathetic understanding of the similarities and dissimilarities of the different ethnic groups within Nigeria, and to studies of the problems of coexistence. The problems of coexistence could be expanded to the African continent and to the world at large. It would make an integrative experience, to which the professors and students could draw from their special disciplines. Such a theme would be more meaningful to the Nigerian graduate than a jet plane tour of the history of western civilization. Many other meaningful themes could be developed.

EDUCATION IN SKILLS

Nigeria relies heavily on the local universities to supply the high-level manpower necessary for her development. National manpower surveys help to determine the areas of need, which in turn help to determine the different broad areas in which the university should provide professional training. Mr. C.F. Carter, Vice-Chancellor of the University of Lancaster, has warned against "using the narrow definition of 'national need' in shapping curricula", arguing that such needs are almost impossible to predict in the present world of complex social and technical development. (12.1) Since, however, no single university has been known to span all possible academic fields, each university has to choose what to offer among many possibilities. National needs form one reasonable yardstick for such selection; they also help to guard against serious over-production of university graduates in any field, something that could cause serious economic and social problems for a poor country. There are, of course, certain areas or academic fields (*e.g.* the physical and biological sciences or the social sciences) which form essential parts of any university offerings.

Having decided what broad areas of knowledge to encompass, these should be grouped into units (call them schools or faculties) which recognize the existence of common or unifying elements. The Robbins report made reference to natural groupings of subjects, and gave as examples chemistry, physics and mathematics (in the sciences), and English, history and French (in the humanities). Some subjects have organic connections; in some cases the jobs into which the graduates go help to establish the common elements. Such broad groupings of academic fields are recommended for Nigerian universities. The establishment at Nsukka of a faculty of biological sciences and the reorganization said to be going on in Lagos aimed at establishing integrated schools are moves in that direction. If Daniel Bell's assessment is correct, some American universities are also moving in the same direction. He suggests that the proposals at the University of Chicago for the establishment of 'area colleges' looks like the 'schools' at the U.K. University of Sussex. (6.4) Asa Briggs, in *Drawing a New Map of Learning,* gives a fascinating account of the thinking which led to the establishment of the Sussex 'schools' and the various measures taken to make the schools effective and meaningful. (13.1)

Division into broad groupings of academic fields with unifying or common elements (as against several independent departments and sub-departments) is not in itself enough. It should influence curriculum planning. Each division—it may be called any suitable name—should select which common or unifying elements should constitute a common or core requirement for all the students within that division. It should be possible to find such unifying elements, otherwise there would be no rationale for associating the different disciplines within that division. Some groupings of unrelated departments within the same faculties in some Nigerian universities are hard to defend. In some cases, different departments within the same faculty grant different degrees, e.g. bachelor of arts and bachelor of science, each with entirely different requirements.

After the divisional common requirements have been determined, the next step would be to organize the different specialties within the division, each of which would be supported by the foundation of common requirements. In determining what goes into the special or major field, account should be taken of what is known in that field, the future role of the student on graduation, and the fact that the university is the apex of the educational pyramid. The recommendation of the UNESCO Tananarive Seminar is also worth bearing in mind:

> It must be admitted that, in certain respects, the economist, the statistician, the lawyer and the sociologist must be more highly qualified in Africa than in other countries, for they will have less data and information (particularly of a statistical kind) at their disposal, they will be more isolated intellectually

and forced to rely principally on their own knowledge and to trust to their imagination and personal judgement in situations in which their counterparts in the developed countries would consult specialists in other branches of study. (14.1)

In addition to the special or major area requirements, it would also be necessary to determine whether the students in these areas need to take some more work from other areas, within or outside their broad divisions, to enhance their mastery of their specialties.

In effect, the curriculum content would take the following pattern:

(i) Common university-wide requirements for all students regardless of their broad divisions.

(ii) Common divisional requirements for all students within each broad division (—school, college, faculty, division, whatever the name), to serve as the foundation for the special or major area.

(iii) Special or major requirements.

(iv) Subsidiary requirements outside the student's major field (where considered necessary), chosen from within or outside his broad division.

The need for educational objectives extends to the divisions (or schools, etc.). Each division should have its own objectives within the framework of the institutional objectives. Going lower down the line, every course which finds its way into the curriculum should have its own objective(s). It must be seen to contribute to the divisional objectives and, finally, to the overall objectives of the institution. It must fit into the curriculum structure as a block fits into the wall of a house.

The objectives should also influence the decision as to what proportion of the curriculum should be assigned to each of the four parts (i)–(iv) above. Decisions as to the length of the degree programme would also be linked to the objectives to be attained. Nigerian universities have hitherto inherited the three-year (for advanced level students) and four year (for ordinary level students) patterns as if they were handed down from above and must not be changed. Universities in the Soviet Union and on the continent of Europe show that other patterns are equally respectable. The length of time for completing each part of the curriculum and the curriculum as a whole should be determined by the minimum length of time it should take to achieve the curriculum objectives. If, in the process of fixing the length of time, it is discovered that successful completion of the curriculum would take either too short or too long a time, then the objectives should be reviewed to find out whether too little or too much is not being attempted.

THE 'GENERAL PRACTITIONER'

During the 1950's a professor of religious studies at Ibadan gave a public lecture on what he called 'The Useless Disciplines'. The term was used to distinguish between disciplines such as medicine, agriculture and chemistry which have obvious uses and disciplines such as religious studies, classics and history whose uses are not so obvious. Such a distinction comes to the fore when employers visit the university campus to recruit prospective graduates for employment. These employers generally distinguish between specialized jobs requiring special training—chemists, doctors, statisticians—and jobs for which no specific university specialty is a requirement. The latter are usually administrative positions for which a knowledge of classics or history or linguistics is to all intents and purposes useless. The graduates who find themselves in these positions therefore have no occasion to utilize the knowledge they spent three or four years acquiring at the university, especially if they studied at universities that gave them no formal education outside their major disciplines and subsidiaries.

Most graduates in arts and social studies (except those in subjects such as economics) fit into this category. Unless they become teachers, they take nothing from their university education to their jobs except the qualities of mind and social interaction which they have acquired indirectly. The claim by Ferguson in his 'Ibadan Arts and Classics' that his classics graduates have fitted admirably into different types of careers does not mean that the knowledge of classics to degree level does anything special to prepare the holders for every conceivable career. The direct link which exists between a degree in pharmacy and the duties of a pharmacist does not exist between a degree in classics and an administrative position in industry or in the civil service. There is no reason why a graduate in religious studies or English should not be as successful as the classicist in the administrative positions cited by Ferguson, granted they have comparable personal qualities. Each could afford to forget his university courses and yet be successful on the job.

The number of graduates turned out annually by Nigerian universities in these 'useless disciplines' is quite large. Even though the universities are now under national pressure to give priority to scientific and technological studies, it is recognized that there will always be a need for these 'general practitioners' for administrative and managerial roles in the civil service, commerce and industry. They would come under the category captioned 'others' in Harbison's 'High-level Manpower for Nigeria's Future'. The estimated number of high-level manpower to be required by Nigeria between 1960 and 1970 in this category was 10% of the total estimated number of university graduates needed during the same period.

It would appear worthwhile for Nigerian universities to design a special curriculum for this group of students which would relate their university studies more directly to their later career. Instead of requiring them, as at present, to major in classics or English or geography, an integrated curriculum could be designed to give them strong background preparation for almost any administrative role within Nigeria. They would still have to learn the peculiar problems and language of their jobs on the job (i.e. after graduation), but they would bring from the university relevant academic preparation to back them up rather than a degree in a subject which they need not be bothered with for the rest of their lives.

The UNESCO Tananarive Seminar made a similar proposal when it recommended the provision of special training for students intending to take up administrative positions. Strong emphasis, it went on, would be placed on the development of personality and character, bearing in mind the responsibilities the students would shoulder after graduation.

Selection and Organization of Learning Experiences

There is a tendency to regard the student's learning or educational experience as something limited to what transpires within the classroom and the laboratory. Although Jacob's *Changing Values in College* has several limitations, some of which Jacob himself admits in the book, the following summary of his findings would agree with the experience of many students:

> Student values do change to some extent in college. With some students, the change is substantial. But the impetus to change does not come primarily from the formal educational process. Potency to affect student values is found in the distinctive climate of a few institutions, the individual and personal magnetism of a sensitive teacher with strong value

> commitments of his own, or value-laden personal experiences of students imaginatively integrated with their intellectual development. (15.1)

Assessing later the influence of college as a whole, Jacob says: 'a combination of factors can produce a distinctive institutional atmosphere, a "climate of values", in which students *are* decisively influenced'. (15·2)

In their own study of Michigan State University students, Dressel and Lehmann found that:

> Although courses and instructors do seem to have some impact on students' attitudes and values—especially in the last two years—peer-group contacts and non-academic experiences are regarded by students as being more important. (16.1)

Both findings tally with Dressel's contention that:

> every practice and policy of a college affects the learning of students. Priorities in expenditures of funds reveal values of boards and administrators and thereby influence the values of students. Scholarship and loan policies, preferential treatment of athletes, social regulations, student government, and all other aspects of an institution constitute educational experiences. (17.1)

Unfortunately there are no similar studies for Nigerian universities to cite. If experience in American universities can be taken as a guide, it becomes imperative to look not only at but also beyond the formal curriculum in selecting and organising the learning experiences which would facilitate the attainment of the educational objectives of the institution.

In planning the learning experiences, it is important to know the characteristics of the students for whom these experiences are being organized. What are the students' expectations of the university? What qualities and experiences do the students have to offer? As Piper rightly suggested in 'Getting the best fit between students and courses' *(course* here referring to curriculum, teaching methods, and the student's whole environment), the educator should design the course (i.e. organize the learning experiences) in such a way as to take maximum advantage of what the student has to offer. (18.1)

Happily, Nigerian universities have recognized all along that the lecture method is not the only teaching method. Laboratory work

is considered an essential component of the student's learning experience in the pure and applied sciences. In the arts, the tutorial has
been an important teaching method, particularly at Ibadan, and
many undergraduates claim to learn more from their tutorials and
the weekly or fortnightly essays they turn in than from their formal
lectures. Field trips are commonly undertaken, particularly by
geography and geology students. Practical, on-the-job experience
is required of many students seeking professional qualifications—for
example in medicine, agriculture, education, accountancy and
engineering; generally it is the non-professional student, the 'general
practitioner' type, who acquires no practical experience.

A few additional recommendations worth consideration by
Nigerian universities are described below. It is, however, important
to emphasize that the educational objectives of the institution and
the content or subject matter of the curriculum should influence the
selection and organization of learning experiences.

Independent research projects
I respectfully disagree with those educational experts who counsel
that the new African nations, like Nigeria, have no urgent needs for
research-oriented graduates. It is possible that these experts are
referring to graduates who will spend their lives beside microscopes
in research laboratories, or in universities where their survival would
be tied to their research capability. If this is what they mean, they
need to say so more explicitly. Every Nigerian graduate cannot hope
to be employed in a full-time research appointment, even if all had
the requisite qualifications, but any Nigerian university that can make
all its graduates research-oriented would be doing an invaluable
service to the nation. Not only is it of importance, as Olubummo and
Ferguson rightly point out, to give every student especially those who
will not be employed in full-time research 'the desire to add to
knowledge and the mental equipment to fulfil this' (2.2), but also
the standards of the public services in the country are not likely to
improve until the men and women who go into them are trained
and willing to bring disciplined originality to their work. It is not
unusual to find many university graduates who consider that their
role is the implementation of existing policy. Many graduate teachers
or administrators regard research as something for research officers
and university professors, even though their everyday work is charged

with research possibilities and would benefit tremendously from research findings.

Some Nigerian university departments require their students to submit research papers. This practice is not, however, widespread. Even in departments where it exists, the requirement is not extended to the general degree students; moreover it is often left until the final year. It might be more meaningful if every student were introduced to research methodology earlier in his career, and encouraged to undertake research on simple but real problems.

Russian higher education provides a ready example of a research-oriented programme. Yelyutin points out that practically every higher school makes it possible for its students to participate in the scientific research being conducted by their respective departments. Many programmes require annual projects from students, which they carry out independently, with the lecturer acting as a consultant. The emphasis is on initiative and originality on the part of the student, who has to defend his project at a public hearing. Students in the humanities present annual theses, choosing from subjects announced by their departments. Before graduating, the students must present graduation projects (e.g. the design of a motor car or locomotive engine—for students in the technical higher schools) or graduation theses (for students in the humanities). (9.2)

After surveying a number of recent attempts in U.S. universities to introduce independent study covering every year of the undergraduate's career, Mayhew suggested that the trend towards independent study was 'based on the educational assumption that no one teaches another anything. Rather change comes about when an individual learns something on his own'. (19·1)

It is doubtful whether Mayhew wants to be taken literally. His aim was probably to emphasize the importance of active participation and interest on the part of the learner. Writing on the same subject but in greater detail, Dearing stressed the necessity for the student to become 'an initiator as well as a participator if he is to continue his intellectual and cultural growth after he leaves the campus'. (19·2)

Continuity, Sequence and Integration

Continuity, Sequence and Integration are three important criteria for effective organization of learning experiences. Continuity involves a continuing and recurring application of the required skills over a period of time, thus ensuring that the student is given adequate exposure to them. Sequence involves arranging the learning experiences in such a way that the earlier experiences prepare the student for the later experiences. The first step leads to the second which leads to the third, each step entailing a higher level of treatment than, and building upon the ideas and principles of, the preceding step.

The three Nigerian university curricula analysed demonstrate both continuity and sequence. The highly prescribed curricula cut down on chance factors by removing from the student the responsibility for picking what courses to take. Where electives are provided, they are not always free; the student is given a range within which to choose. Moreover the overall effect of the electives, free or prescribed, is not enough to cause alarm.

Integration is a much more difficult criterion to evaluate from a study of the curriculum as published in university calendars or catalogues. It calls for an organization of learning experiences in a manner that will ensure that the student comes away with a unified view of his total learning experiences, including both the formal curriculum and the extra-curriculum. With regard to the formal curriculum, it implies an inter-relationship of the different academic fields forming part of the student's undergraduate programme, and a relationship between the principles acquired from these disciplines and the problems of the society.

It is possible that the comprehensive examination which Nsukka required each department to set for its final year students in 1963 was calculated to test such curriculum integration. This was a three-hour examination, designed to test the graduating student's aptitudes for and attitudes to his major discipline, and it carried 20% weight in the computation of his final degree results. The difficulty of stating the objectives of the examination in more comprehensible language (resulting in different interpretations by different departments), coupled with the desire to adopt a pattern of multiple-paper degree finals, led to some changes. The comprehensive paper has been renamed a general paper carrying less than 20% weight. Although its objectives still leave room for different interpretations by different departments, it is increasingly being regarded as a test of the student's grasp of the underlying principles of his major subject.

Integration also embraces the extra-curriculum. For the student's total learning experiences to be unified, his classroom experiences must be related not only to one another but also to his experiences outside the classroom. To achieve maximum results, therefore, his curriculum and extra-curriculum experiences should be so organized as to reinforce each other. This is one facet of university organization in Nigeria which needs serious attention. No Nigerian university senate is known to pay serious attention to the extra-curriculum, except to criticize the appropriate administrative officers for not teaching the students good manners, or to rusticate the students and require them to sign pledges of good conduct before being readmitted.

The Extra-Curriculum

Every Nigerian university makes some provision for what American universities often designate 'student personnel services', though to a much less ambitious extent than a visitor finds in many American universities. Except at Nsukka which has a "dean of student affairs" (an American importation of designation but not of comparable responsibilities) each of the other Nigerian universities entrusts part of these services to the Registrar and part to Masters and Wardens of halls of residence.

A critical appraisal of the services provided shows the lack of a serious attempt to coordinate the student's life after the scheduled classroom hour with his formal curriculum, or to relate the campus life as a whole to the educational objectives of the university. Bearing in mind that most Nigerian undergraduates spend their full careers in residence at the university and even the few who live off campus invariably spend part of their career in the campus as residential students, the universities would appear to be throwing away a golden opportunity of reinforcing the classroom experiences and thereby making a greater impact on their students. Ibadan has tried several British university-type experiments to increase staff-student interaction: a system of moral tutors; associating members of staff to halls of residence; high table dinners; attaching staff apartments to halls of residence to enable the Warden and a few other staff members (usually single) to live within the halls of residence. Unfortunately many of the experiments failed as a result of a lack of mutual confidence between staff and students. Some students doubted the motives of staff members who invited them to their homes for tea, especially when some staff members used such teas to solicit certain types of information from students. Some staff members designated moral tutors had no interest whatsoever in students, and where there were no common academic interests the enforced relationships died a natural death, to the relief of both parties. The term moral tutor sounded objectionable to some, particularly when the private lives of the moral tutors were common knowledge among the undergraduates (who, incidentally, lived on the same campus community with their lecturers and knew many of their questionable activities).

The general feeling among many lecturers and professors is that what happens to the student outside the classroom is none of their responsibility; they do not wish to play the role of wet nurse to any student. There are exceptions, of course, and the fact that they are exceptions makes students sometimes initially suspicious of their motives.

Until studies of the impact of each of the various facets of university life on students are conducted in Nigerian universities, one can only take one's cues from studies elsewhere which show that practically every facet of university life—the attitudes of the academic and the administrative staff, the stewards in the student dining halls, the porters in the halls of residence, and the attitudes of fellow students—all affect the attitudes, values and learning of the students. Even the architectural design of the university buildings and the campus layout affect student attitudes and values.

Reference has already been made in earlier sections to the leadership role of most Nigerian university graduates. It sounds paradoxical that the universities which would not hesitate to recommend their graduating students to employers for very responsible positions demonstrate by their attitudes to their undergraduates that these same students are too immature and inexperienced to shoulder responsibility within the university environment or even to be consulted on matters affecting student welfare. Most Nigerian university students would be stunned to learn that there are universities in America operating an 'honour code', under which a student can take his examination anywhere (including his bedroom or the library) with no invigilator except his sense of honour which binds him not to cheat and to report any other student he finds cheating.

Most Nigerian students would be amazed at the degree of participation in university government enjoyed by students at Antioch College in Yellow Springs, Ohio or at a few other universities where students have a say in even the recruitment and promotion of university professors. These are some examples of serious attempts to convert the extra-curricular life of students into worthwhile educational experiences.

Many universities outside Africa are developing several non-academic experiences for their students, designed to supplement the classroom experiences and facilitate the attainment of the educational goals of the institution. Work-study programmes, study-abroad programmes, off-campus voluntary service projects—all come within this category. Stanford University, through its system of granting 'activity credits', accords recognition to several non-academic student activities. About a third of these activities must consist of physical activity in the freshman and sophomore years; the rest could be physical activity or group activities (such as chorus, band, orchestra, dramatic productions, some journalistic activities) approved by the General Studies Committee. Group activity, as it is referred to in the Stanford University Bulletin Series 17, No. 18 (May 13, 1965), is listed as one of the four basic requirements for all undergraduate students, and only veterans, married students and students over 24 years of age are exempted from that requirement. The six activity units do not, however, earn grades used in degree computation.

Brooklyn College in Brooklyn, New York, uses students to serve as advisers to several student social groups. The student advisers are selected for their superior personal and leadership qualities and prepared for their role through participation in special weekly leadership seminars. In July 1965 the College claimed to have student advisers for approximately 150 groups. The adviser maintains a valuable link between the College and the student groups he advises. No credit is given for attendance at the leadership seminars, even though each student adviser is required to participate in the seminars for as long as he remains an adviser. The seminars are designed in such a manner that a student adviser can move to a more advanced seminar each year, from sophomore to senior year. A syllabus has been drawn up for the seminars, and any student who completes it satisfactorily could be assigned as an Assistant Counsellor or Student Counsellor.

> Real value-laden experiences must be secured outside the classroom, and often outside the campus. At most institutions, this automatically rules them out as integral features of a curriculum. . . . Nevertheless, those institutions which have

been able to build such experiences into their course of study, or to organize aspects of campus life in such a way that their value-implications carry over into the classroom, have usually had an unmistakable influence on students. (15.3)

Direct experience

Whatever may be the educational objectives of the institution, one important principle in the selection and organization of learning experiences is to ensure that the students are given the opportunity to practise the behaviour implied by those objectives. If the Nigerian university aims at producing graduates who will accept leadership roles very early in their careers, the learning experiences should provide opportunities for the students to shoulder responsibility and exercise some leadership. If the university is to produce graduates who will foster political and social cohesion in Nigeria, they should be given the opportunity to put their future roles into practice during their student days. Without providing such opportunities for students, the university would be depriving itself of the opportunity of assessing its impact on the students at a period when the students are still under its control.

Regardless of the divergent views which different educational philosophers might hold on the importance to the learning process of direct experience, there is evidence from many American universities to the effect that direct experience on the part of students has influenced student values. Examples of such experiences include projects on citizenship training, political involvement, and study-abroad programmes. Antioch College students, according to Jacob, consider their cooperative work-study programme the most meaningful part of their education.

> Experimental studies of the means of persuasion and communication also attest to the important effect of vivid experience in learning, particularly at the point of forming or modifying a person's beliefs and standards of conduct. (15.3)

Integrated into the undergraduate programme and made compulsory for all students, the National Youth Service Corps suitably modified could provide an opportunity for such direct experience in Nigeria.

Psychology of learning

In selecting and organizing learning experiences, due account should be taken of the findings of educational psychologists, to avoid avoidable blunders. A few of these findings are:

(i) One learning experience may produce more than one outcome, and these outcomes could be positive or negative or both. In selecting learning experiences, it is therefore important to assess their various possible outcomes.

(ii) Learning experiences which are consistent with each other reinforce each other. On the contrary, those which are inconsistent with each other require more of the student's time and could interfere with each other.

(iii) A student is more likely to be positively influenced by learning experiences which bring him satisfaction than by those which are either distasteful to him or bring him little or no satisfaction. May-hew's statement that change comes when an individual learns something on his own is related to this finding.

Proliferation of courses

Many courses found in university calendars or catalogues are not there because they form an integral and essential part of the curriculum but in order to satisfy the research or scholarly interests of the professors. A classic example cited by Earl McGrath illustrates an extreme case of proliferation. Parsons College (in the U.S.A.) was able, after critical study, to slash down its courses from 755 to 169. (19.3) Nigerian universities may profit from a similar exercise.

EVALUATION

All three universities studied appear to recognize the necessity for a periodic evaluation of their work. The methods of evaluation vary, and some of them will be described below.

(a) The Visitation

Every Nigerian University provides in its enabling legislation for the position of Visitor, a position generally held by the Governor or Head of the Government which established or finances the university. The function of the Visitor is to conduct a visitation or appoint a person or persons to conduct a visitation of the University. The Ibadan and Lagos Visitor (who is the Head of the Federal Military

Government) has other major powers which will be dealt with in the chapter on academic freedom.

The Visitation idea came to Ibadan as part of its British heritage during its period of apprenticeship to London, and it is considered a valuable "stock-taking" device. The visitation generally takes place after intervals of about five years, though this period could be modified. [The University of Ibadan (Amendment) Decree No. 13 of 1972 stipulates that a visitation shall be conducted 'as often as circumstances may require not being less than once every year']. It usually consists of distinguished university people (from outside universities) who spend several days or weeks on the campus and are required to review practically every aspect of the university operations, including the physical plant, the curricula, academic staff recruitment procedures and personnel services, the library, admission requirements and student activities. University publications, reports and statistics are made available to the members as background material, and while on campus, they are free to request interviews with any persons or groups within or outside the university community, if they feel such interviews would be helpful to them in their assignment. At the end of their visitation they submit a report to the governing body of the university, outlining their criticisms and recommendations. Generally, their report influences future development at the university, although the University Council (i.e. the governing body) is not bound to adopt all or any of their recommendations.

It is not clear why the Federal Military Government considers an annual visitation to Ibadan imperative. The Ibadan and Lagos laws confer on the Visitor the power to issue directives to the authorities of the university with a view to implementing any recommendations of a visitation.

(b) The Advisory Committee

Nsukka, prior to the outbreak of the civil war in 1967, used a Joint University Advisory Committee to evaluate its work annually. The committee consisted of two representatives appointed by each of the two universities that helped to guide the young university in its first decade: Michigan State University and the University of London, in addition to two representatives appointed by Nsukka. The Nsukka Vice-Chancellor served as chairman of the committee, but in practice this often meant presiding over the formal sessions of the committee and thereafter leaving the members to break into smaller functional groups which did the evaluation.

The committee met at Nsukka for about one week every year, generally in or about November. Each member served for two years, and the representatives of each university were appointed in a manner that ensured that both members did not retire the same year. Because the committee met annually, it did not attempt to evaluate every phase of the work of the university at any one sitting; the focus shifted from, say, the sciences in one year to, say library facilities the following year. The committee reported to the University Council, and its recommendations, though not binding, influenced development at the university. The integration of the biological sciences at Nsukka owed much of its impetus to the committee.

The Joint University Advisory Committee has ceased to function, and no formal alternative arrangements for regular external periodic evaluation appear to have been made since the end of the war. The University of Nigeria Law does not spell out the duties of the Visitor.

(c) External examiners

The use of external examiners is a means of evaluation used by all Nigerian universities, including Ahmadu Bello, Ife and Benin. The system of external examiners is an importation from British universities, strongly prescribed for each Nigerian university by the National Universities Commission.

The external examiner is appointed by the university on the recommendation of the department in which he is to serve as examiner. He is often a university teacher, though there have been instances in which non-university people have been appointed. It is regarded as a mark of academic recognition to be appointed an external examiner. Although the detailed functions and powers of the external examiner may vary from one university to the other, they generally include moderating the examination questions before they assume their final form for printing, marking at least some of the students' answer scripts, participating in the oral or practical examinations, and membership of the board of examiners which considers the final results of examinations.

The external examiner is required by Nsukka to submit a confidential report to the Vice-Chancellor on the examination. Many of them go beyond the examination alone and report on the curriculum content or structure of which the degree examination is a part.

It is largely for this reason, coupled with the fact that the external examiner is in effect expressing an opinion on whether the prospective graduate qualifies to receive a degree, that the external examiner system is regarded as a means of evaluation. In 1963 an external examiner reported that the entire degree curriculum of one department in one Nigerian university was so inferior that he did not consider anybody passing through it fit to receive a degree. Regardless of the individual performance of each graduating student in the finals, he recommended that none of them should be allowed to graduate. Since as an external examiner he had no veto power, he was outvoted at the board of examiners by the departmental representatives and the students graduated, some with honours. The incident places a serious qualification on the external examiner system as a means of evaluation.

(d) Faculty evaluation

Within each university, the Senate, assisted by its ancillary arms such as faculty boards and departmental boards, is constantly considering major and minor changes to the curriculum. Nsukka, for example, up to 1967, had a curriculum committee as an arm of its Academic Council which was itself an arm of the Senate. It was representative of every faculty within the university, and its broad function was to consider any proposals from faculty boards for additions to or deletions from academic programmes previously approved by the Senate. Its major concern was to avoid duplication of courses, to ensure that each departmental programme conformed to the general university regulations (e.g. for maximum and minimum graduation requirements), and to ensure that every proposed new course had a place in the overall academic programme. The Academic Council has ceased to exist; the curriculum committee reports direct to the Senate.

(e) Evaluation by potential employers

Some university departments, particularly those offering professional training, sometimes seek the views of potential employers of their graduates on the curriculum. This method of evaluation recognizes that students successfully completing the programme would be seeking specific types of employment, and it would be in their interest if their potential employers, especially the major ones among them, endorse their curriculum. It also recognizes that these employers are in a better position than the university to assess the performance of the graduates in their jobs and, therefore, the relevance of their training. Experience so far shows that many employers welcome such consultation and some make valuable suggestions. Problems arise when recommendations from different employers differ in respect of the same programme and the difference is irreconcilable, or when an employer is completely unsympathetic to the broader educational objectives of the institution, for example, by proposing that all the time given to general education should be diverted to further work in the professional area.

(f) Comments on current methods of evaluation

(i) *Use of outside people.* One common factor among the universities is the reliance on the recommendations of persons drawn from outside the particular institution. Part of the rationale for this is that the Nigerian university is still young and inexperienced, and therefore would do better to subject its programmes to the critical eye of experts from the more established universities. Part of it stems from the feeling that the Nigerian University, in its bid for recognition within the world intellectual community, would enhance its image by establishing relationships with academicians and universities which are internationally well known in the academic world. Nsukka, as an example, was able to make some of its programmes acceptable to the Nigerian public by emphasizing that they were recommended by the Ashby Commission or by the Joint University Advisory Committee. Part of it can be traced to the feeling that outside people would be more detached from the problems within the institution and would consequently be more objective in their evaluation and recommendations.

The use of outside academicians to evaluate the work of the university has its advantages. As a result of the autonomy granted to each Nigerian university by law, many university people regard any attempts by the government to question the activities of the university as interference in the internal running of the university which should be the responsibility of the university itself. The University Council, with its outside members, is one check on the excesses of professors and the academic administration. These outside members of the board are often, however, unqualified to pass enlightened judgement on the academic programmes, and more readily than not yield to the professorial point of view that academic matters are a responsibility of the Senate, the recommendations of which body the University Council should generally rubber-stamp. The way the universities are constituted, each university council is answerable to no outside authority. Whatever its members decide becomes law within the institution (except, of course, where it contravenes the university law or the laws of the land and someone is courageous enough to take the university to court). The most progressive proposals on the curriculum could be thwarted by the Council. Although there is no evidence that this has happened, there are instances in which a university council has taken questionable policy decisions on academic matters and compelled the Senate to implement such policies. From this point of view, evaluation by external experts can be a great advantage. The freedom granted them to interview staff and students usually provides an opportunity for staff and students to give expression to pent up frustrations. The outsider has nothing at stake; he can be forthright in his criticisms without jeopardizing his career, and his criticisms can (even if only hypothetically) span the entire university set-up, from the government to the governing board, from vice-chancellor to students. It is true that the Council can reject any adverse report, but there is an Igbo saying that a proverb about a tattered basket makes a person in rags uncomfortable! The powers conferred on the Visitor of Ibadan and Lagos make it possible for the Visitor, acting on the recommendations of a visitation, to take major decisions on the universities over and above the governing councils.

The use of outsiders has weaknesses as well. One major weakness is that many of these outsiders (when appointed from overseas) are not familiar with the Nigerian situation. Their attempts at brain picking offer some help but not often enough. Consequently many recommendations are based either on the situation in the home country of the members or on pre-conceived notions as to what the Nigerian situation should be. It is not unusual for the staff of the institution (who consider themselves better equipped to know the right answers since they live with the problems) to adopt an uncooperative or a hostile attitude to the recommendations, on the grounds that those who made them were unrealistic. The attitude of course is often different when the recommendations are acceptable to the staff member concerned.

A second weakness relates specifically to external examiners. It is common knowledge that professors tend not to invite as external examiners persons they fear may report adversely on their departments. It is not unusual for a professor to invite a friendly professor from another university, who in turn reciprocates by inviting his host to be his own external examiner. It is also known that some professors tone down adverse comments to enhance their chances of being invited the following year.

(ii) Lack of clearly stated objectives. The fact that the universities lack clear statements of objectives must present an obstacle to any serious attempts at evaluation. It is difficult to evaluate a curriculum without knowing what it is meant to achieve. The tendency for the person doing the evaluation is to compare the content and structure of the curriculum with the content and structure of the curricula of related departments within his experience, an experience which may or may not be relevant to the Nigerian situation. External examiners generally compare the level of performance of the students they examine elsewhere with the performance of the students in their own universities. It is largely for this reason that the claim is made that the external examiner system makes for parity or near parity of academic standards among the universities operating the system. What this, of course, means is that the students are judged by standards which may or may not be applicable to them particularly when the different curricula are not aiming at comparable objectives. Many external examiners found it difficult to evaluate the Nsukka comprehensive examination because it was something outside the experience of most of them.

(iii) Neglect of the extra-curriculum. Many of the current attempts at evaluation are confined to the formal curriculum. This is understandable because of the lack of serious attempts to forge significant links between the formal curriculum and the extra-curriculum. Visitations and joint university advisory committees enquire into student welfare services, but other agents of evaluation like external examiners, curriculum committees and potential employers generally confine themselves to the formal curriculum. Universities which use external examiners for final year examinations only, as Nsukka does, automatically impose additional restrictions on the role of these examiners who are not in a position to express an opinion on those portions of the curriculum completed prior to the final year and which do not constitute part of the final year examinations. At Nsukka this would cover the entire general studies programme; at Lagos it would exclude the General African Studies course. Thus

the external examiner is precluded from evaluating not only the extra-curriculum but also those portions of the formal curriculum considered essential for every student of the university.

(iv) Lack of studies. Most of the studies which form a regular feature of the literature of American higher education are non-existent in Nigeria. Nigerian university professors have shown little or no interest in the problems of higher education as possible fields for research, and the administrators either claim they have no time for research or consider research outside their terms of reference or competence, even though they gather relevant data annually which form valuable research material. Just as the findings in Jacob's *Changing Values in College* must have shaken many American university people, so it is possible that the first major study of the impact of the Nigerian university on its students may challenge the claims of many Nigerian university people about the tremendous service they are performing for the country.

(g) Recommendations

Evaluation should be comprehensive. Evaluation, in regard to the curriculum, embraces the educational objectives and the selection and organization of the learning experiences (including both the formal curriculum and the extra-curriculum). Any meaningful evaluation must therefore cover these grounds. The person conducting the evaluation must know the educational objectives, particularly the desired behaviour changes which the educational experience at the university is intended to produce in the students. He also needs to know each of the different learning experiences which are expected to produce these desired changes, and how they are organized into the formal curriculum and the extra-curriculum. In presenting his report, he would need to explain his methods of evaluation.

Effective evaluation is incomplete if limited to the formal curriculum in isolation. Jacob's *Changing Values in College* has shown some of the hazards of limiting evaluation to the formal curriculum alone. It could lead to the hasty acceptance or rejection of the curriculum without regard to other important factors. As Dressel pointed out, failure to produce the desired behaviour changes in students may be caused by one of the following:

(i) the inappropriateness of the educational objectives, which might not be clearly stated and understood or which might be unattainable and therefore unrealistic;

(ii) the irrelevance of the learning experiences selected to the attainment of the desired objectives;

(iii) the inadequate organization of the learning experiences;

(iv) the invalidity or inappropriateness of the evaluation criteria. (17.2)

Evaluation which takes all these factors into account will enable the institution to find out in which respects the whole educational experience it offers needs improvement.

The need of studies. Reference has already been made to the lack of essential studies to facilitate evaluation and decision making. The educational objectives of an institution normally refer to desired patterns of behaviour among the students graduating from that institution. The institution states what it intends to make of its students during their three or four-year undergraduate career, and this is followed by details of the various curricula and other learning experiences designed to assist the student in attaining the objectives. Evaluation of the effectiveness of these educational experiences is therefore in effect an assessment of the extent to which the institutional objectives or the desired behaviour patterns have been attained by the students. Studies of the students therefore form a crucial part of such evaluation.

If the studies are to be meaningful, they must be conducted at different periods in the career of the same group of students. One such period is immediately following the student's entry to the university. By studying the student at that point it would be possible to ascertain what he brings with him to the university. Knowledge of what he brings with him would provide useful information for comparing students entering the university from different educational backgrounds. It would also give the university material for reviewing its educational objectives, with a view to filling important gaps revealed by the study or eliminating objectives that had been adequately met by other agencies outside the university. Above all it would give the university concrete data with which to assess its success or failure in attaining its educational objectives. A random sample of the student body, selected in a manner that would include samples of the major backgrounds from which the university draws its students, would suffice for the study.

A similar study could be conducted at the end of each year of the student's career, to keep track of any behaviour changes throughout his career. This would help to determine whether the changes occur at any particular period in a student's career, say during the first year or later in his career. The results of such periodic studies would be helpful in the organization of the curriculum and the other learning experiences.

It is necessary to conduct a study shortly before the student graduates, to determine how successful the university has been in producing the desired behaviour in him. A comparison of the results of the study with the results of the first year study would help to determine the extent of the impact of the university on that student.

In view of the fact that Nigerian universities are claiming to train future leaders of the country, it is important to evaluate how much of the impact made on these potential leaders by their university during their undergraduate years is retained after graduation. If much of it is retained, then the educational experiences at the university can be said to exercise lasting influence on its graduates. A study is therefore essential some years after the students have graduated from the university, provided allowance is made for significant learning experiences to which the students have been exposed since graduation.

Long-range planning. As mentioned earlier, every Nigerian university has some machinery for handling curriculum problems. Very often, however, the concern of the curriculum committee, or its equivalent in each university, is limited to requests for the addition or deletion of courses from existing curricula and, less frequently, to the introduction of new degree or non-degree programmes.

If the Nigerian university is to provide effective leadership for the society, it must set its sights not only on the present but also on the future, attempting informed predictions of the changing roles of the Nigerian university graduates in the next ten, twenty or more years. To accomplish this, it must project its horizons not only within but also beyond Nigerian boundaries, to probable developments in Africa and the world. Having done so, it must consider what effects such probable developments are likely to have on its educational objectives, and in turn on the selection and organization of its learning experiences.

It is recognized that there are arguments against such excursions into the future. Carter has been quoted earlier as arguing that it is almost impossible to predict national needs in the present world in view of the complex social and technological development now taking place. He did not, however, recommend that the U.K. universities should fold their arms and take what comes to them because it is futile to plan ahead; he argued for the kind of education which he felt would prepare the graduates of the U.K. universities for such complex social and technological development—in this case, for 'a more general education and an imaginative understanding over a fairly wide area'. (12.1) He was, in a sense, predicting the kind of university education to meet the future needs of the United Kingdom.

It is difficult to name any country undergoing more rapid technological changes on a large scale today than the U.S.A. In spite of this the state of California as far back as 1966 had set into motion a machinery charged with the responsibility for designing school curricula for the California of A.D. 2,000. The panel was bound to take into account the serious point made by Carter, plus the possibilities the present human assaults on the moon may open up. It might make some recommendations which later events may prove misguided, but long range planning is one way in which to ensure that the future does not arrive like the unexpected thief in the night.

It is hoped that each Nigerian university will consider creating some machinery for such long-range planning, distinct from the machinery for considering the addition or deletion of individual courses or the interpretation of existing regulations. Such long-range planning machinery should include sociologists, philosophers, psychologists, scientists, political scientists and representatives of other relevant fields; in short it should be inter-disciplinary in scope. The existence of such a machinery would also provide a forum for giving preliminary consideration to major changes in curriculum emphasis, to determine the overall effect of such changes on the educational objectives of the institution and thereby minimise the problems created by piecemeal evaluation.

Student participation. There is no evidence that Nigerian universities make any use of their students for evaluating the curriculum. The general feeling appears to be that the students are not qualified to express constructive opinions on the nature and content of their education. The continued maintenance of such an attitude would seem to deprive the universities of one important avenue for evaluation. It is true that the student's horizon is often more restricted than that of the university, and that some students may not fully appreciate the value of some educational experiences until after leaving the university. There is however no doubt that the student is a major source of information on how much benefit he is deriving from his studies. This likely to become more obvious as his university studies are related more and more to the problems he is likely to face outside the campus.

If student evaluation is to be meaningful, the student needs guarantees that he will not suffer any disabilities as a result of his comments. On the other hand, the student must guard against making malicious comments which have no justification other than the desire to embarrass or hurt his teacher.

Student participation in evaluation should help to keep the students aware of the educational objectives of the university. It should also provide a useful introduction of the student to the need for periodic evaluation of his work after graduation. The Nsukka experience of 1970 shows that, given the opportunity, students could make valuable contributions.

SUMMARY

Methods have been proposed in this chapter for curriculum reform in Nigerian universities. The adoption and implementation of these proposals by Nigerian universities would entail years of arduous work and re-thinking; but it is hoped that it will be a positive step towards the development of truly Nigerian undergraduate curricula. The following curriculum pattern is expected to emerge:

(a) A core of university-wide requirements common to all students, and aimed at preparing the student for his future civic responsibilities. This portion of the curriculum, if properly drawn up, should be unmistakably Nigerian since its aim is to prepare the student for his role as a leading Nigerian citizen. It should also provide an integrative experience by making each student discover how his and other specialties relate to the overall problems of life in the Nigerian, the African, and, to a lesser degree, the world context.

(b) Common requirements for every student within each broad academic division, planned to emphasize the interrelatedness of knowledge and to help the student to place his field of specialty in its wider context.

(c) Requirements within the student's specialty or major discipline, selected from his academic division.

(d) Subsidiary or ancillary requirements, intended to reinforce or supplement the student's specialty, and chosen from within or outside the student's academic division as may become necessary.

(e) Organized extra-curricula experiences, aimed at reinforcing and supplementing the formal curriculum, in order to enhance the possibility of attaining the institutional educational objectives.

The degree of emphasis on each part of the programme would depend on the institutional objectives. In mapping out each degree curriculum in detail, it would also be essential to determine at what points or in what years to introduce the different components of the curriculum and other learning experiences for maximum effect. A university that attaches great importance to education for civic responsibilities might ensure that it features in the student's final year, and probably spread it through the earlier years as well.

REFERENCES

1 Saunders, J.T. & Dowuona, M. (eds.), *The West African Intellectual Community*, Papers and Discussions of an International Seminar on Inter-University Cooperation in West Africa, held in Freetown, Sierra Leone, 11–16 December, 1961, Ibadan, Ibadan University Press, 1962. 1.1: p. 57.

2 Olubummo, A. & Ferguson, J., *The Emergent University*, London, Longmans, Green and Co., Ltd., 1960. 2.1: p. 116; 2.2: p. 47.

3 University of Nigeria Photographic Society, *Graduates Album and Speeches of Convocations, University of Nigeria, Nsukka*. Vol. 1, No. IV, 1966. 3.1: p. 20; 3.2: p. 25; 3.3: p. 57.

4 Denbigh, Kenneth, 'Unwilling Specialists, The College X Plan', *Times Educational Supplement*, No. 2501, April 26, 1963. 4.1: p. 867.

5 'Special Training not enough: wider duty to educate', *Times Educational Supplement*, No. 2609, May 21, 1965. 5.1: p. 1603.

6 Bell, Daniel, *The Reforming of General Education, the Columbia College Experience in its National Setting*, New York and London, Columbia University Press, 1966. 6.1: p. 15; 6.2: pp. 282–285; 6.3: pp. 208–210; 6.4: p. 192.

7 Thomas, Russell, *The Search for a Common Learning: General Education 1800–1960*. New York, McGraw-Hill Book Company Inc. 1962. 7.1: p. 299; 7.2: p. 280.

8 Moos, Elizabeth, *Higher Education in the Soviet Union* New York, National Council of American-Soviet Friendship, June 1956. 8.1: p. 27.

9 Yelyutin, Vyacheslav, *Higher Education in the U.S.S.R.* New York, Bookfield House, Inc., 1959. 9.1: p. 32; 9.2: p. 30.

10 Katz, Joseph & Sanford, Nevitt, 'The Curriculum in the Perspective of the Theory of Personality Development' in *The American College*, Nevitt Sanford (ed.). New York, John Wiley & Sons, Inc., 1962 (4th edition. Sept. 1964). 10.1: pp. 437–439.

11 Mundelein College, Chicago, *Catalogue* 1965–1967. 11.1: p. 9; 11.2: p. 11.

12 'Changing Patterns of Study', The Gulbenkian Educational Discussion, 1964, *Universities Quarterly*, Vol. 19, No. 2, March 1965, 117–161. 12.1: p. 120.

13 Daiches, David (ed.), *The Idea of a New University: An Experiment in Sussex*, London, Andre Deutsch Ltd., 1964. 13.1: pp. 60–80.

14 UNESCO. *The Development of Higher Education in Africa*. Paris, UNESCO 1963. 14.1: pp. 54–55.

15 Jacob, Philip E., *Changing Values in College*, New York, Harper & Brothers, Publishers, 1957. 15.1: p. 11; 15.2: p. 99; 15.3: p. 98.

16 Dressel, Paul L. & Lehmann, Irvin J., 'The Impact of Higher Education on student attitudes, values, and critical thinking abilities', *The Educational Record*, Vol. 46, No.·3 Summer 1965, 248–258. 16.1: p. 256.
17 Dressel, Paul L., *The Undergraduate Curriculum in Higher Education*, Washington D.C., The Centre for Applied Research in Education, Inc., 1963. 17.1: p. 26; 17.2: p. 32.
18 Piper, D.T. Warren., 'Getting the best fit between students and courses', *Universities Quarterly*, Vol. 20, No. 3, June 1966, 317–327. 18.1: pp. 318–319.
19 Baskin, Samuel (ed.), *Higher Education: Some Newer Developments*, New York, McGraw-Hill Book Company, 1965. 19.1: p. 20; 19.2: pp. 52–53; 19.3: p. 38.

CHAPTER 6

ACCESS TO THE UNIVERSITY

University Education for Whom?

TWO APPROACHES TO UNIVERSITY ADMISSIONS

Harold W. Stoke referred to the question 'Who shall be educated' as 'one of the oldest, most persistent, and most pervasive of all educational debates'. (1.1)

The debate continues. On one extreme are the advocates of universal higher education, who maintain that university education should be made available to whoever can reach it, with no predetermined maximum numbers to be enrolled at any one time, and no standard selection procedure aimed at controlling admissions. On the other extreme are those who maintain that university education should be restricted to the carefully selected few who would provide the leadership for society. McGrath called the two viewpoints the 'societal view' (in favour of universal higher education), and the 'scholastic view' (in favour of restricted access). (2.1) Historically, the scholastic view has been predominant for centuries. Serious attempts at making university education universal are much more recent, and have found greatest favour in the United States of America. It would be helpful to consider this recent development in some detail before proceeding to consider the Nigerian experience.

UNIVERSAL HIGHER EDUCATION

The 'societal view' maintains that the purpose of higher education is not only to supply society as a whole with the different categories of trained manpower it requires, but also to provide for each individual an opportunity to develop himself intellectually to the limit of his capability. An admissions policy that is highly restrictive or selective arrogates to the university admissions officers the responsibility for deciding who should and who should not receive university education. Screening out persons who, if admitted, might have become successful deprives such persons of the opportunity to develop themselves intellectually to the limits of their ability. It also impairs their chances of competing on equal terms for leadership roles in their society. The 'societal view' holds that it is unnecessary for the university to assume the responsibility for screening the potential leaders of the society; the leaders of society will be selected by society through the natural processes of competition and survival of the fittest.

Universal higher education has found greatest favour in the United States of America, where there is a deliberate policy to make higher education available to a majority of each age-group of population. One argument advanced in its support is that higher education is within the intellectual reach of many more people than traditionally receive it:

> The American theory is that gold is where you find it—in short, that talent is evenly distributed throughout the whole population, and that it is, on the whole, generously distributed. The American position is that talent is not something given, and fixed, but something that can be discovered, encouraged, and developed. (2.2)

The 1962 norms for general intelligence developed in connection with the General Aptitude Test Battery used by the United States Employment Service appear to support the American theory that talent is evenly distributed among the population. They showed that 50% of the American population have at least the capacity to complete two years of junior college (which is equivalent, at least in respect of the transfer programmes, to the first two years of university education) and many within this group would probably have the capacity to exceed that level; about 31% have the capacity to complete the regular four-year undergraduate programme, and 16% have the capacity to proceed to advanced degrees. (2.3) To restrict higher education to a select few would therefore mean preventing many capable young people from attaining their maximum potential in life and, in the process, a failure to discover some 'mute inglorious Miltons' or the gems 'of purest ray serene' which the dark unfathomed depths of ocean bear.

Underlying the American support for universal higher education is the spirit of American democracy. This spirit is evident in Bowles' definition of the goal of American education as 'the maximum development of every person to the limit of his ability'. (3.1) Access to education, including higher education, is generally regarded as an inalienable right of a citizen in a democracy. Hence the Educational Policies Commission, in 1964, could base its case for the extension of universal education beyond the secondary school on the following grounds:

> Unless the opportunity for education beyond the high school can be made available to all, ... then the American promise of individual dignity and freedom cannot be extended to all. .... In the future, the important question needs to be not 'Who deserves to be admitted'? but 'Whom can the society, in conscience and self interest, exclude'? (4·1)

The Commission held the view that nobody should be excluded from further (i.e. higher) education 'unless his deficiences are so severe that even the most flexible and dedicated institution could contribute little to his mental development'. (4.1) It therefore went on to recommend the establishment of what it described as 'non-selective' colleges in 'every population centre', which would 'admit for at least two years of general study all high school graduates who apply'. (4·2)

Bowles reports that the U.S. target is to make it possible for at least 51% of the age-group population to proceed to higher education. He reckoned that this target would be achieved by 1967, or by 1980 at a conservative estimate. (2.4)

The supporters of universal higher education also put forward the economic advantages to the nation of making higher education universal. D.P. Moyinhan, in *The Impact of Manpower Development and Employment of Youth,* refers to attempts by Dr. E.F. Denison to measure education as a source of economic growth. Denison estimated that the U.S. national product would increase by 1·4% if between 1960 and 1980 40% of the U.S. labour force were to receive one year of education beyond what they normally would have received, and that this would represent a 0·07% increase in the growth rate over that period. The average annual economic growth could be raised by 0·10% percentage points if the additional year of education were extended to the entire U.S. labour force. (2.5)

At the individual level, the data from 1961 life-time and mean annual incomes of U.S. males 25–64 years old, considered in relation to total years of schooling by the individuals, showed that men who received 1–3 years of college education could anticipate a life-time income exceeding $273,000, 22% above that of high school graduates who received no post-secondary education (reckoned at $224,407). Those completing four or more years of college education could expect about $360,604 life-time income, which is 61% above the income of high school graduates without post-secondary education. (2.6) In other words, giving more people higher education increases the national rate of economic growth while at the same time increasing the average annual income of the individuals who receive the education.

The U.K. Committee on Higher Education (the Robbins Committee) also talked about the advantages of higher education even in respect of those who fail to complete it. It argued that:

> the total advantage of higher education to a country or to its people cannot be fully described in terms of the numbers who successfully complete it. Those who abandon higher education in other countries may yet be more useful citizens in the community on account of their experience. (5.1)

Having listed some of the arguments in favour of universal higher education, it is essential to consider some of the problems likely to accompany it. The first major problem is the cost involved. It has been estimated that it would cost the United States anywhere between $15 and $20 billion a year to make higher education fully universal, excluding the cost of facilities. (2.7)

A second problem is the need to create new institutions to offer programmes which may not hitherto have been offered by institutions of higher education. One estimate is that America would need about 2,000 *different types* of institutions if it were to cater for the numerous interests, abilities and talents of its widely broadened student clientele. Thus universal higher education would bring about the diversification of higher education which in turn, would lead to the establishment of different types of institutions offering different types of programmes.

A relaxation of entry standards usually goes with a policy of universal higher education. In some European countries, such as the Netherlands and France, admission to the University (or to higher education generally) is fairly automatic, the only important requirement being the successful completion of secondary education. The French Grandes Ecoles are exceptions to this general rule, being very highly selective. In the U.S.A., the laws of some states require the state-supported universities and colleges to admit any high school graduate of that state who applies for admission. The consequence of this is that these institutions admit many students who, in more selective circumstances, might not have been admitted. W. Kenneth Richmond described the effects of such an admission policy within the U.S.:

> It is as if the biblical eye of the needle had been replaced by a portal wide enough to admit the big battalions, or—to switch metaphors—as if the tariff walls which once protected the formal academic studies had been removed and a new era of free trade begun. (6)

Having relaxed entry standards, a university could either decide to tighten the bolts after the students have been given the opportunity to demonstrate their capability to cope with university studies, or it could help the students to 'get by' by providing what Hutchins called 'an educational cafeteria' designed to cater for various palates. In the former case, the result is often a high drop-out rate— sometimes as high as 50% of each intake. Where the bulk of the drop-out occurs at the end of the first year, it conveys the impression that the universities have merely delayed the selection process by one year, and appears to inflate the average cost of university education. It may, of course, be that the benefit of that year of exposure to higher education, to the individual as well as to the society, could compensate for the material wastage; that is the point brought forward by the Robbins Committee in the quotation above. An annual drop-out of such a high percentage of freshmen in the Nigerian context could create more social, psychological, and economic problems than it could hope to solve. It would be rare to find many Nigerian undergraduates who would readily accept that they failed because they had reached the limit of their ability. The national uproar which followed the dismissal of between 20 and 30 students on academic grounds from University College, Ibadan in 1949 is still within living memory.

Many of the criticisms of American undergraduate education can be traced to some of the adjustments that have been made in order to accommodate large numbers of students of varying ability levels. Emery F. Bacon, in a paper presented to the 17th National Conference on Higher Education held in Chicago on March 2, 1962 under the auspices of the Association for Higher Education remarked:

In our anxiety to provide a college education for as many students as possible, as it may rightfully be argued that a democratic society demands, we have erected over 1,500 institutions of higher learning. Unfortunately, many of these schools today grant a bachelor's degree that has no significance, and a number of colleges may actually be inferior to a few secondary schools.

We have secured for ourselves quantity, but we have sacrificed, to an alarming extent, the quality of education upon which we at one time prided ourselves. Indeed, in the opinion of some Americans and practically all foreign critics, we have structured a program of education from first grade through the senior year in college which, with few exceptions, borders on the trivial. (7.1)

Another problem accompanying universal higher education is that it tends to prolong the overall period of education. When the Educational Policies Commission recommended an extension of universal education to the first two years of college, it proposed the postponement of vocational preparation until after those two years. Very few American university students are required to make their final choice of major subjects until after their first two years in college; many American universities make it clear, in any case, that the undergraduate curricula are not intended to produce specialists in any field but to provide citizenship training. Specialization has been postponed until the student enters a graduate or professional school. This has its effects on the undergraduates. One reads of students who are unable to discover themselves, who lack motivation, and see in the education they receive little relevance to life and a future career. The upsurge in the use by these students of LSD and other hallucinatory drugs is to aid them in discovering themselves. The launching of 'Free Universities' by students in different parts of the U.S.A., or 'The Experiment' by Stanford University students, are manifestations of a dissatisfaction with an education which seems aimed at keeping the youth away from full involvement in society and out of mischief for as long as possible.

Taking into account the great technological advances made by the United States in recent years, which have resulted in a five-day working week and may yet lead to a further reduction in working hours and days, it is difficult to dissociate the decision to extend universal education to higher education from the labour situation in the country. There is no urgent necessity for so many young people in the labour market, so it helps the labour situation to keep them away from it as long as possible. An increase in the years of education is one very effective means of achieving this, regardless of the relevance of the education provided to the present or future lives of the students. A.D.C. Peterson summed up the point in these words:

> It is certainly a widely accepted principle in the sociology of education that however much educationists have pressed on cultural grounds for the gradual raising of the terminal age of secondary education, the decisive factor in bringing about this gradual rise has been the employment situation. Either there were no jobs for the adolescent in farm or factory, or organized labour was anxious to keep him off the market. (2.8)

RELEVANCE TO NIGERIA

Placed alongside a policy of highly restricted access to higher education, the idea of universal higher education sounds admirable. It is democratic; it is fair. It should lead to the discovery of many flowers which might otherwise be left to blush and perish unseen. When the politician, Chief Nanga, in Chinua Achebe's *A Man of the People* assumed the unearned degree of M.A. (Minus Opportunity), he symbolized in some respects, many others who might have earned M.A. or higher degrees with minimum effort if only the opportunity to do so had been made available to them. Many of our accomplishments can be attributed to the availability to us of opportunities which we made good use of; there might be many other people who have comparable talents and abilities but have accomplished much less because similar opportunities were not available to them for one reason or another. Universal higher education would help to equalize some of these opportunities.

Having paid this tribute to universal higher education, I must quickly add that it would be daylight madness to accept it as the immediate target for educational planning in Nigeria. Universal education should begin from the bottom rather than the top of the educational pyramid. The educational targets recommended by the Commission on Post-School Certificate and Higher Education in Nigeria (the Ashby Commission) during the ten-year period 1960–1970 illustrate how far away Nigeria is from universal education, even below university level. The Commission recommended that out of 1,000 children in Northern Nigeria aged about 12, about 250 should receive primary education, 25 should receive secondary education, and 2 or 3 should go on to a university. For the rest of the country, all the 1,000 should receive primary education, 70 should receive secondary education, and 5 to 6 should go on to the university. (8.1) The conclusion from these targets is that by 1970 universal education was not expected to have been achieved throughout the country, even at the primary school level. At the secondary level, only 2·5 to 7% of the age-group population was to be covered. No one could seriously contemplate making higher education universal in these circumstances.

The low targets do not mean that Nigeria does not recognize the importance of education. She certainly does, perhaps even more than many developed countries, but she also recognizes the budgetary limitations on development plans. There are few governments in the world that channel a higher *percentage* of their total annual budgets into education than the Nigerian governments, particularly the state governments. Some regional governments before the creation of 12 states in 1967 had ploughed as much as 40% of their budget into education alone. It is impossible to exceed this level of expenditure on education, or even to maintain it, if the governments are to ensure a balanced development of the country. The former Eastern Nigerian government radically modified its plans for universal primary education some years ago when it discovered the immensity of the problems and costs involved.

An expansion in educational facilities and opportunities must be matched by a comparable expansion in employment opportunities for the products of education. Unfortunately this has not always been the experience in Nigeria. The expansion of elementary and secondary education has led to a higher incidence of unemployment among products of those levels of education. The phenomenal expansion of university places in the 1960s resulted in an apparent glut of graduates in arts and some of the social sciences. Limited industrialization and limited openings for university graduates in the private sector of the economy has turned the civil service and more recently the secondary schools into the major employers of university graduates. The establishment of competitive examinations for graduates seeking appointments to certain positions in the civil service is undoubtedly a sign of things to come. Graduates, particularly those with pass degrees, have been known to spend up to twelve months in a frust-rating search for employment.

David Potter remarked that by promising equality of educational opportunity for all, a democracy educates people without pausing to consider whether suitable jobs would be available for those receiving the education. The expectation is that a society which is constantly raising its level of education would also constantly generate enough positions for those being educated. Even those who drop out are not a write-off to society; the fact that they have been enabled to develop to their maximum intellectual and personal abilities is enough to justify the social cost of their education. He, however, goes on to suggest how this line of reasoning would run aground when applied to poor countries:

> All this is very well and works admirably if the country following these practices has the necessary physical resources and human resourcefulness to raise the standard of living, to create new occupational opportunities, and to find outlets for the abilities of an ever increasing class of trained men. But it must have this endowment to begin with, or it is certain to suffer intensely from the social waste that results from giving training which cannot be utilized and from the psychological damage that results when a competition has an excess of participants and a paucity of rewards. (9.1)

EDUCATING AN ELITE

The current Nigerian approach to university education is a man-power approach: the high-level manpower needs are assessed from time to time, and each Nigerian university is required to align its enrolment figures to the national manpower targets, including the distribution of students to the different courses of study. As an example, the universities were requested to ensure that about 75% of their total enrolment by 1967/68 were in scientific and technological fields; in addition, maximum enrolment figures were pre-determined for each university. Consequently students are offered admission to (and government and other scholarships are offered for) specific courses of studies.

The targets for university education by 1970, already cited, work out at 0·2% to 0·3% of the age-group population for Northern Nigeria, and 0·5% to 0·6% for the rest of the country. Statistics provided for the UNESCO Tananarive Seminar on the Development of Higher Education in Africa, if they are accurate, give the position in Nigeria at the time the targets above were proposed by the Ashby Commission. The population aged 20 to 24 years in Nigeria in 1960 was estimated at 3,095,000. (10.1) The total number of Nigerians in higher education within and outside Nigeria during the 1960/61 academic year was estimated at 2,207. (10.2) This approximates to 2,000 enrolled out of an age-group population of 3 million, or 1 per 1,500 or about 0·07%. (These percentages must be treated as approximations; they probably ignored the fact that many Nigerian undergraduates at that time entered the university after the age of 24, and some still do). The UNESCO seminar recommended a minimum target of 1·5% for Middle Africa, including Nigeria by 1980 or earlier. (10.3)

One immediate reaction to these statistics is that Nigeria is spending millions of pounds annually for the education of less than 0·5% of the age-group population. This brings with it the concept of the elite, with all its distasteful connotations. The Nigerian university is undoubtedly educating an elite, if that is the only description for the persons being equipped to provide intellectual, professional, and cultural leadership for the country. There is hardly any alternative to this in the present stage of Nigeria's development, and the Nigerian university need not be apologetic about it if it can formulate admission procedures that would eliminate at least some of the distasteful connotations of eliticism.

University education, by its very nature as the apex of the educational pyramid, is not within the intellectual reach of every member of the society. John Gardner once stated that 'Everyone does not have a right to be a college graduate, any more than everyone has a right to run a four-minute mile'. (11.1) Therefore, as Clark Kerr remarked, 'The great university is of necessity elitist—the elite of merit'. (12.1) The high rate of wastage found in countries which grant fairly automatic access to higher education to every high school graduate and the very existence of wastage among the more selective university systems tend to support this view. In the Netherlands, the wastage rate in the 1960s was estimated at about 40%. In addition many students often spent seven years on courses of study that should normally take 4 to 5 years, with the result that a third of all university students were above the age of 25. The wastage rate in France was estimated at over 50%, except in the Grandes Ecoles which had very low wastage. The highly selective American universities have low wastage, while the rate is high in the less selective universities; the overall average was about 45%. For comparative purposes, universities in the Soviet Union which are selective in their admissions had about 20% wastage in their full-time courses, which was about as low as in Britain. (5.2) The following statistics, which are *approximations* extracted from a graphical chart in *Access to Higher Education,* show that in 1959 only a small percentage of the age-group population had access to higher education in even the most highly developed countries:

Country	Completing primary schl.	Entering sec. schl.	Completing sec. schl.	Entering higher educ.
Japan	98	95	46	15
U.S.A.	96	94	64	35
New Zealand	96	94	15	14
U.S.S.R.	95	75	40	16
United Kingdom	94	25	6	5
France	94	20	10	8
Israel	60	42	10	13
India	42	17	7	4
United Arab Republic	30	24	10	4
Ghana	22	16	2	2

The high figure recorded for the U.S.A. calls for two observations. First, of the 35% entering higher education in 1958/59, only 17% completed it in 1961/62. (5.3) Secondly, because the bachelor's degree has come within the reach of so many, higher degrees or evidence of graduate studies are now required for many top positions; consequently, the graduate schools are in a sense taking over the role of educating the elite. The figures for France are also significant. Although France grants virtually automatic admission to the university, only 8% of the age-group population enter higher education. This is because the screening has been done lower down the educational pyramid: only 20% enter the secondary school, with 10% completing.

Compared with the figures above, and with the UNESCO target of 1·5% for Middle Africa, the Nigerian targets appear appallingly low. It is doubtful however whether the country has the funds to do significantly more at present. The Ashby Commission demonstrated the immensity of the problem involved in hitting even such a low target in 1970:

> Lest these objectives seem too modest, let us add that to build educational pyramids of this shape will require something like an additional 130,000 secondary school places and about 4,500 more teachers, more than 100 sixth form streams and at least 350 more sixth form teachers, more teacher-training colleges, greatly enlarged technical institutes, and a seven-fold increase in the capacity of universities. (8.2)

In a country in which university education is to be so highly selective, admission procedures assume tremendous importance. If care is not taken, admission could become the privilege of the influential or wealthy people. Fortunately, the laws establishing each Nigerian university provide that no person shall be denied admission on discriminatory grounds. It is important to buttress this provision with an effective admissions policy which will guarantee equality of opportunity to all who seek admission to the institution. That way, if an elite is educated, it will be an elite of merit. When Ikejiani pleaded in *Nigerian Universities and the Nation* that 'University places should not be reserved for the privileged few alone' (13.1), it was not clear whether his emphasis was on *privilege* or on *few*. It could not be on *privilege* when it is common knowledge that the wealthy and the ruling classes in Nigeria are often more interested in sending their children to foreign universities than in getting them into local universities. The Nigerian university is anything but the exclusive preserve of young people from privileged homes.

THE ROLE OF SECONDARY SCHOOLS

Before considering improvements to methods of selection to the university, it is important to consider the very major role which the secondary school should play to assist the university in the overall task of ensuring that admission is offered to the best qualified candidates in each academic field.

Henry Byer wrote an article entitled 'Changing Roles in College Admissions' (14) which illustrates one major role of the secondary school which may not be obvious to many people. In it, he contended that the role of the school in the admissions process would not only grow but might outstrip the role of the college or university itself. He used the 1963 admissions statistics of Harvard College to illustrate his contention. During that year, Harvard College received a little over 5,000 applications, out of which it considered 3,750 fully admissible. These figures cover the admission process as they appear to most people, and convey the impression that the process was under the absolute control of Harvard College which could decide whom to admit or reject. Byer, however, asserts that this impression is erroneous. He states that in 1963 about 150,000 of *all* college-bound students would have been considered fully admissible to Harvard, which works out at about 40 times the "fully admissibles" (3,750) who actually applied. About 145,000 of these were never considered by Harvard, and Harvard probably never knew of their existence since they never applied to it for admission. The decisions as to whether they should go to Harvard or not were not made at Harvard but by the secondary schools and the homes of those students. They may have been right or wrong decisions, but that is irrelevant here; the important thing is that the illustration emphasizes the role of the secondary school in the choice of colleges by its students.

There is evidence that the Nigerian secondary school also influences choice of university by its students. Enquiries by one Nigerian university revealed that it was not receiving many applications from one of the best secondary schools in the country because of some adverse remarks the principal of that school had made about that university to his students. The position changed only after the principal visited the university campus to attend a meeting of secondary school principals and was shown the facilities at the university. What he saw was so surprisingly better than what he had gathered previously that he spontaneously called on the registrar to enquire whether late applications could be considered from his school that year.

In many parts of the world, the secondary school exceeds this role by being assigned the formal responsibility for selecting who proceeds to higher education. Bowles estimates that about three-quarters of the world's educational systems (which enroll half the students who annually enter higher education) rely on the results of the final secondary school examinations for determining eligibility for entrance to higher education. (3.3) Nigerian universities rely completely on secondary school examinations (in respect of students admitted with the Higher School Certificate), or use them as a screening device (in respect of the School Certificate) for selecting candidates to sit the university entrance examinations. The secondary school examinations are, however, run by independent examining boards, but with the students relying heavily on the schools to advise them on what subjects to take in addition to preparing them for the examinations.

Many universities elsewhere have recognized the important role of the secondary schools and established effective liaison with them. American universities deserve particular mention in this respect; the close liaison between university admissions officers and the secondary schools is very striking to a visitor. I had the opportunity of seeing this co-operation between the university and the secondary schools in practice in 1962 when I attended the Principals' Chewing Match, an annual conference of Principals of Secondary Schools in Michigan held at Higgins Lake. The academic and personal qualific-ations of the secondary school leavers were of mutual interest to both groups, and so was their performance after their admission to the university. The degree of liaison has been much less pronounced in the United Kingdom. The tendency among the older universities in that country was that good students would apply to them. It was often the new universities which found it necessary to go to the schools. The recommendations of the Robbins Committee and the emergence of the newest universities are likely to lead to greater liaison.

In Nigeria, prior to 1967, only the University of Nigeria had evolved a deliberate policy of liaison with secondary schools, begin-ning in October 1963 when it organized visits by members of the university academic and administrative staff to 119 secondary schools in different parts of Nigeria. Regular periodic contacts were main-tained with the secondary schools throughout Nigeria between then and the out-break of the civil war in 1967, through the exchange of visits, the publication by the Registrar's Office of a *Newsletter to Secondary Schools*, through regular supply to the schools of relevant university publications, and through arranging special sessions at conferences of principals of secondary schools. Surprisingly enough, a few schools considered it degrading for a university to go to the schools; they maintained it should be the other way round. Many schools, however, applauded the idea as something worth emulating by the other universities. It was a welcome sign that the university had at last recognised the important role of the secondary school.

Many Nigerian secondary school students and staff know very little about many of the courses of study available at the Nigerian universities. They know there are faculties of medicine, engineering, agriculture, and law; they know they can study many of the subjects offered at the School Certificate/General Certificate of Education examination. But they know little about the various specialties within the faculty of medicine, engineering or agriculture, and they know next to nothing about many university studies which have no secondary school equivalent: for example, business administration, education, home economics, political science, journalism, sociology, or psychology. They know little about the opportunities for higher education outside the university—say, at the advanced teacher training colleges or the colleges of technology. As a result, many of the students apply for courses of study for which they are either not qualified or for which they stand little chances of gaining admission. The impression is also created that the university is the only respectable and effective avenue for self-development.

A great deal of general and academic counselling already goes on in Nigerian secondary schools, even though none of these schools has the kind of full-time professionally trained counsellors one finds in most American secondary schools. Within a typical Nigerian boarding school counselling goes on all the time, shared jointly by the staff and the prefects and senior students. Where urgent attention is needed is in careers advice, even though in saying this I do not ignore the serious questions raised in *The Educational Decision-Makers* on the role of secondary school counsellors, especially in determining whether a student goes to college and to which college. (15) A few Nigerian secondary schools have designated some teachers careers masters, but many of them are handicapped by lack of adequate information on the different universities. Universities can help here by sending to each school copies of the regular official publications of the university, particularly those which would be of interest to the schools. Visits by university representatives to the schools to speak to staff and students, and of secondary school staff and students to the university to see what it has to offer would supplement the information contained in the publications. Periodic conferences of careers masters could also be arranged, at which the members could be brought up to date with latest developments within the universities, and, hopefully, other sectors of higher education.

The reports of secondary school principals on their former students seeking admission to the universities could be modified so as to transform them into a more effective selection criterion. This will be considered in greater detail later.

METHODS OF SELECTION

University systems everywhere are selective in one way or another; invariably the selection is left either to the lower schools or to the university. Bowles reckons that formal responsibility for selection is left at the level of secondary education in about three-quarters of the world's educational system. In such systems, eligibility for entry to the university is based on the results of the final secondary school examinations. He, however, adds that about twenty of these systems superimpose a selection examination administered by the universities on the final secondary school examination, thereby transferring part, if not the entire responsibility for selection to higher education. On the other hand, about one quarter of the world's educational systems (including the Soviet Union and the United States which constitute two of the largest systems) enrolling nearly the remaining half, have transferred formal responsibility for selection to higher education. Among these systems, most selections are made at the point of entrance to higher education, *i.e.* prior to entry (as in the Soviet Union), whereas several systems grant virtually automatic admission to all secondary school leavers thereby deferring the final selection until the end of the first year of studies. (3.3) Even among this group, the secondary school still plays a part in the selection process by indirectly screening out the students who drop out during the secondary school career; however it allows the marginal students to get in, which might not be the case where selection is based on high performance in the final secondary school examinations.

Bowles went on to say that selection within secondary education is the least expensive, followed by selection through entrance examinations conducted by the universities prior to entry. Deferred selection after one year at the university is the most expensive as it necessitates providing for many students who will never complete any university programme. (3.4)

Nigeria combines both methods. As has been stated earlier, some students are admitted entirely on their results at the Higher School Certificate (H.S.C.) examinations taken at the end of the two-year sixth form. Admission to the sixth form itself (which is regarded as part of secondary education) is normally dependent on acceptable performance at the School Certificate taken at the end of five years of secondary education. Students seeking university admission with only the School Certificate or its equivalent are required to sit a university entrance examination, in which case the responsibility for selection rests with the university, with the School Certificate results serving as a screening device for selecting the persons qualified to sit the entrance examination. In addition to the two broad groups of candidates, Nigerian universities handle a third group—the private candidates who receive no secondary education but who qualify either for the university entrance examination or for direct admission (like holders of the H.S.C.) as a result of their performance at the ordinary or advanced levels of the General Certificate of Education (G.C.E.) examinations conducted by London University and the West African Examinations Council.

SELECTION CRITERIA
(a) Performance in subject matter examinations

This is the major selection criterion adopted by Nigerian universities, as well as universities in many other parts of the world. Bowles says it serves as virtually the sole selection criterion by all educational systems except the American system. The assumption behind its widespread use is that superior work in such subject matter examinations is a sign of the student's capability to do satisfactory work at the university, while poor performance is a sign that the student cannot cope with university work.

This assumption has led to widespread and continuing controversy. On the one hand, one comes across statements such as this: '"A" (i.e. advanced) Level marks offer the best prediction of success in university courses'. (16.1) The author of that statement, like many other university people in the British Commonwealth, considers performance at the advanced level subjects taken at the G.C.E. or H.S.C. examinations as an effective predictor of performance at the university. On the other hand one also comes across university people holding contrary views. Brock, for instance, in *Admissions: An Oxford View*, justifies the Oxford University entrance examination on the grounds that the G.C.E. advanced level tests performance rather than promise, and might not be an efficient predictor by itself in arts subjects. Oxford University uses the G.C.E. results only as a supplement to its entrance examination which is designed for the boy or girl who is 'ceasing to think as a sixth-former and beginning to think as an undergraduate'. (17.1)

The middle of the road university people would acknowledge some shortcomings in the use of subject matter examinations for university

selection, but hasten to add that the results of its use have been sufficiently encouraging, and that no system of selection could be perfect,
anyway.

Discussions on the suitability of subject matter examinations
per se as predictors of success at the university often shift to consideration of the appropriateness or inappropriateness of specific examination papers. Not uncommonly, also, they shift into a discussion
as to the wisdom of basing university selections on the results of examinations set and graded by bodies external to the particular university.
An element of this can be seen in Brock's proposal for a reform of the
G.C.E. Special Papers. He proposed that the universities and the
schools should be involved in setting the examinations, and that the
universities each candidate wishes to enter should be given an opportunity to see his scripts prior to his selection. He hoped the papers
could be made predictive if handled this way. (17.2) Some professors
in a Nigerian university had expressed a similar desire to see the
G.C.E. or H.S.C. scripts of the candidates applying to the university
for admission before deciding whether or not to select them; they
were reluctant to accept results handed out by an external body.

One major problem in the use of performance in subject matter
examinations as the only or major selection criterion is that a number
of university disciplines have no direct subject matter equivalents in
the secondary schools. Law, for instance, is not studied in any form in
a Nigerian secondary school, nor are some other subjects like
sociology. There are some university studies not taught in secondary
schools but which have acknowledged links with some secondary
school subjects, performance in which is often used as predictors
of performance in the university studies. For example, physics and
mathematics are often used as predictors of performance in engineering, while physics, chemistry and biology are regarded (rightly or
wrongly) as predictors for medicine. There are, however, university
studies, like law, in which such predictors have not been found (at
least in Nigeria) and for which knowledge of any specific secondary
school subjects is not a requirement. In such cases, some other
selection criteria need to be found as there would be no point in
requiring high performance in specific subject matter examinations
unless this is considered a predictor of success in university law studies.

A second major problem, at least in Nigeria, is that even in the
subjects studied in the secondary schools, the subject matter examinations on which candidates are now considered for admission

(except with the university entrance examinations) are not necessarily constructed with university entry in mind. Methods of study
vary between the secondary school and the university; history taught
in the secondary school may focus on the acquisition of historical
events whereas at the university level it may focus on their interpretation. A student distinguishing himself at the acquisition of
historical data at the secondary school may not necessarily distinguish
himself when acquisition gives way to interpretation. Students who
have gained high marks in English Language at the secondary school
(where it was separated from the study of English Literature and
consisted primarily of composition writing and some comprehension)
have encountered difficulties at the university when English expanded to include English literature, literary criticism, linguistics and the
like. One possible solution might be for the Nigerian universities
to design their own subject matter entrance examinations, designed
with university entry in mind, for advanced level candidates, just
as they have done for ordinary level candidates. The possibility of
a joint entrance examination for all the universities was mentioned
in the 1960s but appears to have been dropped.

The general experience in the educational systems which rely on
subject matter examinations is that they have proved generally
satisfactory predictors, particularly with the students who obtained
superior results in the examinations. Mediocre performance may or
may not lead to satisfactory work at the university. Most failures in
the examinations are unsuitable for university studies, but some have
proved capable of satisfactory work. The fact that some failures have
proved capable of satisfactory work at the university suggests the
possibility of some errors in selection if these examinations are used
as the sole criterion, provided that the examinations themselves had
been carefully prepared.

It is necessary to conduct a study of the different subject matter
examinations used by Nigerian universities as selection criteria, to
assess their effectiveness as predictors of success in university studies.
No such study has been done; if any has, the results have not been
published. Meanwhile, in view of some of the problems raised earlier
on, it would be helpful to utilize additional selection criteria to
supplement these subject matter examinations which are set and
marked by bodies external to the Nigerian universities. (It should be
mentioned that Nigerian and West African university staff are
becoming increasingly involved in the setting and marking of these

examinations, now that the West African Examinations Council has assumed responsibility for them).

(b) Tests of academic aptitude

Academic aptitude tests are used primarily in the United States where several batteries of tests have been and are still being developed. American universities which belong to the College Entrance Examination Board are obliged to select their students on the basis of the batteries of achievement and scholastic aptitude tests developed by the Board, except where state laws prohibit this. State universities which are required by the state to admit all residents of that state holding high school diplomas administer some of these tests *after* the student has been offered admission. The results of the tests provide material for counselling the student when he enrolls.

Aptitude, achievement and other standardized tests have a special place in the American educational system. Owing to the tremendous diversity in American education at every level, and the difficulty of comparing the quality of the thousands of high school diplomas (which are in no way standardized) there is need for some standardized yardstick by which one candidate can be compared with another candidate from another school or state. The standardized tests constitute this yardstick; they equate the candidates to the same score-board, regardless of the differences in their previous education or background. This need does not exist in Nigeria because the School Certificate/G.C.E. Ordinary level and the H.S.C./G.C.E. Advanced level are public examinations taken by all students regardless of their schools as well as by private (i.e. non-institutional) candidates. These examinations make it possible, therefore, to compare one candidate with another.

There is increasing opposition to the use of these tests in the United States, though, paradoxically, the number of test batteries has also been increasing. Felix Robb foresees a decline in the enthusiasm for the tests among American universities: 'Apparently a number of colleges. . . . are challenging the use of objective test scores; the rumbling is sufficiently loud to suggest that a significant shift in thinking (or wondering) is taking place. This will bear watching closely'. (18.1) He stated that there was an increasing recognition that test results *alone* do not provide an adequate basis for admission to university studies. Moreover there was some unhappiness about the preponderance of objective testing in America, with less and less attention being paid to the essay type examination 'which requires the individual to express himself in his own terms'. (18.2)

The erstwhile Nigerian Aptitude Testing Unit (which has since become part of the West African Examinations Council), assisted the law faculties of three Nigerian universities in the 1960s to develop and administer some aptitude tests to candidates for admission to those faculties. Attempts by N.A.T.U. to extend the tests to other university faculties failed because of the practical problems involved. If the results were to be meaningful, the tests had to be applied to *all* candidates for admission to any particular field of study and not only to the candidates already offered admission. Because most candidates are admitted on their performance in the advanced level G.C.E. or H.S.C. examinations, to subject these candidates to the N.A.T.U. tests would have meant organizing special examinations prior to final selection. No university was prepared to take on the trouble and expenses such a decision was bound to entail. The ordinary level or School Certificate candidates who are normally required to take university entrance examinations appeared a less problematic group. Here also the N.A.T.U. request could not be met because it would have meant subjecting the candidates to more examination hours a day than was considered equitable, or running a two day examination, with the expenses and problems involved both for the universities and for the candidates. N.A.T.U. did, however, test some students in some faculties *after* their admission to the university, to determine the correlation between performance at the tests and performance at the university.

An official of N.A.T.U. acknowledged that N.A.T.U. was working on the unproved assumption that the present subject matter examinations were not reliable predictors of success in university studies. The universities needed something more than a hunch to swing over from one set of examinations to another which had also not proved its reliability in the Nigerian setting, and the adoption of which would increase the cost of university admission. If Bowles' claim is valid, that aptitude tests achieve about the same results as subject matter examinations when used as the only selection criterion, there might be little wisdom in trying to *replace* the existing examinations with aptitude tests. Even if the N.A.T.U. tests above established a positive correlation between aptitude scores and performance at the University, this need not mean that aptitude tests are better or poorer predictors than the present subject matter examinations.

What seems needed is some systematic research into the reliability of the School Certificate, H.S.C., and G.C.E. examinations as predictors of performance at the university. Such systematic research should cover more than one of the six Nigerian universities, and several disciplines, including those not taught at secondary school level. The degree of correlation should help to determine the extent of radical action the universities should take in revamping their selection criteria. The research is bound to take some years to accomplish. In the interim, the universities could explore other avenues for improving their selection techniques. School reports provide one possibility.

(c) Secondary school records and reports

A member of the Conference of Principals of Secondary Schools in the former Eastern Region of Nigeria once asked a university official what use the university made of the confidential reports which they (the principals) were supposed to write for each former student of their school seeking admission to any of the universities. The reaction from the other members showed that they were equally concerned about the outcome of the time consuming reports they were constantly required to write. Unless these reports actually influenced the selection process, it was a sheer waste of time to write them and hypocrisy to demand them.

The university official gave a frank answer. He said his university would like to attach greater weight to the reports if only it could be convinced that the reports from different principals were equally reliable. Experience had shown that they were not. Some principals appeared honest and objective; some considered each of their former students a priceless gem, while some saw no good in most of theirs. To attach much weight to the reports might therefore give an unfair advantage to some candidates while exposing some others to an undeserved handicap.

In addition, it would be difficult to fit the large numbers of private candidates who did not attend any secondary schools into the scheme. Generally these private candidates qualified for university entry while in full time employment, by taking correspondence courses from overseas or local correspondence establishments. Their employers know practically nothing about their academic ability or potential, and their reports are often couched in vague language. In a number of cases some employers are antagonistic towards the candidates for seeking admission to the university (and consequently intending to resign their appointments); the malicious reports some of them turn in reflect this. Candidates have therefore been known not to pass their application forms through their employers, for fear of antagonising them when they are not certain that their application would be successful.

The Nigerian university is thus confronted with the dual problem of the unevenness of the reporting from secondary schools on the one hand, and the problem of fitting in the private candidate who deserves an equal opportunity to compete for the few university places available every year. Its attitude has been to request these confidential reports but not to make use of them for selection. The reports, however, become part of the admission records. By so doing, the university is, unfortunately, throwing away the opportunity of developing what could be a valuable addition to selection criteria.

The unevenness of school reports is not a Nigerian phenomenon; there is no reason why it could not be reduced and the reports made more reliable. Bowles reported that studies conducted in some countries supported the finding that past performance in studies is the most reliable basis for estimating future performance in studies. (3.5) By basing their selection on the results of the School Certificate and the H.S.C. the Nigerian universities have in a sense endorsed this finding. Unfortunately they base their entire judgement on performance in one final examination rather than on the student's academic records and the pattern of his progress during his secondary school career. This appears contrary to the fact that these universities now assess their undergraduates for degrees on their performance in the final year examinations and some work or examination taken in preceding years. The same principle could be applied to the admissions process.

The report from the secondary school could be modified to include the student's position in his class during each year of his secondary school career, e.g. in the upper 5% of class, with relevant comments by the principal or class teacher. Any secondary school that keeps records should have little difficulty in assembling such data. Where the student's School Certificate or H.S.C. results are known at the time the forms are completed, these should also be included, with comments by the principal relating the actual

results with the anticipated results based on the student's performance in class. (It is recognized that the comments may not be possible
in cases of students who left the secondary school many years before
the report is requested, in which case the results alone would suffice.)
Where the results are not known, *i.e.* have not been released, the
expected results should be given. Such data, which give the student's
progress graph during his school career, would be more objective
and meaningful to the selection process than the subjective opinions
now requested from school principals. The School Certificate and
the H.S.C. results would provide a common denominator for all
students and help to determine how much weight should be attached
to class position, especially as a top student in one school might
not emerge as a top student in another school. The data from the
schools could be used either as further screening devices or be made
part of a general scoring system for arranging the candidates in an
order of merit.

The problem of the private candidate remains outstanding. One
hopes that as the present backlog of private candidates is reduced
and with the expansion in secondary education, the number of
private candidates who have had no secondary education would
decrease and finally disappear as in many developed countries.
Private candidates of future years are likely to be more in the category
of persons who could not enter the universities straight from the
secondary schools, and who would therefore have secondary school
records. Until the situation changes, the universities have no alternative but to accept that it is not possible to receive the additional
selection criterion based on school records in respect of private
candidates without formal post-primary education. This need not,
however, prevent the use of the criterion where it is available. A
university that uses the scoring system for selecting students could
incorporate the additional criterion where it is available and through
an appropriate method of computation still arrive at scores which
would enable it to place both categories of candidates on one order
of merit. The use of a scoring system will be considered later.

(d)   The Interview

The importance attached to interviews as selection criteria
varies from university to university. Some universities in the United
States and the United Kingdom interview all candidates for admission, while many do not believe in interviews and hold none. Some

interview only borderline candidates, while some interview only candidates with exceptional academic qualifications. Some confine the interviews to professional courses like medicine and forestry where they feel the personal qualities of the candidate affect his chances of success in the profession, and only personal interviews could test these qualities. No two universities I have visited in the United States and United Kingdom, or Nigeria agree definitely on how much weight should be attached to interviews.

The general experience, confirmed by Bowles in his international study of university admissions (3.5), is that the interview is not a very reliable selection yardstick, especially when used alone. The reasons for this are too obvious to need elaboration.

The faculty of education in a Nigerian university at one time interviewed all its prospective students as a pre-requisite for selection. Some years after these interviews had been discontinued by the entrance board, the faculty brought up the case of a student it felt it could not certify as a teacher because of his unsatisfactory behaviour (the student was probably a psychiatric case). The dean of the faculty used the occasion to revive his case for personal interviews as a condition for selection, arguing that his staff would have spotted traits of the unsatisfactory behaviour had the student in question been interviewed before he was selected, thereby saving the university the embarrassment of refusing to graduate a student who had completed the academic requirements but who lacked the personal qualities for the teaching profession. When the records were checked in the registrar's office, it was discovered that the student was in fact interviewed by the faculty prior to his selection, and that no reference had been made to any abnormality in his behaviour at the time!

Interviews are costly in time and money, and I would not recommend their use for all candidates unless some research findings justify such use. There might be a case for interviewing marginal candidates who score about the same overall points on the scoring system and are hardly distinguishable on the basis of their records alone. This would involve fewer candidates and the interview would be more meaningful. Wherever interviews are used, it would be important to agree before hand what weight (or maximum score) should be attached to interviews. It is easy to forget all other important selection criteria and base the selection entirely on the interview.

Use of a Scoring System

The mechanics of selection vary from one institution to another. In some universities, decisions are taken virtually intuitively. Someone reads through the application forms, studies the examination results, the principal's report and any other relevant material, and then decides on the basis of his overall impression whether the candidate should or should not be admitted. He then moves on to the next candidate's application form. In some universities, two or more persons do this independently, and their recommendations are later compared and reconciled.

The mechanics of selection in Nigeria need to be more systematic than that. The Nigerian university should adopt a selection procedure which would remove any shadow of doubt that admission is based on merit. The intuitive method, like the interview, becomes less reliable when large numbers of candidates are involved. Moreover it is hard to defend when a candidate claims that a less qualified candidate in his field has been admitted and he has not, and the Nigerian university is often called upon to defend specific offers of admission. A Roman Catholic archbishop once reported a university registrar to the chancellor of that university on the charge that the registrar (who was a Protestant) rejected the application of a Roman Catholic priest on religious grounds. This incident, in which a highly respected religious head ignored every protocol in order to peddle a blatant lie aimed at discrediting and, hopefully, getting rid of the registrar, illustrates the magnitude of the problem facing any person responsible for admission to a Nigerian university. One way to protect him and also to guarantee fairness to all candidates is to adopt a scoring system.

What makes up the scoring system depends on the selection criteria used by each institution, and the selection criteria are determined to a large extent by the objectives of the institution and the nature of its courses of study. My major argument in favour of a scoring system is that it compels the university to give serious thought to the qualities it considers essential in prospective students if they are to derive maximum benefit from its courses of study, and further to determine what weight should be attached to each quality in relation to the others. In practical terms, a score is assigned to whatever factor is considered important as a selection criterion other than those criteria which all candidates are required to have and which serve as screening devices. The scores vary in magnitude, depending on the weight attached to that particular criterion in relation to other criteria.

As an example, a Nigerian university may decide, particularly in respect of the advanced level G.C.E., that ability to pass a certain number of subjects at one sitting rather than in several sittings is evidence of superior academic ability, in which case a score is given to any candidate who achieves that. It could decide that Grade I (Excellent) at the H.S.C. or advanced level G.C.E. is evidence of high ability and potential for university success; consequently it could work out a scale of scores for different levels of achievement in each of the subjects taken at the qualifying examination. It may decide that between two candidates who had identical results at the G.C.E. advanced level, the candidate who also had a specified number of ordinary level passes or equivalent results had a better foundation for university studies; in that case a score could be given for possession of that number of ordinary level passes.

This principle could be expanded to include any experience or factor considered sufficiently important as a predictor of success at the university. If, as in the Soviet Union, work experience is considered essential, this could be included in developing the scoring system. Where personal attributes are considered important predictors, they could also be incorporated into the scoring system. The actual form taken by the scores is immaterial: they could be expressed in decimals, with 1·00 as the highest attainable score, or they could be in whole numbers. What is much more important is to determine the different criteria and sub-criteria and how much weight to attach to each of them. When the scores for the candidates have been added, it becomes easy to arrange the candidates in any course of study in order of merit. Offers of admission would follow that order.

Years of experimenting will help each institution to review its selection criteria, together with the weight (and therefore the score) for each criterion or sub-criterion. Whitla's account of the experience of Harvard University is pertinent here. Harvard used to give equal weight to academic abilities and personal attributes; it did so with the students admitted in 1954 (i.e. the class which graduated in 1958). It now attaches greater weight to personal attributes. With the students admitted in 1964 (who graduated in 1968), 0·78 weight was given to personal attributes and only 0·06 to academic abilities. The correlation between personal and academic factors had been reckoned at 0·46 which, according to Whitla, illustrates that 'those two dimensions do have some common properties'. (19.1) One obvious conclusion on reading through the article is that the students who apply to Harvard are so homogeneous in terms of high academic ability that some other factors are necessary to help to spread them out. Moreover with such a group, high academic ability is assumed a constant (the SAT median rose from 560 with the class which graduated in 1958 to 654 with the 1968 class). In developing a scoring system, therefore, academic ability is given reduced weight. As Whitla acknowledges, the 'broad base of academic strength. . . . enable us to expand our expectations of quality to personal characteristics that add diversity and style to our undergraduate body'.

THE QUOTA SYSTEM

As a result of the uneven educational development in Nigeria, there is an imbalance in the number of candidates qualified for university education who are produced annually by the twelve States making up the country. This is reflected in the number of students from each State enrolled in the six universities: the bulk of them invariably come from the States better developed educationally. To make for a more even distribution, the call has been made by the States with fewer educational facilities that admission to Federal universities should be on a quota basis, a specified number of university places being alloted to each State each academic year.

The 'quota-system', as it has since been designated would create serious administrative problems for the Nigerian university, especially in relation to the distribution of students to faculties, schools or departments. More importantly, its adoption would be a contravention of an important provision in the law establishing each of the universities—the provision that (quoting from the University of Lagos Decree 1967):

> No person shall be required to satisfy requirement as to any of the following matters . . . . race (including ethnic grouping), ... place of birth or of family origin . . . . as a condition of becoming . . . . a student at the University.

The application of a quota system would result in admission being denied a brilliant candidate in a Federal university in his own country, in preference to a less brilliant student, purely on grounds of place of birth. Apart from the legal implication already referred to, a Federal Government adopting such a policy could not expect a high degree of loyalty from the former candidate.

Fortunately, the Nigerian Federal Military Government has rejected the quota system. There must be other less repugnant methods of correcting the educational imbalance, including assisting the States affected to build and operate more schools.

REFERENCES

1 Stoke, Harold V., *The American College President*, New York, Harper & Brothers Publishers, 1959. 1.1 : pp. 167–168.
2 McGrath, Earl J., (ed.), *Universal Higher Education*, New York, McGraw-Hill Book Company, 1966.
3 Bowles, Frank, *Access to Higher Education*, Volume 1, Paris, UNESCO and the International Association of Universities, 1963. 31 : p. 141; 3.2 : p. 77; 3.3 : p. 158; 3.4 : p. 159; 3.5 : p. 160.
4 Educational Policies Commission, *Universal Opportunity for Education Beyond the High School;* 1964. 4.1 : p. 5; 4.2 : p.25.
5 Committee on Higher Education, *Higher Education*, Report of the Committee appointed by the Prime Minister under the Chairmanship of Lord Robbins 1961–63, London, Her Majesty's Stationery Office, 1963. 5.1 : p. 44–45; 5.2 : pp. 38–39; 5.3 : p. 44.
6 Richmond, W. Kenneth, *Education in the U.S.A., A Comparative Study*, New York, Philosophical Library, Inc. 1956.
7 Bacon, Emery F., 'What will be the implication for American higher education of the growing concentration on the superior student'?, in Association for Higher Education, *Current Issues in Higher Education* 1962: *Higher Education in an Age of Revolutions*, Washington D.C., National Education Association, 1962, p.189.
8 *Investment in Education*, The Report of the Commission on Post-School Certificate and Higher Education in Nigeria, Lagos, Federal Ministry of Education, Nigeria, 1960· 8.1 : p. 10; 8.2 : p. 11.
9 Potter, David. M., *People of Plenty*, Chicago & London, The University of Chicago Press, 1954 (9th impression 1965). 9.1 : p. 116.
10 UNESCO, *The Development of Higher Education in Africa*, Paris, UNESCO 1963. 10.1 : p. 245; 10.2 : p. 256; 10.3 : p. 28.
11 Gardner, John W., *Excellence : Can we be equal and excellent too?* New York, Harper & Brothers, 1961. 11.1 : p. 81.
12 Kerr, Clark, *The Uses of the University*, Cambridge, Massachusetts, Harvard University Press, 1963. 12.1 : p. 121.
13 Ikejiani, Okechukwu (ed.), *Nigerian Education*, Ikeja, Longmans of Nigeria Ltd., 1964. 13.1 : p. 185.
14 Dyer, Henry S., 'Changing Roles in College Admissions', *Phi Delta Kappan*, Vol. XLVI, No. 7, March 1965, 318–321.
15 Cicourel, Aaron V. & Kitsuse, John I., *The Educational Decision-Makers*, Indianapolis, The Bobbs-Merrill Company Inc., 1963.

16 The International Study of University Admissions, *Access to Higher Education*, Vol. II, National Studies, Paris, UNESCO and the International Association of Universities, 1965. 16.1 : p.581

17 Brock, M.G., 'Admissions: An Oxford View', *Universities Quarterly*, Vol. 19, No. 3, June 1965, 259–266. 17.1: p. 261; 17.2: p. 264.

18 Robb, Felix C., 'What Factors should determine Admissions Policy', in Kenneth M. Wilson (ed.), *Research Related to College Admissions*, Atlanta, Southern Regional Educational Board, 1963. 18.1: p. 6; 18.2: p. 7.

19 Whitla, Dean K., 'Admission to College: Policy and Practice', *Phi Delta Kappan*, Vol. XLVI, No. 7, March 1965, 303–306. 19.1: p. 305.

Other Sources

Benjamin, Harold R.W., *Higher Education in the American Republics*, New York, McGraw-Hill Book Company, 1965.

Harbison, Frederick & Myers, Charles A., *Manpower and Education* (Country Studies in Economic Development), New York, McGraw-Hill Book Company, 1965.

Silcock, T.D., *Southeast Asian University* (A Comparative Account of Some Development Problems), Durham, N. Carolina, Duke University Press, 1964.

Working Papers prepared by different task forces for the Committee on Education and Human Resources Development, Education and World Affairs, New York.

Smith, George B., 'Who would be eliminated'? in *The coming crisis in the selection of students for college entrance*, Washington D.C., National Education Association, 1960.

Committee of Vice-Chancellors and Principals, *Report of a Sub-Committee on University Entrance Requirements in England and Wales*, April 1962.

Ashby, Eric (in association with Mary Anderson), *Universities: British, Indian, African*, A Study in the Ecology of Higher Education, Cambridge, Massachusetts, Harvard University Press, 1966.

James, E., 'Forty-eight from four hundred', *Universities Quarterly*, Vol. 19, September 1965, 378–390.

Hunt, J.B. and Line, M.B., 'School and university'; an experiment in closer relations, *Times Educational Supplement*, 2617, p.117, July 16, 1965.

Lockwood, G., 'Admissions to Harvard and Yale' *Universities Quarterly*, Vol. 19. September 1965, 365–377.

Hanson, C., 'Continental university stakes', *Universities Quarterly*, Vol. 19, September 1965, 361–364.

Crossland, F.E., 'Politics and policies in college admissions', *College & University*, Vol. 41, 23–31, Fall 1965.

'Undergraduate admissions, image and reality; panel discussions', *College & University*, 40, 414–417, Summer 1965.

Willingham, W.W., 'Application blank as a predictive instrument', *College & University*, 40, 271–281, Spring 1965.

Jackson, M.L., 'Needed: some new rules in the college admission game', *Phi Delta Kappan*, Vol. XLVI, 336–339, March 1965.

CHAPTER 7

THE SIXTH FORM CONTROVERSY

It is not for lack of a sense of proportion that a whole long chapter is being devoted to sixth form education as a prerequisite for university education in Nigeria. It is because the sixth form controversy presents an excellent example of the utter confusion into which an African country can be thrown by a slavish attempt to copy another system, and the uncritical acceptance of the recommendation of a commission. It is a controversy which is already older than a decade, but which need not have arisen at all had Nigerian universities and ministries of education asked a few basic questions.

Entry requirements to Nigerian universities were initially dictated by the requirements for entry to English universities. As Silcock remarked, it was natural for the colonial government (and this included the French and the Dutch as well as the British) establishing a university in its overseas territory to set the same criteria for admission to the university or to specific degree programmes as would obtain in the 'home' universities. (1.1) At the time University College, Ibadan admitted its pioneer students in January, 1948, the London Matriculation Certificate satisfied entry requirements to the English provincial universities, including London. The certificate was normally obtained by sitting the London Matriculation examinations, but it was also possible to obtain exemption from the examination by attaining a stipulated level of performance at the Cambridge School Certificate examinations, taken at the end of normal secondary education. Thus a brilliant student could move straight from the normal secondary school to the university, without any intermediary step.

The degree programme was, however, divided into an 'intermediate' stage (lasting two years) and a final stage (lasting two years for general, and three years for honours degrees). In 1951 the entry requirements for English universities were raised to what they now are—the possession of at least two subjects at the advanced level of the G.C.E. or at principal standard in the H.S.C. With this action, the undergraduate curriculum was shortened by the removal of 'intermediate' work from the university, the secondary schools taking over this responsibility and accomplishing it through their two-year sixth forms'. Because sixth forms were at that time practically non-existent in Nigeria, and because it would have been impossible to fill Ibadan with the relatively few Nigerians—generally in their 30s—who had passed the intermediate examinations of London University through private study, London University kindly allowed Ibadan to continue admitting the old level of students—*i.e.* students holding the School Certificate. The one proviso was that the "intermediate" work must continue at the college, in order to raise the level of the students to the new entry requirements in England before they could commence degree work. The 'intermediate' examinations continued at Ibadan until the 1956/57 academic year, when they were replaced by 'preliminary arts' and 'preliminary science' examinations. The period of study was also reduced from two years to one year when it became obvious that the students could complete the work in one year. To make it abundantly clear that students admitted at this level were not qualified for university education, they were said to be offered 'concessional entry' and subjected to a university entrance examination, while the qualified students (holding the advanced level G.C.E., the H.S.C., or the old London intermediate arts or science) were offered 'direct entry' without an entrance examination.

The concession granted Ibadan by London was not for all time. It was to enable the country to develop sixth form education. After consulting the federal and regional ministries of education on the expansion of sixth form facilities, Ibadan announced that it would discontinue concessional entry after 1962, by which time it was generally expected that there would be enough candidates with the H.S.C. or G.C.E. at advanced level to satisfy the very modest need for students.

The Commission on Post-School Certificate and Higher Education in Nigeria (Ashby Commission), in its report released in September 1960, came out in dogmatic support of sixth form education as the *only* proper preparation for university education, and recommended large scale expansion of sixth form facilities. The Commission announced that 'University College, Ibadan, will soon have abandoned the preliminary courses which represent an equivalent standard to Higher School Certificate and General Certificate of Education Advanced level courses, since already the number of applicants for admission holding the full minimum entrance qualifications exceeds by a considerable margin the number of places for new entrants to the College'. (2.1) Unfortunately it seemed to have ignored two important considerations: first, that it had recommended a *sevenfold* increase in university places, which is a long way beyond the modest numbers that were generally admitted annually by Ibadan up to that date (usually never exceeding 300 in one year); secondly, it did not consider the composition of these surplus highly qualified candidates to which it referred. If it did, it would have discovered that the bulk of them qualified through the G.C.E., not through the sixth form, and that most of them were in arts and social science fields, not in scientific and technological fields. Their existence in large numbers did not therefore help in a situation in which the universities were required to adapt their student intake to ensure that 75% of the total enrolment were in scientific and technological fields.

The sixth forms failed to supply the required numbers of candidates, particularly in the sciences. In the circumstances, the Nigerian universities had no alternative but to continue the practice Ibadan had followed under similar circumstances—to admit two levels of students: the 'concessional entry' group and the 'direct entry' group. Admission statistics supplied by Dr. C.W. de Kiewiet and Dr. Eldon Johnson in an unpublished paper for the Committee on Education and Human Resource Development, Education and World Affairs, New York (January 1966) revealed that of the 1965 intake at Ibadan, 'concessional entry' accounted for 9% in arts, 22% in science, 22% in agriculture, and 44% in medical studies. Statistics for Nsukka for the same year show that a little less than 50% of the entire student body entered the university with the School Certificate or ordinary level G.C.E., the highest percentages coming from science (80%) and agriculture (90%). The UNESCO Commission on the establishment of the University of Lagos, while expressing support for the sixth form as the proper preparation for university education, recognized that for some years it would be necessary to admit the two levels of students as the other universities were then doing.

Many principals of secondary schools in Nigeria have denounced the universities for taking the two levels of students. The Conference on the Development of Sixth Forms in Nigeria held at Ibadan on December 15–22, 1961 strongly urged the universities to discontinue concessional entry. Although their resolution to that effect was tantamount to requesting the universities not to fill vacant places in the sciences and related fields, it had some rationale behind it. The continued admission of the two levels of students was an indirect way of stifling and eventually eliminating the sixth form. The boy who opts for sixth form work spends two years at school beyond the School Certificate. If all goes well with him he proceeds to a university where he may graduate after studying for three more years, making a total of five. His classmate who decides to proceed straight to the university without going through the sixth form can graduate after four years at the university, thus gaining a university degree and moving into the labour market a year before his former colleague. This alone is sufficient to discourage students from going in for sixth form work, or to make the lower sixth form students sneak out to sit university entrance examinations without the knowledge and approval of their schools. The fact that an appeal to the universities to help in stopping this unauthorised exodus from the sixth form featured among the resolutions of the 1961 conference on the sixth form is evidence that it was widely practised. The matter is made even less tolerable by the fact that it is generally the brilliant students who are retained by their schools or are accepted by other schools for sixth form work. The less brilliant ones are thus free to sit university entrance examinations and, if successful (which often means if they shine brighter than other available candidates) they are often admitted for four-year degree courses. This is certainly not the best atmosphere in which to make sixth forms thrive.

What then are the alternatives? The Ashby Commission saw no room for alternatives. If the account in an article in the *West African Journal of Education* is accurate, the dogmatic emphasis on the sixth form by the Commission was intended to forestall any attempts 'to replace traditional sixth forms with some other educational expedient, junior colleagues for example'. (3.1) The 1961 Conference on the Development of Sixth Forms in Nigeria recorded general agreement on the educational importance of the sixth form, believing that its function 'could not so effectively be undertaken by any other institution'. (3.2)

RECOMMENDATIONS OF THE ASHBY COMMISSION ON SIXTH FORM EDUCATION

It is the Ashby Commission more than any other body of people that has influenced the expansion of sixth form education in Nigeria.

It is therefore in order to examine first their reasons for complete faith in the sixth form.

The Commission's major argument for recommending sixth form education is that the work covered in the sixth form properly belongs to the secondary school and not to the university, the work being 'unsuitable for university teachers'. (2.2) This is a generalization which should be considered against the following comment from the Robbins report: 'The specialised sixth form, like the British honours degree, is the exception in the world and not the rule'. (4.1) The impression left by the Ashby Commission is that the sixth form is an indispensable prerequisite for university education. To pontificate on the place of sixth form work as the Commission did also displays very short memory of the development of university entry requirements even within the United Kingdom, the citadel of the sixth form. What is now called sixth form work and consequently said to belong to the secondary schools was originally university work in England. The sixth form idea began in England between World War I and World War II. As the schools began to establish more and better sixth form teaching, the universities had to raise their entry requirements. The Report of a Sub-Committee on University Entrance Requirements in England and Wales, published in April 1962 on behalf of the Committee of Vice-Chancellors and Principals of the Universities of the United Kingdom which set up the Sub-Committee, pointed out that the universities were slow in turning over to the sixth form work which had hitherto been done at the university: 'The universities slowly accepted this change and began to concede what had once been first year work in the University to the sixth form'. (5.1) The Report went on to state that 'This transition was prolonged and untidy, and it was not until after 1950 that almost all those entering universities from English and Welsh schools came after completing at least two years in a sixth form'. (5.1) It is therefore clear that sixth form work was university work in England until 1950 when the universities slowly turned it over to the secondary schools. It remains university work in most other parts of the world.

Some data provided in Appendix two (B) of the Robbins Report show that many U.K. universities still continue to teach sixth form work:

Some students in the Undergraduate Survey also reported that they had repeated sixth form work while at the university.

Students in their second year or later (other than those studying medical subjects) were asked if they had repeated at
university any of the subject matter which had already been
covered in the same way at school. About half (51%)
replied that they had . . . . A higher proportion of students in
science (58%) and applied science (59%) than in the
humanities (45%) or social studies (35%) had repeated
school work while at university; a lower proportion of students
at Oxford and Cambridge (44%) than at other universities
(54%) had done so. (6.1)

The Survey also disclosed that for 47% of the students, the school
work repeated at the university occupied one term or less, for 23%
more than one term but less than two terms, while for 30% it occupied
more than two terms, meaning that for nearly a third of the students
surveyed, the first year at the university was a repetition of sixth
form work. A third of the students surveyed felt they could have
passed the university examination given to them at the end of their
first year while still at school. 25% of such students were at London,
30% at Oxford and Cambridge, and 35% at other universities. (6.1)

These data should provide food for thought for those who argue
that sixth form work belongs to the secondary school rather than to
the university. They also illustrate how much confidence the universities involved have in the quality of sixth form work. My experience
in Nigerian universities, confirmed by my discussions with some
U.K. professors, is that many professors would prefer freshmen with
less specialization in their proposed university studies but a more
amenable approach to studies. In any case, why go through the sixth
form at all if many universities will devote their first year to a repetition of sixth form work?

The second argument by the Commission was that pupils without
sixth form education (i.e. holders of the School Certificate or ordinary
level G.C.E.) are not 'adequately prepared or sufficiently mature
for the university environment with its greater freedom and its
view of students as young adults possessing a developed or growing
sense of responsibility about the disciplining of their time and study
rather than as schoolboys whose work at every point needs the
closest supervision'. (2.3) Regarding maturity, Nigerian universities
stipulate a minimum admission age of 17 years, undoubtedly
intended to prevent the admission of babies. In any case, the major
problem at the Nigerian university has not been one of admitting

too many babies but of how to lower the average age of the students. Very few School Certificate or G.C.E. ordinary level students enter the university in Nigeria before they are 18 or 19.

The comment about lack of maturity might be more appropriate in the United Kingdom, where, in order to allow longer preparation for the advanced level examinations (which are more crucial for university entry), the schools now try to get the ordinary level examinations over with as early as possible. The Robbins Report states that in 1961/62, about 29% of all undergraduates in universities in England and Wales, and 53% of those at Oxford and Cambridge had gained 5 or more ordinary level passes before they were 16 years old and some before they were 15. (4.2)

The statement about inadequate preparation is probably based, not on the situation in Nigeria but on the widespread criticism of the adequacy of the ordinary level G.C.E. preparation in the United Kingdom, the blame for which has been placed largely on sixth form education. In the hurry to get over with the ordinary level 'chore' as quickly as possible so as to concentrate on what is much more important—sixth form work, preparatory to the advanced level examinations—the ordinary level G.C.E. course is being abbreviated to the first four years of secondary school, particularly in the boys' schools. Consequently many institutions of higher education complain about the poor preparation given to these students in English language, elementary mathematical principles, and modern languages. 'We think that there is substance in these criticisms and we believe that an abbreviated general education is one of the causes of these shortcomings', commented the Robbins Report. (4.2)

One could argue that sixth form education is not itself adequate preparation for university education. Apart from the data quoted earlier on the extent to which U.K. universities repeat sixth form work, one could also severely question the necessity for moving the students into specialization at sixth form level if they are moving thereafter to a university which emphasizes integration of studies and wishes to begin its freshmen on a foundation of courses that stress the interrelatedness of learning. Sixth form education might have had direct relevance to university education when the single subject honours was the pattern in Nigeria and the United Kingdom. The early specialization which it encourages is now under heavy attack in the United Kingdom. Surprisingly, the Ashby Commission, in recommending the curriculum for the Nigerian sixth form, warned against any experimental curricula. So we have, on the one hand, universities which are being encouraged to be experimental, while on the other hand they are to be fed by sixth forms which have little if any scope for experimental curricula, and yet the Commission emphasized that the purpose of the sixth form is to prepare for university work. It is not surprising that a strong body of opinion at the University of Nigeria opposed granting any exemption from the General Studies courses to direct entry students, their argument being that sixth form education was not the equivalent of General Studies which the university considered essential for all its students.

A gap undoubtedly exists between the secondary school and the university, just as a gap exists between the primary and the secondary school in Nigeria. A chapter on admission problems in France admitted that fact but considered it an inevitable fact of present day life: 'In the present state of civilization it is impossible for the secondary schools to turn out pupils of the standard required for higher education, which is constantly rising owing to the progress of science'. The writer held the view that higher education must acknowledge this and take any remedial measures necessary when the students are admitted:

> The higher education system must therefore devise its own means of making good certain deficiencies, take up the task of preparing students at the point where the secondary schools relinquish it, and devote a transitional year to initiating the young baccalaureat holders into higher education. (7.1)

The French universities meet this by organising the propaedeutical course which (a) acts as an 'indispensable supplement to the secondary cycle', as well as (b) providing 'further education which has a value of its own'. (7.1) The Ibadan preliminary courses, to my experience, did a splendid job with the School Certificate students and even the British-oriented professors who grumbled about the indignity of handling sixth form work at the university felt happier with these students at the end of the preliminary year than they did with direct entry students. The Ashby Commission was so convinced that the sixth form was the only mode of entry to the university that it did not seem to have attached any importance to the Ibadan experience. Those who studied or taught at Ibadan in the early 1950s would recollect that many departments (including history, English, geography) required students admitted with advanced qualifications (H.S.C., G.C.E. 'A' level, and even the London University intermediate arts) to spend a preliminary or preparatory year at the college before proceeding to the degree programmes, because of the inadequacy of their external qualifications for the courses of study at the college. Nsukka, which came into being less than a month after the Commission issued its report, has had no problem in handling its School Certificate entrants.

The third important argument advanced by the Commission in favour of sixth form education is financial: it is cheaper to provide that kind of education at the secondary school than at the university:

> Furthermore, unless a drastic and dramatic change comes over the financing of universities, there can surely be no justification for continuing to travel by the most expensive vehicle to a destination which can be reached by a method on which the method of progress is at once less expensive and undeniably more satisfactory. (2.4)

This argument has always been used to deliver the knockout blow to any critic of sixth form education in Nigeria. It is likely to have influenced the Nigerian Federal Government when it accepted the recommendations of the Commission and decided on an all-out effort to increase sixth form streams to 350, the total number of students to over 10,000, and to make grants for the development of sixth form work throughout the country. One question which few have bothered to ask is on what grounds the Commission based this assertion. Was it acting on the report of a cost accountant or on mere supposition?

It was only many years after the Commission had reported that I saw the results of any attempt to compare the costs of sixth form education with the costs of a preliminary or 'concessional' year at the university. These-results appear on page 5 of an unpublished paper, 'Preliminary Memorandum on the Economics of Education in Nigeria', prepared for the Committee on Education and Human Resource Development, Education and World Affairs, New York. If these results are reliable, then the cost argument would immediately be defeated.

Total Marginal Recurrent Costs per Student of alternative patterns of university entry

		UNIVERSITY:
FIELD	SIXTH FORM: 2 YEARS	1 CONCESSIONAL YEAR
Arts and Social Sciences	₦800 (@ ₦400 a year)	₦700
Sciences	₦800 @ ₦400 a year)	₦1,000

The figures were based on the assumption that the marginal costs per student per year in the sixth form are equal to the average costs of ₦400 per year, but it is mentioned that marginal costs may in fact exceed average costs. The figures do not take into account the capital costs of expanding sixth forms, particularly if expansion follows the lines recommended by the Commission.

If the figures are accurate, a year at the university would be less expensive than two years of sixth form education for arts and social sciences, but vice versa for the sciences. Even in the sciences where the year at the university is 25% more expensive, this cost is more than compensated by the difference in the quality of university work when compared with the quality of sixth form work in Nigeria. Moreover the figures have not taken into account the benefit to the individual and the national economy of entering the labour market one year sooner, thereby adding one year of productivity to his life span. Fafunwa contends that the ₦800 recurrent unit cost is inaccurate, and proceeds to advance figures to show that in the science subjects alone the sixth form is several times more expensive than a year at the university. (8.1)

The next argument by the Commission in favour of sixth form education need not be taken very seriously. The Commission argued that 'in a world in which the relative shortage of good university teachers is a constant source of anxiety' it is neither 'politic' nor 'sensible to make them direct their energies to work of a preparatory nature associated with sixth forms'. (2.4) The Nigerian sixth forms are experiencing a more acute shortage of *qualified* teachers, especially in the sciences, than Nigerian universities, and Nigerian governments have had to recruit sixth form teachers from as far afield as India, Pakistan, the United Kingdom, the U.S.A. and Canada. The Ashby Commission recognized that it would be necessary to look outside Nigeria for these teachers. Present experience is that most of these teachers who feel qualified to teach at University level seek university appointments at the earliest opportunity. Most

Nigerians with high academic qualifications would hardly consider sixth form teaching as a life career; they may be compelled to do so only after the universities and outside research or specialist positions have become glutted.

The last argument put forward by the Commission was that 'a sixth form strengthens the rest of the school and gives tone to the whole of secondary education'. (2.2) When I relate this argument with earlier enrolment targets proposed by the Commission, I cannot help wondering whether the sixth form is, in fact, part of secondary education. Consider these targets. The Commission estimated that 63 students would complete the School Certificate course in Southern Nigeria (i.e. Eastern Nigeria, Western Nigeria, Lagos). Out of this number, only 5–6 can hope to go to the university, implying that the sixth form is designed for only these 5–6 out of 63 students since the purpose of the sixth form is to prepare for university education. Recognizing that somewhere in the report the Commission also recommended some pedagogical training within the sixth form, we might liberally accept that the sixth form was also intended to provide intermediate training. This liberal acceptance will add only 10–11 more students to the sixth form. Thus out of 63 who successfully complete the School Certificate course, only 16–17 could be retained, while 47 are expected to seek employment. (2.5) What this means in effect is that for the great majority of the student population, secondary education is over with the School Certificate. It is difficult to appreciate the kind of tone or strength which this elimination of the majority in each class gives to the rest of the school.

The sixth form has so far created more problems in Nigeria than many of the secondary schools are prepared to tackle adequately. First, the Nigerian governments have required some of the few good schools offering sixth forms to admit students from the less fortunate schools. This has flooded the sixth forms in schools such as Government College, Umuahia with boys used to different disciplinary codes in their respective schools, creating serious disciplinary problems for the schools. Secondly, since all reference to terminal education at the sixth form has not led to any change in the nature of sixth form education, the sixth form students consider themselves lined up for university education. They have each spent five years in secondary education prior to their entry to the sixth form, and many of them would be 17–19 years of age. They see the privileges enjoyed by their former classmates who have either gone into the university or obtained employment after the School Certificate, and naturally demand some of these privileges. Many schools fail to grant them these privileges for fear of the harmful effects they might have on discipline throughout the rest of the school.

To conclude the arguments in favour of sixth form education, I quote the supporting views of the Ibadan Conference on the development of sixth forms in Nigeria, as reported by the editors of the *West African Journal of Education*:

> First there was general agreement upon the educational importance of the sixth form. Its function, it was believed, could not so effectively be undertaken by any other institution. It could serve as a bridge between secondary school and university and also as an appropriate terminal course for those who did not wish to proceed to the university. It could provide more individual education than could be given at either a junior college or in a university class. It could entrust its sixth formers with responsibilities towards both themselves and the rest of the school which would form the best type of preparation for using and not abusing the greater freedom that they would know when they left school. (3.2)

One important function of the sixth form, which the Conference must have felt awkward to add, is that it bestows prestige within the secondary school world to the schools that have it and the sixth form teachers. This certainly carries much greater weight than most of the so-called functions above. Reference to the provision of terminal education, for instance, is simply tagged in to produce a more impressive list of paper functions. Which sixth form in Nigeria provides terminal vocational education? Not one! The present sixth form education is terminal only in the sense that a number of the students who complete it fail to gain admission to the university for one reason or another and therefore seek employment.

The Conference saw in the sixth form an effective bridge between the secondary school and the university, without pausing to consider whether and why such a bridge was necessary in Nigeria. How many countries (apart from Britain and some of her former dependencies) find it necessary to erect such bridges to link secondary with university education?

RECOMMENDATIONS

It is unfortunate that the Ashby Commission left Nigeria with a controversy over sixth form education which might have been simple to resolve but for the fact that there are many Nigerians who are prepared to swallow hook, line and sinker any recommendation in the Ashby Report. To many of them the report is practically sacrosanct. Moreover, the sixth form is the pattern in Britain, therefore it must be the ideal pattern. If the Commission had pleaded for the establishment of the junior college, which is typically American, the recommendation would certainly not have received such enthusiastic support.

The entire argument on whether sixth form education should or should not be the proper entry qualification to the university appears misguided and unnecessary. The overall educational pyramid in most parts of the world consists essentially of elementary or primary education, secondary education, and higher (including university) education; hence university education is referred to as tertiary education. In a well co-ordinated educational system, a capable student should be able to move up from one level of education to the next, without the necessity for a superstructure or bridge. The sixth form is obviously an attempt to superimpose another level of education between the secondary school and higher education. It is true that the United Kingdom has done precisely that, but, as the Robbins Committee aptly pointed out, this is an exception in the world educational context rather than the rule. Moreover it is the intense competition to get into U.K. universities, more than anything else, which is forcing standards up and making many pupils spend three instead of two years in the sixth form so as to obtain very good results at the G.C.E. advanced level. As the Robbins Report observes:

> The actual qualifications of most of those entering higher education bear less and less relation to minimum requirements. This is strikingly illustrated by the fact that about 80 per cent of English and Welsh university students have at least three passes at the advanced level and about half of them have passed with marks of 60 per cent or more in at least two subjects. (4.3)

It would have sounded much more meaningful if the Ashby Commission and the advocates of sixth form education had focussed their searchlight on the quality of Nigerian secondary education vis-a-vis university education. If they concluded that the quality of Nigerian secondary education is low, they should have recommended how to improve it rather than propose the imposition of another structure which is regarded in one breath as part of the secondary school, giving tone to it, and in another as something different, intended for a select few after others have been eliminated. It would seem that the Nigerian secondary school should consider it much more important to inculcate the excellent qualities enumerated in the recommendations of the 1961 Ibadan Conference on sixth form education ('responsibilities towards both themselves and the rest of the school which would form the best type of preparation for using and not abusing the greater freedom that they would know when they left school') on the 47 or more students who were not destined for higher education than on the few lined up for higher education. The latter have the opportunity of proceeding to a higher institution where, one hopes, they will have greater opportunity of acquiring these and additional qualities.

If the thinking could move in the direction of considering the quality of Nigerian secondary education, it would make more sense than having to toss a coin to decide whether or not the country should have sixth forms. If the quality is considered good enough, well and good. If the quality is considered low, then steps should be taken to improve it. Even if these steps include adding an extra year to secondary education (to make it six years as in many parts of the world) it would still be a more rational approach than having to decide whether a bridge is necessary between secondary and university education, regardless of the quality of each.

A gap invariably exists between secondary and university education. K.O. Saiyidain and H.C. Gupta, writing about admissions problems in India, drew attention to the impression formed by Dr. Frank Bowles that in many of the countries he visited a gap of about one or two years existed between the secondary school and the university in the subject matter covered, and in the methods and standards of teaching. Dr. Bowles expressed the view that the upper third of the secondary school students could leap over this gap on their own, while the average student needed at least one year's remedial work. (7.2)

Dr. Bowles' views, based on his study of admission problems and practices in several countries (excluding Nigeria), agree in essence with the recommendations I circulated to Vice-Chancellors of Nigerian Universities in mimeograph in the 1963/64 academic year but which did not appear to have been discussed by their Committee. I quote these recommendations in full:

I recommend that every brilliant secondary school boy or girl should be eligible for University admission without being required to go through the sixth form. Holders of the West African School Certificate in Division I should be eligible for admission without even the necessity of an entrance examination. The Division II candidates recommended by their schools might be subjected to a University entrance examination which would determine their eligibility for admission. These brilliant students would thus have the opportunity of proceeding direct to the University and graduating in four years. The Universities would get only the best from the secondary schools by these channels. The fear of premature babies finding their way into the Universities expressed by the Ashby Commission should be taken care of by the minimum age requirement stipulated by each University, usually 17. The big problem in Nigerian Universities now is to lower the average age of students, not to raise it as in Britain.

The facilities already provided for sixth form work could be used to give an intensive two-year course to holders of Division III and the weaker Division II students, together with holders of the G.C.E. at ordinary level in 4 or 5 subjects who passed the examination by private study. The curriculum would be so designed that the students would be prepared for University admission. I would suggest a panel of University and Secondary School representatives to design the curriculum which need not lead to the present H.S.C. or G.C.E. 'A' Level. Efforts might be made to remedy the students' deficiences and raise their academic level in the subjects they hope to study at the University. The West African Examinations Council could be invited to administer the examinations taken at the end of the 2 years. Students who complete the course successfully would be offered admission to the University for a three-year degree course. The less brilliant student thus has the opportunity of attaining the same goal as his more brilliant colleagues, but at a slower pace. If he fails to make the grade after the two years then the University is not the place for him. (9.1)

I went on to propose broadening the categories of students admitted to the two-year preparatory courses, to include brilliant teachers holding the Teachers' Grade II Certificate but without secondary education and who plan to study education at the university, and students from commercial schools and trade schools who have the potential for courses such as industrial arts, education, engineering, business administration and business education which are offered by some Nigerian universities, but who may not have received a sufficiently broad general education. I pointed out that the categories could be broadened; the intention was to cater for some brilliant young people whose professional qualifications would not normally channel them to the university even if they wanted university education, unless they neglect their responsibilities and swot for the General Certificate of Education examination under conditions that are often adverse. My recommendations concluded as follows:

The two-year courses could be called University Preparatory Classes or any other suitable name. It would be misleading to call them Junior Colleges because even though in some ways they may resemble the American Junior College they differ from the Junior College in many important respects. Within a few years of the operation of this plan the Universities would be drawing students from the following sources:

(a) Top boys and girls straight from secondary schools;

(b) Students successfully completing the University Preparatory Classes;

(c) Candidates who obtain G.C.E. 'A' level by private study;

(d) Foreign students.

The programme would be subject to periodic review; it could be abandoned or replaced by another programme when the country is ready for the change.

The University Preparatory Classes should adopt an academic year similar to that followed by the Universities, thus making it possible for fifth formers in Secondary Schools to know their School Certificate results before deciding whether to seek admission to the University or to the University Preparatory Classes. (9.2)

I would consider the major principles of those 1963 recommendations still tenable today. The brilliant students completing the regular secondary school should be allowed to proceed to the university without two years of further detention in a sixth form. Experience at both Ibadan and Nsukka has shown that such students can cope with university studies. If any students need further preparation before entry to the university, they are the doubtful secondary school leavers and the young people of promise whose talents are needed by the country but whose educational background is deficient in one way or another and who, through the inadequacies of national educational planning, find themselves in blind alleys. The Grade II Teacher is the ready example. The preparatory classes would naturally pay special attention to those fields of study for which the universities experience difficulties in recruiting students.

In view of the fact that the university preparatory classes (or whatever they are called) are strictly speaking not part of secondary education, I would modify that part of my 1963 recommendations and propose instead the creation of special facilities such as the Federal Emergency Science School (now the Federal School of Science), away from the secondary schools, to be responsible for these classes. The arrangement is bound to be temporary. The expansion of secondary schools is likely to produce enough brilliant pupils to fill the limited places available at the universities. Moreover educational reforms are likely to eliminate some of the categories of potential students for the classes, for example, the Grade II teacher.

A further modification to my 1963 recommendations is in respect of the years of study. It would probably be best to keep the period of university studies the same as for the brilliant pupils who go straight to the university, to avoid equating work at these preparatory classes to work at the university. The preparatory classes should take the pupils to the point from where they can move on to the four-year university studies (or whatever the duration may be). The duration of the preparatory classes should depend on the length of time it would take to accomplish this. For most students of the type I have in mind, one year should be enough.

The sixth form is a bottleneck which Nigeria cannot afford. In the November/December 1963 School examinations held in Nigeria, 15,890 candidates entered for the School Certificate, as against 1,857 for the H.S.C. Of the School Certificate entries,

1,719 came out in Division I, and 3,480 in Division II. Of the H.S.C. entries, only 634 satisfied the minimum requirements for direct admission to the universities, by passing in at least two subjects at principal standard. To insist that the Nigerian universities must limit their intake to the latter category is to place the cart before the horse. Experience in the United Kingdom—the citadel of the sixth form—is that the universities have raised their entry requirements in response to what the schools have been able to produce. They did not begin by setting arbitrary standards and then waiting without students until the schools had caught up with them. According to the Report of a Sub-Committee on Entrance Requirements in England and Wales, 'The universities other than Oxford and Cambridge have always drawn a high proportion of their students from grammar schools in the state system, and the level of the requirements they have been able to set for entry to their first degree courses has been dictated by what the majority of such schools could provide'. The majority of Nigerian schools can provide only students with the School Certificate. Nigerian universities should accept the best of these students without distilling them through the sixth form bottleneck. Bowles' survey of the world situation and the experience at Ibadan and Nsukka indicate that these students can succeed at the university. Nigerian secondary schools should divert their energies from the sixth form to an improvement of the quality and content of secondary education generally. It is possible to give 'tone' to a school without the sixth form.

Some people argue that standards will fall if the universities accept School Certificate students, and unfortunately many Nigerians readily succumb to that argument. There is no substance in the argument unless it is intended as an indictment on the quality of secondary education in Nigeria. In any case, Ibadan acquired its international reputation for high academic standards while taking School Certificate as well as H.S.C. and G.C.E. 'A' level students. When the National Universities Commission joined the controversy by proclaiming that they could not see how a student admitted to Nsukka with the School Certificate could emerge after four years with a degree comparable in quality with that received by an H.S.C. entrant after three years, the members disclosed a blissful ignorance of the nature of the Nsukka degree curriculum. Harvard University is one of the most highly respected universities throughout the academic world. Not only are the Harvard undergraduate curricula designed primarily for the School Certificate level of entrant, but Harvard even admits a few pupils with high potential who have one more year to go at the high (i.e. secondary) school. Entry qualifications affect standards, but they alone do not determine standards. And, as stated earlier, if the brilliant Nigerian student cannot move straight from the secondary school to the next step of the educational ladder—the university—without the aid of a bridge, then either the quality of secondary education must be stepped up or the university needs to review its entry requirements.

It ought to be mentioned also that the sixth form is a waste of time for pupils planning to proceed to courses of study at the university like law, sociology, or business administration which have no secondary school equivalents.

Nigerian educational authorities should acknowledge that they plunged into sixth form education unwisely, and pull out before committing more funds into it. The facilities already provided for sixth form education in some schools would help to improve the facilities for the regular secondary school programmes. Perhaps some day when economic, social or other considerations make it necessary to keep Nigerian youth away from the labour market some years longer, I might become an advocate of the sixth form!

It is gratifying to observe that the June 1973 (Nigerian) Seminar on a National Policy on Education recommended as follows on sixth form education. 'The sixth form as at present constituted should be abolished. Pupils should go direct from secondary school to university'.

REFERENCES

1 Silcock, T.H., *Southeast Asian University*, A Comparative Account of Some Development Problems, Durham, N. Carolina, Duke University Press, 1964. 1.1: p. 7

2 *Investment in Education*. The Report of the Commission on Post-School Certificate and Higher Education in Nigeria, Lagos, Federal Ministry of Education, Nigeria, 1960. 2.1: p. 73; 2.2: p. 12; 2.3: pp. 73–74; 2.4: p. 74; 2.5: p. 10.

3 'The Ibadan Conference on the Development of Sixth Forms in Nigeria 15th to 22nd December, 1961', *West African Journal of Education*, Vol. IV, No. 1, March 1962, 3–4. 3.1: p. 3; 3.2: p. 4.

4 Committee on Higher Education, *Higher Education,* Report of the Committee
   appointed by the Prime Minister under the Chairmanship of Lord Robbins
   1961–63, Her Majesty's Stationery Office, 1963. 4.1: p. 41; 4.2: p. 76;
   4.3: pp. 75–76.

5 *Report of a Sub-Committee on University Entrance Requirements in England and Wales,*
   London, April 1962. 5.1: p. 8.

6 Committee on Higher Education, *Higher Education,* Appendix Two (B) to the
   Report of the Committee appointed by the Prime Minister under the Chairmanship of Lord Robbins 1961–63, London, Her Majesty's Stationery Office, 1963.
   6.1: p. 25.

7 The International Study of University Admissions, *Access to Higher Education,*
   Volume II, National Studies, Paris, UNESCO & the International Association
   of Universities, 1965. 7.1: p. 142; 7.2: p. 215.

8 Fafunwa, A. Babs., *A History of Nigerian Higher Education,* Lagos, Macmillan & Co.,
   (Nigeria) Ltd., 1971. 8.1: pp. 248–249.

9 Ike, V. Chukwuemeka, 'Entry Requirements for Nigerian Universities' (unpublished mimeograph), 1964. 9.1: pp. 5–6; 9.2: p. 7.

CHAPTER 8

THE UNIVERSITY AND THE STATE

UNIVERSITY AUTONOMY

If there is any point on which the weight of foreign advice to Nigerian and African universities is heavily on one side, it is on the absolute necessity for the autonomy of each university from government control. As Ashby put it, 'Every foreign adviser, any visiting working party, every international commission tells them that universities must be autonomous and free from government control'. (1.1)

Ashby himself was among these foreign advisers, although he appeared to have modified his stand in his 1964 Godkin lectures at Harvard University, from which his words above were extracted, and later still, in his *Universities: British, Indian, African* (pp. 320–343). The Commission on Post-School Certificate and Higher Education in Nigeria (of which he was Chairman) recommended that

> a university has to be insulated from the hot and cold winds of politics. Responsibility for its management must be vested in an autonomous council. The council must include representatives of the public, but these representatives must attend as individuals and not as agents for some sectional interest or party line. (2.1)

The theme of university/state relationships was discussed at length at the international seminar on Inter-University Co-operation in West Africa held in Freetown (Sierra Leone) from December 11 to 16, 1961 under the joint auspices of Fourah Bay College (then the University College of Sierra Leone) and the Congress for Cultural Freedom. The seminar declared that West African universities cannot maintain their dual loyalty to 'the standards and traditions of universities all over the world' and also to 'the intellectual and cultural aspirations of their own countries' unless they are given 'autonomy within the framework of the State'. This autonomy in academic affairs should be acknowledged by the state, especially in view of the dependence of these universities on the state for financial support. It accordingly recommended that to ensure this autonomy the existing constitutions of West African universities should be interpreted in such a way that the academic body is responsible for:

(1) the admission, teaching and examination of students;
(2) the appointment, promotion and tenure of academic staff;
(3) the allocation of funds to the different categories of their budgets;

and that where universities are controlled by governing bodies which are not composed exclusively of university teachers, these bodies should be responsible for the interpretation to governments of the needs of the university, and for the interpretation to the university of the demands which the nation is making upon it, but should leave to the academic body the functions specified above.

The Seminar believes that these conditions are essential if higher learning is to flourish in the nations of West Africa. (3.1)

It is hardly surprising that a seminar comprising largely university teachers should adopt such a recommendation. In a 'republic of scholars', it is only logical that the major decisions should be taken by the scholars. Where lay members happen to be included in the governing boards, their role should be severely restricted to public relations or liaison between the 'inner city' or the 'republic' and the outer city or 'society'. What is surprising is that the seminar did not appear to recognise that it was advocating a set interpretation to *existing* constitutions, regardless of the legal provisions of those constitutions, and that it was giving the erroneous impression that universities elsewhere are generally controlled by governing boards composed exclusively of university teachers.

Undoubtedly as a result of the kind of advice above which had been drummed into Nigerian ears right from the establishment of University College, Ibadan, the Nigerian governments granted autonomy to each of their universities. As the National Universities Commission pointed out in its report,

The independence of Nigerian universities to teach what they will, to whom they wish, without any discrimination on grounds of race, tribe, religion or colour has not only been widely accepted, but it is enshrined in the laws under which everyone of them is established. (4.1)

Dr. Mellanby records that the first meeting of the provisional council of University College, Ibadan (held on April 22, 1948) was held in a room in Lagos lent by the British Council for the occasion. 'We decided to meet there rather than in a Government office, to emphasize the fact that we were an independent organization'. (5.1)

In its reaction to the report of the Commission on Post-Secondary and Higher Education in Nigeria, the Nigerian Federal Government announced its support for university autonomy: 'Universities should have autonomy in the management of their affairs . . . . . The university is established by a statute which gives it freedom and autonomy'. (6.1) This support was affirmed in 1965 during the crisis in the University of Lagos when some members of the Nigerian Parliament urged the Federal Government to intervene in the dispute between the Council and the Senate of the University. The Federal Minister of Education replied:

> This Parliament, in its wisdom, passed the Lagos University Act 1962, and under that Act the Provisional Council (of the university), acting within its powers, takes certain decisions. No matter what one may feel about the decision of this Council on the Lagos University, the Provisional Council which is a statutory body, acting within its powers and having every right to do what it did, cannot be challenged validly. (7.1)

The law establishing each Nigerian university provides for a university council which acts as the supreme governing body of the university, and is responsible for the general management of the property and the affairs of the university. The majority of members of the council are appointed by the government and are generally lay (i.e. non-university) people. The vice-chancellor is by law a member of the council, and some representation is granted the academic staff through the Senate and, in some universities, the congregation. The Commission on Post-Secondary and Higher Education in Nigeria recommended the inclusion of some experienced academics from overseas universities on each council, but the recommendation has not received general acceptance. The university is in no way part of the civil service and, once the council acts within the powers conferred upon it by the university law, it is not answerable to the government for its decisions, neither can the government nullify any of those decisions. The case of the University of Lagos has been cited; the Federal Government considered itself without any legal power to intervene in a situation in which an attempt had allegedly been made on the life of the new vice-chancellor and the university was on the verge of collapse a few months before it was due to turn out its first crop of graduates.

As further illustration of the Nigerian Federal Government's proclaimed reverence for university autonomy, the Federal Government rejected a recommendation by the National Universities Commission (in 1963) that the Federal Government should be represented on the council of each Nigerian university, in view of its financial contribution to the capital and recurrent expenditures of each of these universities.

Does the foregoing mean that the Nigerian university is completely free from government control? Any person unfamiliar with events in Nigeria, especially since 1962, might conclude from the preceding paragraphs that each Nigerian university enjoys complete autonomy and freedom from governmental intervention of any kind. Compared with some universities elsewhere, the Nigerian university enjoys a good measure of autonomy. Events have, however, shown that the establishment by law of autonomous governing bodies is not necessarily a guarantee that the universities will be 'insulated from the hot and cold winds of politics' (or of military rule, one would hasten to add)! The fact that the government appoints both the chairman and the lay members who constitute the majority of each governing council has proved a potent weapon in the hands of politicians. As Law pointed out, 'Governing boards, for the most part, seem to represent the view point of the groups that have the power to place them in their positions'. (8.1) The action of one of the Nigerian Regional governments some years ago demonstrated that a council that refused to dance to the tune of the body which placed it in power could very easily be replaced.

It was not surprising to many people that one of the first actions of the Nigerian Federal Military Government early in 1966, following the January 1966 coup, was to appoint an entirely new council for the University of Lagos. Many who were shocked by the removal of the first vice-chancellor of the university by the provisional council doubted whether some politicians in the Federal Government were not using the council to achieve political ends. They doubted whether in different circumstances the Federal Government would have proclaimed itself as utterly impotent to intervene even when there was a serious threat to life and to the very existence of a university that had cost the government millions of pounds to build.

It is also significant that the rejection by the Federal Government in 1963 of the recommendation of the National Universities Commission referred to above has been reversed by the post-1966 Federal Military Government. The Federal Government is now represented on the council of each Nigerian university.

The Premier of Eastern Nigeria once remarked in an address at the University of Nigeria that he recognised that the university had the freedom to do as it pleased, even if this meant providing for every conceivable discipline regardless of their relevance to national needs. At the same time those of them controlling the government recognised their responsibilities as representatives of the tax-payers; as interpreters of the needs of the people, they felt bound to support only those university programmes which they considered relevant to these needs. The remarks were taken in good faith. Not long after, meetings were held between representatives of the university and the government to explore avenues for co-operation between the university and the government that established it and gave it sustenance.

A similar attitude must also have existed within the federal government, its remarks on the Lagos University crisis notwithstanding. It is significant that while affirming its support for the autonomy of Nigerian universities, in its reaction to the Report of the Commission on Post-School Certificate and Higher Education in Nigeria, it included the statement that 'Such external control as may have to be exercised should be mainly financial'. (6.1) As will be elaborated upon later, actions taken by the Head of the Federal Military Government as well as by some State Military Governors show that the subtle approach can readily be abandoned for outright and illegal intervention, if circumstances so demand.

In my view, the experts, foreign and indigenous, who preach the doctrine of complete autonomy of the Nigerian (or African) university, honest as their intentions may be, have been utopian. For one thing, all six Nigerian universities have been established and are being financed by government for a purpose, and it sounds utopian to expect the government to turn each of these universities loose to university councils and professors who would be free to request as much money as they consider appropriate and to spend what they receive as they deem proper, without being answerable to anybody outside the university circle. As the National Universities Commission pointed out, Nigerian universities:

> are among the most potent instruments by which our national aspirations, whether these be social, economic or cultural, can be fulfilled. We, therefore, hold that all the governments of the Federation have a special responsibility to concern themselves not only with providing the funds necessary to maintain the universities, but with the positive task of planning and developing a national and coherent system of higher education to meet the needs and aspirations of the nation. We hold, further, that investment in higher education is more than a social overhead. It is the very bedrock upon which all economic and social development must rest. The strength of any nation is in its professional and scientific manpower. (4.1)

A second reason why the doctrine of complete autonomy from the state is considered utopian is that it exposes either disturbing ignorance or deliberate distortion of practice in other parts of the world. This point might not have been made but for the fact that many of these experts or commissions justify their recommendation by generalising about practice among the established world universities. The Freetown Seminar, for instance, has already been quoted as declaring that West African universities cannot measure up to 'the standards and traditions of universities all over the world' unless they are given 'autonomy within the framework of the State'. A brief survey of state-university relationships in other parts of the world will demonstrate that the doctrine of complete autonomy for *state-financed* universities has hardly any adherents; if it has, they would represent the exception rather than the rule.

W.H. Cowley, in his unpublished manuscript, *Professors, Presidents and Trustees*, dismisses as 'delusive half-truths' the commonly quoted statements that the medieval university consisted of 'a free republic of scholars' with no external controls, and that European universities have since remained such republics. Because of the striking contrast between the medieval universities and present-day universities in Europe or elsewhere, I shall confine my survey to present-day universities, beginning with Europe.

Universities in France (home of the University of Paris, one of the most influential medieval universities) are *controlled* by the state. The University of Paris was declared a secular institution under the royal power in 1574. Later all institutions of higher learning were merged during the French Revolution into a centralized educational system. Mountford summarizes the current status of the universities:

> In France the school-leaving *baccalaureat* gives a student a right to register at a university without more ado; most academic appointments are within the control of the Minister of Education, who also approves the curricula; and the budget of universities is subject to detailed supervision. (9.1)

Universities in Sweden are also controlled by the state. Mountford describes the position in Holland:

> In the Netherlands the appointment of professors and lecturers is the prerogative of the Crown, which also makes the appointments to the Board of Curators, who are responsible for the administration of the university. (9.1)

German universities are controlled by the state which also founded them. They enjoyed autonomy in their internal administration until the Nazi regime. The current position is again summarized by Mountford:

> In the Federal German Republic the universities are publicly controlled; professors, while enjoying freedom in their choice of curriculum, are civil servants and are 'called' to their posts by the Minister of Education of the state (Land) where the university is situated. (9.1)

The position in the United Kingdom is different. British universities have not come under the same degree of state control as universities in France, Sweden, Holland or Germany, but it would be inaccurate to state that they enjoy absolute autonomy from governmental control. Carr-Saunders points out that quite often the staff of overseas universities, in their concern for university autonomy and through inexperience in the relations between the U.K. universities and the British government and public bodies, tend to regard as interference certain actions by the overseas government which universities in Britain would not have resented.

> The British universities are not leading lives insulated from the outside world, official or lay, and they do not conduct

their affairs guided only by an estimate of their functions founded on a monastic-like concentration on their special duties as they understand them. (10.1)

Without going far back into history, it is a fact that the British government 'has always felt itself at liberty to institute special enquiries into the affairs of particular universities by way of royal commissions and the like'. (10.2) The range of salary scales for U.K. university staff is settled by the government and announced in Parliament. In 1946, the Committee of Vice-Chancellors and Principals of U.K. universities acknowledged the necessity for a measure of governmental control over the universities in the following words:

> the universities entirely accept the view that the Government has not only the right, but also the duty, of satisfying itself that every field of study which in the national interest ought to be cultivated in Great Britain is, in fact, being adequately cultivated in the university system, and that the resources which are placed at the disposal of the universities are being used with full regard both to efficiency and economy.... The universities may properly be expected not only individually to make proper use of the resources entrusted to them, but also collectively to devise and execute policies calculated to serve the national interest, and in that task, both individually and collectively, they will be glad to have a greater measure of guidance from the Government than until quite recent days they have been accustomed to receive. (11.1)

In more recent years, the nature of the relationship between the state and the U.K. universities has evoked considerable discussion. One main issue has been how far he who pays the piper should call the tune. The Robbins Report summarized the problem as follows:

> Until the closing stages of the last century, apart from the granting of charters, the role of the State in regard to universities was limited to setting up an occasional Royal Commission and the passage of legislation to make possible the carrying out of its recommendations .... The urgent question is whether in the conditions of today the freedom from control that the universities have enjoyed in the past, and to which such importance has been attached, can be expected to persist unchanged; and whether it can be extended in various

degrees to other institutions of higher education. Will it be possible to secure the advantages of co-ordination while preserving the advantages of liberty? The question is of critical importance. (12.1)

The (Robbins) Committee on Higher Education, while recognising the advantages of giving a university freedom to develop as it considers best, also recognised that such independent determination of its own affairs by each institution was unlikely to produce 'a pattern that is comprehensive and appropriate in relation to the needs of society and the demands of the national economy'.

There is no guarantee of the emergence of any coherent policy. And this being so, it is not reasonable to expect that the Government, which is the source of finance, should be content with an absence of co-ordination or should be without influence thereon. (12.2)

The Committee recommended 'the principle of control through general block grants administered by an independent committee or commission appointed for its expert qualifications, not for its political affiliations'. (12.3) The University Grants Committee, which was already in existence, exemplified in their view the type of committee they had in mind.

A front page 'Comment' in the *Times Educational Supplement* of July 8, 1966 referred to a House of Commons debate on higher education in which a Member of Parliament had asked for more parliamentary control of the universities, recommending the incorporation of the University Grants Committee into the appropriate government department since it might not be easy to abolish it. Lord Robbins is quoted as saying that the principles of academic freedom had 'never been in greater peril than they are at this moment'. (13) Mountford reports that:

It is being argued with increasing emphasis that a national system of education is one and indivisible, that in their undergraduate function (whatever may be said about their research) the universities represent a final or 'tertiary' stage after primary and secondary education, and that the government has a clear responsibility to the community to see to it that the universities, no less than the schools, fill this role efficiently. (9.2)

The argument may, no doubt, continue. The important thing at this point is that the principle of some measure of control by the government was established as soon as the government began to play a significant role in financing the universities. From present indications it would appear that the measure of control will be retained, if not enlarged. The transfer of the University Grants Committee from the Treasury under which aegis it had functioned since its establishment in 1919 to the new Department of Education and Science in 1964 could be interpreted as indicative of a growing feeling that the universities should be considered as part of the national educational system. What people like Lord Robbins were advocating is not complete autonomy from governmental control but protection of the universities from 'the cruder incursions of politics'. (13)

Enough for the situation in the United Kingdom. We move to other parts of the world. In the Union of Soviet Socialist Republics and China, the university is state controlled, as would be expected in communist regimes.

The United States of America, with its numerous universities, presents a less homogenous picture than Russia or China or the European countries mentioned above. American universities can be grouped into two major sectors—public and private. Within each of these sectors, however, there are recognisable differences. In view of the fact that Nigeria does not have private universities, I shall concentrate my observations on the public sector of American higher education. Suffice it to say that the private university can enjoy complete autonomy from governmental control and many of them do. The best known of them are, however, losing a great deal of this autonomy as they welcome alluring research grants from the Federal Government. As Clark Kerr summed up:

> the federal colossus had the power to influence the most ruggedly individual of universities. A paradox emerged: the better and the more individual the university, the greater its chances of succumbing to the federal embrace. Washington did not waste its money on the second-rate. (14.1)

But the private universities which receive these grants and those which do not are under constant pressure from the sources of their income. One needs only to read American newspapers or to talk to American university administrators to acquaint oneself with the several conditions (some of them hardly credible) which the major benefactors of these universities attach to their endowments. Therefore while the strings may not be pulled by the government in respect of private universities, they are often pulled by their sources of financial support. The principle is the same.

Because higher education in the United States is a state rather than a federal responsibility, the pattern of governmental control of the public universities is not uniform throughout the country. Seven public universities (Oklahoma State University, University of Michigan, Michigan State University, University of California, University of Colorado, University of Idaho, University of Minnesota) in six states are regarded as constitutional corporations or universities, granted constitutional status, virtually as the fourth branch of the government (the legislature, the executive, and the judiciary being the first three). This places them at par with the legislature and exempts them from state executive control as well as from direct legislation by the legislature. The intention was to insulate them from the pressures of state partisan politics.

Malcolm Moos and Francis Rourke report that this hard-won autonomy of the 'constitutional' universities is fast disappearing. The dependence of the universities on the legislature for funds gives the latter power over the former and provides a loophole for applying pressures. Because these universities depend on the legislature and public goodwill for their finances and public image, it is not always in their best interests to challenge what they consider legislative infringements of their constitutional rights in court. If they did, they could be construed as wilfully going against public opinion, and any victory won in court could turn out to be a Pyrrhic victory. On the other hand, failure to challenge such infringements over a period of time could later be interpreted by the courts, as was done in an unsuccessful attempt by the University of Utah to defend its constitutional immunity from legislative control, to be acquiesence in and compliance with those legislative infringements. The universities also recognize that attempts could be made to amend the constitutions, as was attempted unsuccessfully in California in 1957. (11.2)

Most American public colleges and universities do not enjoy this constitutional recognition. The state legislatures have power over higher education, and this power can legally extend to practically every detail of university operation except where prevented by constitutional safeguards. Whatever independence these institutions enjoy is often derived from their public relations and the extent of legislative restraint, since the institutions are for practical purposes agencies of the state.

One important conclusion from this survey of practice elsewhere is that in each of the countries mentioned the government exercises some measure of control on the publicly supported universities. In view of the important role which the university plays in the political, social and economic development of any nation, and the large amount of public funds consumed by universities, hardly any responsible government, especially in a poor developing country, can afford to abdicate complete responsibility for what goes on inside the universities to university professors. To expect the Nigerian governments to do so is therefore naive. The governments may accept the advice, especially when they have been advised that this is the practice in the developed countries. Having accepted it and broadcast their acceptance, they soon discover that it is impracticable and begin to seek loopholes for injecting their control.

A story I picked up in 1970 illustrates the point. A Military Governor, unable to use constitutional means to remove a university vice-chancellor, hit on a novel idea. He is alleged to have summoned the vice-chancellor to his office. Having seated the vice-chancellor, he pulled out a drawer from which he produced a revolver. He assured the vice-chancellor that there was no need to be afraid; he only thought it fair to let him know that he had a revolver in his drawer. He then looked the vice-chancellor in the face and demanded his resignation. The vice-chancellor, visibly frightened, wrote his resignation there and then!

On the other side of the coin, any Nigerian university administrator knows the hazards that could follow if the university becomes transformed into an arena for partisan politics. The frequent changes in the top management of many of the Nigerian public corporations, to ensure that the spoils of election battles go to the victors, would cause untold harm to the universities unless adequate safeguards are provided.

It is important to establish healthy relationships between the Nigerian university and the government, which would assure the government that the university is cognizant of national needs and playing an effective role towards meeting these needs, while on the other hand allowing the universities elbow room within which to perform their role to the best of their ability. A well defined partnership between the university and the state is necessary. The aim of this partnership should not only be to enable the government to control the university; it should also enable the university to influence the government. It should not result in subservience of the university to the government; it should recognise that the university is in a position to provide guidelines for the government and positive leadership for society as a whole. The pages that follow suggest how such partnership can be established.

THE MANAGEMENT OF THE UNIVERSITY

The idea that the management of each university should be in the hands of a governing body known as the university council has become widely accepted in Nigeria. The idea is not restricted to the university: most Nigerian secondary schools and other post-primary or post-secondary institutions have boards of governors or whatever other names they may be called, responsible for their management. This system makes it possible for outside talent to be drawn into the management of the institution, while it also acts as a check on the excesses of the employees of the institution. I would support a continuation of the system, but with some important modifications.

COMPOSITION OF THE UNIVERSITY COUNCIL

The University Council has so far generally consisted of a chairman or pro-chancellor appointed by the government, the vice-chancellor of the university, persons appointed by the government (who usually make up the majority), and representatives of the senate, which is the academic body within the university. There might be isolated cases in which representation is also granted to the congregation, usually a meeting of all academic and graduate members of the administrative staff, to the convocation (which includes members of the academic staff and graduates of the university), or to alumni of the institution. In the initial years of some of the universities, overseas universities or bodies were represented on the council.

Although the majority of the members are appointed by the government, only a few are civil servants; most of the government nominees do not have to be closely associated with the machinery of the government. Thus more often than not most of the government nominees are not in a position to present or interpret the intentions of the government at council meetings, neither are channels of communication clearly established to facilitate their presenting or interpreting the university to the government. This results in having a preponderance of government appointees who cannot speak for the government.

As mentioned above, the Commission on Post-School Certificate and Higher Education in Nigeria recommended that persons appointed to the council should attend as individuals and not as 'agents for some sectional interest or party line'. In most cases this advice has been followed, with the result that most lay members of the different councils represent themselves. With the exception of the civil servants, each owes his appointment to the appropriate government but does not attend as a representative of the government.

While recognizing possible dangers in 'sectional' representation on the council, at the same time I see some merits in it.

It is a most effective method of eliminating the dangers of the 'spoils system' or political jobbery as it is better known in Nigeria, while at the same time ensuring wider representation on the Council. The government would be represented, but it would not have the power to appoint or remove all lay members of the Council as at present, a method which is more likely to remove the harmful effects of politics from the institution than the present method.

There is a strong reason for proposing wider representation on the Council. If a university is not to remain an island unto itself, it would benefit from the wisdom of the various important segments of the public which constitutes its clientele. These important segments would also profit from close association with the university. The management of the Nigerian university should be a tripartite responsibility, shared by the state or government (which has overall responsibility for national development), the public (which supplies the state with the funds for development, including the funds for running the universities, supplies the universities with students, and along with the state absorbs the products of the universities), and the university (which has the professional competence and experience in university education). All three must be represented on the Council, and each should decide who should represent it.

I shall deal first with university representation. Hitherto the representatives have been elected by the Senate, usually from among its members. Because of the restrictive nature of the Senate, which is essentially restricted to full professors, deans of faculties and departmental heads, I would propose that the election be made by the entire congregation (which comprises the academic staff and members of the senior administrative staff holding approved qualifications). Even if the university decides for various reasons, to prescribe certain qualifications for eligibility (for instance holding of specified minimum ranks) every member of the academic and senior administrative staff should be given the opportunity of participating in the actual election. The Vice-Chancellor and his deputy should normally be members of Council *ex officio*.

As for government representation, it might be preferable to draw them largely, if not entirely, from top civil servants, representing the government ministries or departments most directly connected with university affairs, *e.g.* education, finance, economic planning. The government representatives should not be granted veto powers, and their limited numbers should make it impossible for them to form a majority; it is not expected that the government would have more than a third of the total membership. As civil servants, they are unlikely to be affected by changes in political parties. Their official positions would on the one hand ensure that the government is constantly aware of major academic developments within the university, and on the other hand it would give the Council first hand information about government intentions and development plans. Experience has shown that the university and the state could unnecessarily be acting at cross purposes owing to lack of effective communication. Under the kind of arrangement proposed, the state would be in a position to influence and be influenced by developments at the university. It is a welcome development to find that the Permanent Secretaries of the Federal Ministries of Education and Finance have recently been injected as members of the council of each Nigerian university. As has been suggested earlier, some other areas of Government may also merit representation.

Public representation presents greater difficulties, the public being so diverse and all-embracing. Rather than hold an election to choose the representatives of the 'public', I would suggest identifying and granting representation to some important and relevant elements of the public. Possible eligible 'elements' are: the conference of principals of secondary schools (representing secondary education), the major professional associations, the Nigerian Employers' Consultative Association, the alumni association. Whatever 'elements' are granted representation would be responsible for selecting their own representatives. This should eliminate political influence in the appointments, and at the same time ensure that representation is accorded to essential arms of the public which might not always be recommended when appointment of all non-university members is in the hands of politicians or military rulers. The West African Examinations Council has derived great benefit from such representation of essential interests.

The chairman of the council should be elected by the members of the council for a term of about four years. The person elected need not be a member of the council at the time of election; it would be preferable if he is elected from the public sector rather than from among the state or the university representatives.

The council could be empowered to co-opt a limited number of persons whose special training or experience might facilitate its work.

POWERS OF THE COUNCIL

In a Foreword to *The Truth about the Change in Vice-Chancellorship*, E. Njoku remarked that the crises which occurred first at the University of Ife and later at the University of Lagos, both within a short period of five years, though tragic in many ways, should be of educational value to Nigeria. "If their lessons can be properly learnt, then the rapid developments in the field of higher education in Nigeria may be matched by the necessary experience in University government". (15.1)

The events at Ife and Lagos have led to the proposals above for the composition of the council. Another important lesson to be learnt from the Lagos crisis is the need to define the powers of the council so clearly that it leaves no doubt that the council is the supreme governing body within the university. The following extract from a statement issued by the Senate of the University of Lagos gives the impression that the powers of the council were not so clearly stated:

Status of Senate and Council

2. The Provisional Council is not, and is not stated in the University of Lagos Act to be, the "supreme governing body of the University". The Act, in accordance with normal academic conventions, establishes two bodies, the Senate and the Council. The Senate consists of persons of academic distinction, mainly the Professors and heads of faculties of the University. It is entirely responsible for academic affairs

and is empowered by section 3 (2) of the Act to 'give such directions as it thinks fit for the administration of the University'.

The Council, on the other hand, is essentially a body of eminent laymen. It represents the public interest in the University and is 'charged with the general control and superintendence of the property of the University' section 6 (1).

3. The Council and the Senate are sovereign within their respective spheres; obviously they must work harmoniously together if there is to be a University. (16)

While the action of the Lagos University council in removing the first Vice-Chancellor of the University for what appeared to be purely political reasons is deplorable, it would be dangerous to advocate a situation in which a university is to be controlled by two sovereign bodies as enunciated above. To say so is not necessarily to take sides with Ruml and Morrison who observed that the liberal college in America had deteriorated under the system whereby the academic staff held responsibility for the administration of the curriculum and methods of instruction, and recommended that the Board of Trustees which has the final responsibility and authority for the educational programme as well as the property of the institution 'must take back from the faculty *as a body* its present authority over the design and administration of the curriculum. The Trustees must take back this authority, but not because the Trustees *as a Board* are able to exercise it better than the faculty as a body'. (17.1)

Such a proposal would sound utter heresy in British and Nigerian university circles in which the academic staff play a greater role in the management of the university than in many American universities. Ruml and Morrison are not the only critics of faculty participation, particularly in the United States. Corson regards as 'one of the deadliest hazards to higher education' 'the resistance of faculties to change in subject matter and in method'. (18.1) He goes on to state that 'Every faculty member believes it is his right to participate in decisions of importance to higher education, yet few understand the nature of higher education outside their own departmental activities'. (18.2) Law comments that 'Faculty members are too close to certain problems to render objective services'. (7.2) Granted there is some validity in these criticisms, all the same it would be chaotic not to involve the academic staff in the formulation of academic policy, especially in the current Nigerian situation where there are as yet no more than a handful of retired professors and few lay members of the council who have had previous experience of curriculum planning at university level. Moreover Nigeria does not have the special universities which an American speaker claimed have been established in the Soviet Union and where new ideas on university education are tried out and, if found suitable, are channelled down to the regular universities for emulation.

The senate or whatever other name the academic body within each university answers to should continue to be involved in the development of academic policy within the university. It should, however, be made abundantly clear that the council is the supreme governing body with authority not only over the property of the university but also over academic and other matters. As the supreme governing body, the council should have the authority to override any decision of the senate or the administration if it has good reason for so doing. The fact that the academic staff are represented on the council (a privilege many American universities have never enjoyed, and which an American professor of higher education told me he was stoutly against) should reduce the possibilities of conflict and enable the academic staff to influence the final decisions.

The military regime in Nigeria appears to have successfully wrested from the university councils a function crucial to the existence of the university—the power to appoint the Vice-Chancellor. During the political era, a Vice-Chancellor was appointed by the council of the university. Some universities stipulated detailed procedures for selecting a Vice-Chancellor, often involving a joint effort by the senate and the council. Whatever influence politicians had on the appointments was indirect, invariably through pressures on the chairman and some members of council. No head of government in Nigeria prior to 1966 had the power to appoint or remove a Vice-Chancellor.

Reference has been made earlier to the unconstitutional method adopted by a military governor to remove a Vice-Chancellor. Following the opposition of the Ibadan senate to attempts by the Federal Military Government to use unconstitutional methods to appoint a Vice-Chancellor for the university in 1972, the Federal Military Government amended the laws of the two Federal Universities, Ibadan and Lagos, transferring from the Council to the Visitor the power to hire and fire the Vice-Chancellor of each university.

The amendment reads, in each case, as follows:....'the Vice-Chancellor shall be appointed or removed from his office by the Visitor acting after consultation with the council'.

Having amended the laws, the Visitor (who, by law is the Head of State) held consultations with the Ibadan and Lagos councils after which he authorized the appointment of a Vice-Chancellor for each university.

Legal experts attach little weight to the words 'after consultation with'. The Visitor is not bound to accept the opinion of the council on any candidate, and he is free to decide on the mode of consultation. However it is significant that the Federal Military Government had to amend the Laws in the first instance, to confer the necessary powers on the Visitor before he proceeded to exercise them. The situation at Nsukka was different.

The University of Nigeria Law stipulates that 'The Vice-Chancellor shall be appointed by the Council....' That Law was in operation in November 1970 when Prof. H.C. Kodilinye was appointed Vice-Chancellor of the university. It was, however, common knowledge that the newly appointed council was instructed by the Administrator of the East-Central State to appoint Prof. Kodilinye vice-chancellor, and the council complied 'with acclamation'. Prior to that, the Administrator had instructed the Council to appoint Prof. J.O.C. Ezeilo acting Vice-Chancellor which the council did. The Administrator and the Military Governor of the South-Eastern State (which was at the time joint proprietor of Nsukka with the East-Central State) went further to issue directives on who should be appointed Bursar and which State should field candidates for the major administrative positions, thereby encroaching on the powers of the council. Luckily no other Nigerian university has followed their lead that far.

Having captured the power to appoint Vice-Chancellors, neither the military leaders nor the politicians who will succeed them some day are likely to give it up. Nigerian universities are not unique in having their vice-chancellors appointed by government. The East African universities had a taste of this some years earlier. Examples have also been cited of state controlled universities elsewhere in which not only vice-chancellors but even the staff are appointed by the state. With the best of intentions all round, one advantage in the system is that it could improve the working relations between the university and the state.

However, knowing that intentions are not always the best, having charted Nigeria's history for the past few decades, and considering the crucial role of the vice-chancellor in a university, I do not consider it in the best interests of the Nigerian university to turn the vice-chancellorship into a political appointment, which is what it has now become. The government appoints the chancellor, the pro-chancellor (or chairman of council), as well as several members of council. The Visitor has powers to institute visitations or commissions of enquiry into the university. These are adequate channels for bringing government influence on the university. To turn the vice-chancellorship into a political appointment is to create room for instability where it would cause the greatest harm. If government sees wisdom in insulating civil service, police and judiciary appointments from the cold winds of politics, it is difficult to justify adopting different standards with the universities. If permanent secretaries in the public service are appointed by the Public Service Commission rather than by the political party in power, it does not sound proper to leave the appointment of so crucial a post as vice-chancellor in the hands of politicians, the style and colour of their attire notwithstanding.

A university council could abuse its powers or fail to discharge its responsibilities satisfactorily. As a safeguard against this, and also as a means of ensuring that the university takes periodic stock of its work and development, I would propose that the state should be required once every ten years to appoint a competent team of experts (including representatives of other universities) to examine and report on all facets of the work of the university, making appropriate recommendations. If this periodic review is made a requirement, it would lose any political overtones and each university would look upon it as a constructive means of evaluation rather than a malicious commission of enquiry. Unlike the visitation, referred to in an earlier section, which reports to the university council, the commission should report to the government which finances the university.

One need which the University of Lagos crisis revealed was for a disinterested party which could intervene legally should there develop an impasse such as that between the Lagos council and senate at the time. One would hope that such impasses do not become a regular feature of university administration, and that nothing should be done to encourage routine appeals to another authority against decisions of the council, otherwise the council would soon cease to be the supreme governing body. The law courts are always available to the person or group of persons who may need redress in the event of an unjust decision, but the personnel regulations of some of the universities make it impossible to go to court against the university and continue on its staff thereafter. The laws establishing the universities make no provision for government intervention. The Visitor of the university or the Chancellor would seem an appropriate possibility for this kind of responsibility which, one hopes, may never be exercised. Each of them, by current university laws, owes his office to the state rather than to the university council. Each of them is generally a person of considerable experience who either commands wide respect or wields great authority; even more importantly, each is regarded as part of the university without being deeply involved in its detailed administration. It would be necessary to agree on the types of problems that could necessitate their intervention and the power to intervene should be written into the law.

The shortlived strike of university lecturers in practically all Nigerian universities in April 1973 and the action taken by the Head of the Federal Military Government in his capacity as Visitor of Ibadan and Lagos should underscore the need to reach a clear understanding of the situations under which the Chancellor or Visitor may intervene. The action of the Visitor on this occasion, ordering the staff of both universities to return to work on a given date or regard themselves as sacked, was not based on any powers conferred on the Visitor by the law of either university. As things would have it, the staff developed weak knees and obeyed, thus averting an awkward situation.

REFERENCES

1 Ashby, Eric, *African Universities and Western Tradition,* Cambridge, Massachusetts, Harvard University Press, 1964. 1.1: p. 97.
2 *Investment in Education,* Report of the Commission on Post-school Certificate and Higher Education in Nigeria, Lagos, Federal Ministry of Education, Nigeria, 1960. 2.1: p. 31.
3 Saunders, J.T. & Dowuona, M., (eds.) *The Wsst African Intellectual Community,* Ibadan, Ibadan University Press, 1962. 3.1: p. 346.

4   Federal Republic of Nigeria, *University Development in Nigeria:* Report of the National Universities Commission, Lagos, Federal Ministry of Information, 1963. 4.1: p. 20.

5   Mellanby, Kenneth, *The Birth of Nigeria's University,* London, Methuen & Co. Ltd., 1958. 5.1: p. 123.

6   Federation of Nigeria, *Educational Development* 1961–70, Lagos, Sessional Paper No. 3 of 1961. 6.1: p. 8.

7   University of Lagos, *Change in Vice-Chancellorship,* an offcial publication, 1965. 7.1: p. 28.

8   Law, Glen Charles, *The Urgency of New Leadership in Higher Education,* Stamford, Connecticut, Press-Tige Publishing, 1962. 8.1: p. 39; 8.2: p. 45.

9   Mountford, Sir James, *British Universities,* London, Oxford University Press, 1966. 9.1: p. 149; 9.2: p. 150.

10 Carr-Saunders, A.M., *New Universities Overseas,* London, George Allen & Unwin Ltd., 1961. 10.1: p. 194; 10.2: p. 193.

11 Moos, Malcolm & Bourke, Francis E., *The Campus and the State,* Baltimore, The Johns Hopkins Press, 1959. 11.1: p. 349; 11.2: pp. 30–33.

12 Committee on Higher Education, *Higher Education:* report of the Committee appointed by the Prime Minister under the Chairmanship of Lord Robbins, 1961–63, London, Her Majesty's Stationery Office, October, 1963. 12.1: p. 228; 12.2: p. 233; 12.3: p. 275.

13 *Times Educational Supplement,* No. 2,668, Friday July 8, 1966. p. 61.

14 Kerr, Clark, *The Uses of the University,* Cambridge, Massachusetts, Harvard University Press, 1963. 14.1: p. 50.

15 Berrie, O.K. et al, *The Truth About the Change in Vice-Chancellorship,* Lagos, 1965. 15.1 :p. 1.

16 'The University of Lagos Crisis': A statement by the Senate, *Daily Times,* April 6, 1965, p. 4.

17 Ruml, Beardsley & Morrison, Donald H., *Memo to a College Trustee,* New York, McGraw-Hill Book Company, Inc., 1959. 17.1: p. 13

18 Corson, John J., *Governance of Colleges and Universities,* New York, McGraw-Hill Book Company, Inc., 1960. 18.1: p. 103; 18.2: p. 99 (quotation at footnote).

CHAPTER 9

ACADEMIC FREEDOM

Although autonomy (from government control) and academic freedom are closely related, they are not necessarily synonymous. It is for this reason that academic freedom is considered separately. The greatest threats to academic freedom in many parts of the world have in the past generally come from the state, but all threats to academic freedom do not emanate from the state alone.

The concept of academic freedom has featured prominently in the writings and recommendations of many experts on Nigerian and African higher education, who have emphasized its absolute necessity, if a university is to develop into a proper university. Here are some of their views and recommendations:

The UNESCO Tananarive Seminar on the development of higher education in Africa included the following statements on academic freedom:

> In order to perform their tasks effectively, African universities must enjoy the traditional academic freedom to the fullest extent possible. They must have the fullest freedom to teach, to advance the frontiers of knowledge through research and to disseminate as widely as possible the results of their research. Like other universities, African universities must keep these principles intact and consolidate and defend these rights as may be necessary. (1.1)

The conference also stressed that:

> The principles of academic freedom are the basic tenets of university existence without which all true values in the academic community are lost. The African university must, therefore, preserve those principles inviolate, assure their prerogatives and defend them without regard to pecuniary considerations. Higher education institutions in developing nations should, therefore, take measures to ensure that the principles of academic freedom to inquire, to debate, and to disseminate as well as acquire knowledge in its ramifications should be held unimpaired for students, staff and

other members of the academic community. For if by chance the African university loses its freedom to learn, to work for and to disseminate the results of its research, it loses its *raison d'etre*. (1.2)

Sir Eric Ashby placed academic freedom among the three 'universals in academic life which will not become firmly established in Africa without the benefit of expatriate help'. (2.1) He conceived of academic freedom in the following terms:

> This does not mean benefit of the clergy for the dons. It means *Lehrfreiheit* as the Germans developed and refined it in the nineteenth century. It is not a personal privilege: it is an essential freedom to enable university teachers to do their jobs with integrity. It guarantees that no teacher shall be victimized in any way by reason of what he teaches or writes, unless it is contrary to the laws of the country. The strongest argument for it is not the appeal to tradition; it is the appeal to empiricism. Where academic freedom is disallowed, universities will fail. If the country's laws are inimical to freedom of speech, then academic freedom is eclipsed in that country. The academic, whether a citizen of the country or not, must resist, or leave, or forfeit his freedom. (2.2)

It is striking that Ashby believes (without giving any reasons) that academic freedom cannot be established in the new African countries without the help of foreign professors. In this regard, it is possible that he based his belief on the views expressed by a Nigerian scholar, Professor Eni Njoku, in 1959, views which Ashby has cited in his writings and which were also quoted extensively by Carr-Saunders:

> The modern university scholar is an entirely new type of person in Nigeria, not identified with any traditional role. The conditions for such a type to flourish, such as academic freedom, is therefore an entirely new conception. Nevertheless, the principle of academic freedom has been accepted in Nigeria, not by itself, but as part of a university organization. Nigerians demanded a university as good as those existing anywhere else in the world. If academic freedom is a necessary element in such universities, then it must exist in the Nigerian institution too . . . . Although the principle of academic freedom is accepted, it is important to realize that it has to justify itself in the Nigerian context. It is not easy to argue that acade-

mic freedom is necessary in order to train the professional manpower required by the Nigerian society. On the contrary, ...
that is the very reason why an insufficiently perceptive university should be given directions by the Government to ensure
that the needs of the country are met. The really cogent
arguments for academic freedom, such as its being a necessary atmosphere for scholarship to flourish, although applicable to Nigeria, are derived from other situations. The scholar
has not yet fully arrived in Nigeria, and the advantages to be
gained by giving him freedom are not yet obvious . . . . At
present it (academic freedom) is merely one of the embel-
lishments attached in its country of origin to an imported
product. It is necessary to consolidate and give local content to
the principle if it is to be successfully defended in times of
crisis. (3.1)

Carr-Saunders went on to discuss the problems facing political
leaders in the new nations, and the co-operation these leaders
expect from every person and every institution within the nation
if their development plans are to succeed. In such circumstances,
to initiate discussions at the university on the merits and demerits
of these plans could be construed as indiscipline. Consequently
'academic freedom comes to be regarded first as unnecessary,
next as a nuisance and finally as objectionable'. (3.2)

The recommendations of the Freetown seminar on Inter-University
Co-operation in West Africa have been quoted in the section on
autonomy. Examined in detail, these recommendations also embrace
the seminar's views on academic freedom. How far has the concept
of academic freedom taken root in Nigerian soil? A release in August
1965 by the International Association of University Professors and
Lecturers conveyed the impression that the soil in Nigeria had not
been ideal for a healthy growth of academic freedom. Part of the
release announced: 'We are sorry that we have once more to report
an infringement of academic freedom in Nigeria. This time it
happened at the University of Nigeria at Nsukka . . . .' (4)

It is easy to infer from the release that at least one infringement
of academic freedom had occurred in Nigeria before August 1965.
I propose to analyse the alleged infringement leading to the August
1965 release, together with an earlier case to which I believe the
release was referring, to see whether academic freedom was in fact
infringed in each case and, if so, to determine possible reasons for
the infringement and from these to comment on the future of academic

freedom in Nigerian universities. Before doing so, however, it is essential to consider some definitions of academic freedom.

Russell Kirk quotes Hook who declared in *Heresy, Yes; Conspiracy, No* that 'there is more sloppy rhetoric poured out per page about academic freedom both by those who believe that they are supporting, and those intent on criticizing it, than on any other theme with the possible exception of democracy'. (5.1) He then goes on to quote the following definition of academic freedom from Couch which he considers the best he had seen: 'Academic freedom is the principle designed to protect the teacher from hazards that tend to prevent him from meeting his obligations in the pursuit of truth'. He continued: 'The obligations of the teacher are direct to truth, and the teacher who, in order to please anybody, suppresses important information, or says things he knows are not true, or refrains from saying things that need to be said in the interests of truth, betrays his calling and renders himself unworthy to belong to the company of teachers'. (5.2) He points out that academic freedom is not usually guaranteed statutorily; it is more often a natural right conferred by social convention. He argues that 'Academic freedom, like every other prescriptive right, has its boundaries and its corresponding duties . . . . There are times when the persons who pay a professor would be derelict in their duty if they did not endeavour to restrain the man who violates his own privileges; and . . . . it is prudent and necessary that there should sometimes exist a control upon the academy besides the control of . . . . "the rational methods by which the truth is established".' (5.3) This appears to harp on the same note as Ashby—that academic freedom is not the same as the benefit of the clergy.

Robert MacIver defined academic freedom thus:

> Academic freedom is . . . . a right claimed by the accredited educator, as teacher and as investigator, to interpret his findings and to communicate his conclusions without being subjected to any interference, molestation, or penalization because these conclusions are unacceptable to some constituted authority within or beyond the institution. *Here is the core of the doctrine of academic freedom. It is the freedom of the student within his field of study.* (6.1)

To safeguard this freedom, appointment and promotion procedures must not be such as to favour some teachers on the basis of their views on controversial issues. MacIver however points out that the educator enjoys his freedom in the context of the university. It is 'the freedom of the scholar within the institution devoted to scholarship'. (6.2) 'In his relations outside his institution the educator has the same liberty as other men, except that he should be careful not to associate his institution in any way with his extra-academic utterances or actions'. (6.3)

These quotations have concentrated, as many professors do, on the rights or freedom of the teacher, 'the student within his field of study'. This is an important aspect of academic freedom, but not the only aspect. The concept of academic freedom also embraces the university as an institution. Mountford's definition covers institutional as well as individual freedom:

> With university autonomy as its foundation, the principle of academic freedom ensures the right of the institution itself and of each member of its academic staff to teach, research, and make public the results of scholarly work in the interests of truth and the advancement of learning alone, uninhibited and unfettered by any extraneous considerations whatsoever. (7.1)

Freedom of *scholarly* investigation regardless of where it may lead, and freedom to communicate the results of such *scholarly* investigation, no matter whether they conflict with the views of the power structure (be they within or outside the university) —these more than anything else constitute the essence of academic freedom. Thomas Jefferson's statement in 1820 in connection with his creation, the University of Virginia, aptly expressed this essence: 'This institution will be based on the illimitable freedom of the human mind. For here we are not afraid to follow truth wherever it may lead, nor to tolerate any error so long as reason is free to combat it'. (8.1)

In any consideration of academic freedom, emphasis must however be placed on *scholarship*. While the university scholar may claim protection in respect of scholarly findings that may prove unpalatable or even heretical, he cannot expect such guarantees for pronouncements which do not stem from scholarly investigation. The only *raison d'etre* for the concept of academic freedom is to safeguard the quest for truth and the advancement of learning.

The Robbins Committee took the trouble of defining what it considered the components of academic freedom as it applies to the institution, namely the freedom to appoint its own staff without reference to any external authority, freedom to determine the content of curricula and to establish and maintain its own standards without reference to any external authority, freedom to determine its rate of growth and to choose its own students, freedom to determine the balance between teaching and research, and freedom to determine the shape of its development, including which subjects to develop in preference to others. (15.1)

I do not consider it necessary to go to such details here. First, it would be difficult to reconcile some of those 'freedoms' with my concept of partnership between the university and the state, a concept which is not necessarily inimical to academic freedom. Secondly, it would appear more profitable to get at the essence of academic freedom than to carve out spheres of influence in which the university must operate without government intervention. As will be illustrated shortly with a case of an alleged infringement of academic freedom in Nigeria, the threat to the freedom of the scholar can come from within the university as well as from the state. Moreover, a university could give up some of the Robbins' freedom, without sacrificing its academic freedom. If I may illustrate what I mean, the academic staff of overseas university colleges and universities were virtually chosen for them by the Inter-University Council located in London, which was as external a body to, say, University College, Ibadan as the Federal Public Service Commission located in Lagos. Yet nobody considered this an infringement of academic freedom. The crucial consideration is that selection was based on qualifications (academic and personal) and merit, rather than on grounds of race, religion, sex, ethnic group, political affiliation, or any kind of pressure from extraneous quarters.

The two alleged infringements of academic freedom in Nigerian universities will now be considered. I am aware they have been discussed by other writers before me, including Nduka Okafor in *The Development of Universities in Nigeria*. I do not, however, share some of the conclusions of these writers.

THE UNIVERSITY OF IFE CASE
The University of Ife, as stated in an earlier section, was opened in 1962 by the then Western Nigeria Government. By design or

accident, most of its initial senior Nigerian staff were members or supporters of the Action Group, the political party then in power in Western Nigeria. A major political crisis in Western Nigeria in mid-1962 brought tribulation to the Action Group. Its leader and many of its top members were jailed on charges of treasonable felony. Its deputy leader, however, remained Premier after clever political manouvering which culminated in the emergence of the Nigerian National Democratic Party (N.N.D.P.) as the political party in power. The new party which had come into power without having to contest an election, was sensitive to criticism, particularly the type that challenged its legitimacy. The Nigerian lecturers at Ife who had remained loyal to the Action Group in spite of its vicissitudes, were naturally critical of the new leaders of Western Nigeria, and so were many undergraduates; a measure of this opposition was the fact that the Premier of the Region who was named Chancellor of the University could not be so installed for fear of the violent reaction to such a ceremony on the campus. The NNDP Government was openly concerned about the mounting opposition to it at Ife, and some of its members made statements (which were later denied) that if the university continued to serve as the sanctuary for subversive elements and to indoctrinate students against the Government, the university might be closed down. Actions of the Government such as the replacement of the members of the Provisional Council of the university, and the appointment of a full-time Civil Servant as its chairman—a precedent in Nigeria— did not improve the position. It was clear that the Government expected the university authorities to clamp down on its staff and student critics who took shelter under the cloak of academic freedom, realising that only the university authorities had any powers of discipline over them.

On December 19, 1963, the Pro-Vice-Chancellor of the University—the Vice-Chancellor was away in the United Kingdom— summoned a special congregation of the academic and senior administrative staff 'in order publicly to declare the stand of the University in the current controversy which revolves round it'. (9·1) He enjoined everyone to prove by their actions their loyalty to the Government as the founder of the university. 'The events of the last two or three days have indicated forcibly that the University must declare a more positive stand'. (9.2)

He then went on to declare the positive stand. 'I wish to say most categorically. . . . that the authorities of the University have only one policy and that is to support the Government of the Day to which the University looks for sustenance'. (9.3) The crucial part of his declaration followed:

> This University, therefore, has implicit faith in the Government of Western Nigeria. Its duty is to support the Government and offer its services to it in all the various fields of talent represented therein. This is the *CREDO* of the University and anyone who does not subscribe to it must have the courage to leave its service. If any one disagrees with the fundamental policy of the University the remedy lies wholly in his hands: to resign! . . . . The regulations (recently approved by the University Council) provide a clear statement of the rights of the individual member of staff to express his views within the limits that he should not thereby endanger the very existence of the University. I wish to state categorically again that the Council will enforce the present regulations most rigorously. . . . (9.4)

He proceeded to a definition of academic freedom:

> A good deal has been said about "academic freedom" in this controversy, I think we should stop confusing the issue. Members of academic communities have no inherent right of free speech which are different from those of other citizens. All freedoms must be exercised by all citizens within the provisions of the Law. In fact, well trained academic minds are expected to bring their superior training to bear upon the exercise of their freedom of speech, and their criticisms are expected to be balanced and fair-minded and their assessment of any situation objective and analytical. Withall, they are exercising the same right to free speech as any citizen. (9.5)

After quoting the Freetown recommendations which he himself had helped to formulate at the seminar, he attempted to absolve the university and the government from any charge of trampling on academic freedom. 'We believe and hereby declare that as far as this University is concerned, the Government of Western Nigeria has left us to operate in the *spirit* of these (i.e. the Freetown) recommendations. We, therefore, have autonomy and academic freedom in the fields judged by the consensus of opinion of representatives of the leading universities in West Africa to be essential and for this we are grateful'. (9.6)

As an immediate response to his statement, a Nigerian lecturer in English resigned from the staff of the university, and an N.C.N.C. member from its Council. (10)

Later the appointment of a Nigerian professor and dean of the Faculty of Agriculture (who was one of the 'critics' of the government) was terminated for 'a gross act of insubordination to the University Council'. He was alleged to have refused to apologize for an act of rudeness to the chairman of the Council and to the Vice-Chancellor of the university. Immediately the news of the termination became known, three Nigerian lecturers and one expatriate lecturer gave notice of their intention to resign from a university they said was fast being rendered a 'servile instrument of the reactionary Regional dictatorship'. Four of them were ordered to leave the university immediately, that is without serving the period of their notice. The dean's allegation that his dismissal had a political motive was denied by the chairman of the Council. (11)

The President of the Federal Republic of Nigeria and then Chancellor of the University of Nigeria made a statement that the termination of the dean's appointment was unfortunate, and offered his good offices to effect an amicable settlement. The Minister of Education (Western Nigeria) regretted the President's statement, repeating that there were no political motives in the dismissal, which was 'strictly a question of discipline'. (12) The dean and the four lecturers left the university.

THE UNIVERSITY OF NIGERIA/LINDSAY CASE
On May 12, 1964, Dr. J.K. Lindsay, Professor of History at the University of Nigeria, Nsukka circulated a memorandum (13.1) to members of the Senate of the university. In the memorandum he expressed unhappiness that the university had decided to admit students to a new degree programme in Archaeology without first consulting the Senate, and gave notice of a motion he hoped to table at the next meeting of the Senate: 'that the Council is urged to consult the Senate before establishing new institutes, departments, or programmes of study as these are as much academic matters as ones of policy'.

On May 14, 1964 the Vice-Chancellor of the university suspended Lindsay from his duties as professor, acting in accordance with the provisions of the University of Nigeria Law 1961 pointing out that he was reporting his action to the University Council as required by the law. He charged Lindsay with abusing the privileges of his appointment as professor, as member of the department of History and Archaeology, and as member of the Senate. He was also charged with circulating or causing to be circulated in his name 'a memorandum containing erroneous statements about the University of Nigeria, intemperate criticisms of University policy and statements attributing grandiose, naive, and improper motives to alleged actions of authorities of the University including the Council of the University'. (13.2)

On May 21, 1964 the Secretary of the University Council invited Lindsay to submit within 72 hours his reply to the four charges above for transmission to the Council. Lindsay complied with this. In his reply dated May 23, 1964 he claimed he could make no defence to the first three charges as he was not aware that he had abused any of the privileges referred to, and that no person (including the Vice-Chancellor) had informed him of any such abuse. Regarding the circulation of his memorandum, he claimed he did so in confidence to Senate members only, by virtue of his statutory membership of the Senate. Any criticism of the university in his memorandum was made in good faith, and he was willing to retract any erroneous information contained in it.

He was invited to discuss the matter with the University Council at a meeting on June 5, 1964. On June 11, 1964 the Vice-Chancellor wrote to inform him that his suspension had been lifted with immediate effect. The Secretary to Council followed this up with a letter on June 12 informing him that the Council had supported the suspension action but had asked that it be lifted for certain reasons (not specified). The letter stated that the Council had, among other things, made him 'aware of the universally accepted meaning of academic freedom (not licence) which Council encourages and guarantees'. (13.4) He was warned that in the event of a recurrence of similar attitude on his part in future, 'Council would justifiably feel itself obliged to terminate your appointment'. (13.4) He was also informed that he was offered appointment as a professor of History, not as Head of the department of History.

The headship of the department of History added another dimension to the Lindsay case. In a letter to the Secretary to Council on June 18, Lindsay expressed surprise at a news item in the campus newspaper that one of his Nigerian colleagues had been appointed to the headship of the department with effect from September 1, 1964, stating that he was hired specifically to be professor and head of the department of History. He stated that even though he had arrived at the university to assume duties as head of department, he had voluntarily agreed that the headship should go temporarily to a British colleague 'without relinquishing my right to assume the Headship of the Department of History when the time came for him to return to the University of London'. (13.5)

On July 31 he wrote a long letter to the Secretary to Council in reply to the latter's letter of the June 12. In it he raised the constitutional issue that the Senate to which he addressed his memorandum should have been the body competent to take any punitive action on him. He recounted that the reaction of the Senate to his suspension had been to pass a 'motion of censure' on the Vice-Chancellor. He refuted the statement that his letter contained any errors, except one insignificant error about dates. If the Council truly expected repentance from him, 'it can only mean that the Council is astonishingly misinformed about the affairs of this university. The statements, I feel, are reasonably accurate. In addition they deal with only part of the story. The memorandum was restricted to the planning of new departments and new programmes of study. It did not refer to planning in other areas'. (13.6) He then gave five long paragraphs of further instances of poor planning and action by the university, including a critical statement on the excessive powers of the Council and its Chancellor. His last paragraph, devoted to the issue of his right to the headship of the department, ended with a statement suggesting he might take legal action against the university. In August 1964 the Acting Vice-Chancellor (the substantive incumbent having left Nigeria for good) exchanged further correspondence with Lindsay; the two letters dealt exclusively with the issue of the headship of department.

On August 31 the Secretary to Council wrote to inform Lindsay that his appointment had been terminated by the Council at its meeting on August 29. He was to receive six months pay in lieu of notice as stipulated in his terms of appointment, and he should leave the campus within one week, *i.e.* on or before September 7, 1964. He replied on September 3, stating *inter alia*:

> When even constructive criticism given in the course of duty is thus ruthlessly crushed none of us can longer hope for much

reform from within the University. With reluctance I am forced to conclude that we must now turn to the authorities of the Eastern Region to which the University of Nigeria is ultimately responsible and of whose money it has already spent so many millions of pounds. .... Those of us who, in one way or another, have been pressing for changes at Nsukka were aware that the cost to ourselves would be the ill-will of one or two of the most influential persons in the present regime of the University. That we have continued, and will continue to press for them is a measure of our respect for the University and our faith in its long-term prospects. (13.7)

He left Nigeria when his efforts to mobilise public support did not produce immediate results. However on March 2, 1965 he wrote to the Secretary to Council from Kingston, Jamaica, announcing:

We were perhaps foolishly optimistic when we decided six months ago to give the University additional time in which to show that it had embarked on the road to reform. .... What has been done, has been done—but the six wasted months make it the more imperative that all persons concerned with the quality and reputation of Nigeria's universities should be given full information about conditions at Nsukka without further delay. As a first step in this direction it is now decided to make available to them the correspondence between the University and myself which has taken place since last May. (13.8)

OBSERVATIONS

The University of Ife case demonstrates what appears to be the greatest threat to academic freedom in Nigerian universities, a threat that is not however peculiar to Nigeria. The trial and condemnation to death of Socrates in ancient Greece posed essentially the same problem, namely: how much can a democratic state entertain criticism of itself? Ife happened to have had among its academic staff and students some who did not see eye to eye with the politicians in power in Western Nigeria and who were accordingly critical of that government, to the continued embarrassment of the latter. The lecturers and students were however acting within their rights as citizens of a country that guarantees its citizens freedom of speech. Nigerian civil servants are not permitted to criticize the government openly and retain their civil service positions. University lecturers are not civil servants, but like civil servants they depend on government appropriations for their salaries. Similarly the university students, whether on government scholarship or not, are receiving an education heavily subsidized by the government. I doubt whether any politician would deny the freedom of the lecturer under the constitution to criticize the government; what the politician questions is whether the government should guarantee the lecturer a regular salary to enable him to do this. Politics could be lucrative in Nigeria; it could also lead the way to penury. Most Nigerian politicians recognized this, and therefore considered it unfair to be at the receiving end of isolated or organized attacks by ivory tower politicians who were not daring and honest enough to give up their well paid and tenured jobs and join those who were braving the chilly winds of politics in the open.

This is one way of looking at the problem, largely from the politician's viewpoint, but it is not the only way. Another point of view is that it is in the overall best interest of the society that improper decisions and actions of the government should be subjected to the searchlight of informed criticism, even by persons who derive their sustenance from the public treasury. After all the brand of democracy which Nigeria inherited from the British attaches great importance to the presence of organised opposition. Each Nigerian government prior to January 1966 not only accorded recognition but also paid a handsome salary to a 'Leader of the Opposition'. Such a designation would, however, be out of place in a true university community because it presupposes a predisposition to every government action—the disposition to oppose, often with the intention of scoring a political victory which may pay off at the next election and make the leader of the opposition the leader of government business. University scholars are in a position to apply their scholarly minds and methods to current civic or political problems, even when these problems are outside their particular disciplines. The outcome of this exercise need not always lead to criticism or denunciation of the government, but when it does the power structure ought to regard this as one of the gains the society derives from the existence of its universities. The scholars are not only exercising their civic privileges but rendering a service to a country which is still building up enlightened public opinion. The university scholar who, however, sees a dichotomy between his scholarly and his political roles, and gladly renounces the methods of scholarship in his criticisms of the government may invoke his rights as a citizen in his defence, but not the concept of academic freedom.

Then, from the institutional point of view, there is the problem of the professor or student whose political actions are a constant embarrassment to the university authorities. For example, in 1965 two students of the University of Nigeria (Nsukka) instituted legal action against the President and the Prime Minister of the Republic in connection with the conduct of the 1964 federal elections. The university authorities heard of the action on the radio. To further complicate matters, the President was also the founder of the University, its Chancellor and Chairman of Council. In such tight situations a university could act rashly, to appease the powers that be and thus safeguard its source of livelihood. The action of the University of Nigeria in this situation shows that Nigerian universities are capable of safeguarding academic freedom even on delicate occasions and in spite of their dependence on the government for funds. The university maintained that the students acted within their rights as individual citizens of the country, and that the university did not have to approve or disapprove of their action.

Whether the Ife Pro-Vice-Chancellor knew it or not, his declaration that the only policy of his university was to support the 'Government of the Day' was an infringement of the freedom of the university he was defending. Such a Vicar of Bray attitude or policy is inconsistent with the goals of a university—the quest for truth wherever it may lead—unless the government of the day happens also to be the only source of truth. It has been suggested that Plato's idea in designing a Republic in which philosophers would be kings was inspired by his aversion to the condemnation of Socrates. Such a tragedy could not occur in a state ruled by philosophers! Unfortunately neither Nigeria nor any country I know of in the present world is blessed with the philosopher kings contemplated by Plato— whose rigorous academic and philosophical training qualify them to determine the Good. Consequently, one must reject the Vicar of Bray policy.

When the Pro-Vice-Chancellor went on to require the Ife professors to subscribe to his CREDO or resign, he also infringed the freedom of the professors and students in about the same way as the loyalty oaths infringed the freedom of academics in American universities within living memory. Likewise, when during the civil war the Vice-Chancellor of the 'University of Biafra' (as it was then called), requested members of staff of the university to engage in war activities or forfeit their salaries, he infringed the freedom of the staff.

The University of Nigeria/Lindsay case is in a different category. The pamphlet of correspondence is understandably silent on many important factors. It would appear that the Vice-Chancellor had no justification for suspending Lindsay when he did. Lindsay's May 12 memorandum was based on many false premises—something one would not expect from a university professor or scholar. For instance, no admission had at that time been offered to any person for any course; there was no attempt to admit students for fisheries or forestry that year, nor to establish a school of librarianship. He was therefore pouring invectives on the university authorities for 'crimes' not yet committed. Moreover Lindsay's department had already taken a decision on the proposed Archaeology degree for transmission to the Vice-Chancellor, a decision that was later implemented. All the same, his memorandum was circulated to members of the Senate only; the Vice-Chancellor, as chairman of the Senate, was in a position to put his sins before him on the floor of the Senate. The University Council wisely decided to lift the suspension. Lindsay's case would have ended at this juncture had he not decided to raise an entirely different issue, unrelated to his suspension.

The dispute over Lindsay's claim to the headship of the department of history led to the termination of his appointment. It would appear that he was appointed to assume duty as professor and head of the department. On his arrival at Nsukka, it became obvious that he would not be competent to build up such a new and important department. As an interim measure, a visiting senior lecturer from London University was asked to act as head. As Lindsay would (according to the terms of service at the time) have received no additional stipend as head of department, the decision did not result in any financial loss to him. Shortly before the acting head was due to return to London, it was still clear that it would be a great mistake to hand the department over to Lindsay. The University Council was therefore *advised* to appoint Lindsay's Nigerian colleague to succeed as head of the department. It is debatable whether the university should have kept to its initial decision to offer the headship to Lindsay even when it was clear that it would not be in the interests of the young department to do so; I do not however see that academic freedom is the issue here. The advice came from Lindsay's fellow scholars at the university, not from the lay council or other external source.

As to whether Lindsay's appointment should have been terminated, it is pertinent to mention that he was still serving a three-year probationary period during which he could leave the university or the university could terminate his appointment, provided each side gave the other six months notice or cash payment in lieu of notice. It is questionable whether it was in anybody's interest to leave a man who had set himself up as head of department and who, as his letters show, had launched an all-out attack on practically every facet of the operations of the university to remain at the university doing nothing constructive, all in the name of academic freedom.

As has been mentioned earlier, the laws establishing all Nigerian universities include provision that there shall be no discrimination against any staff member or student of each university, neither will they suffer any disabilities on grounds of race, religion, or political persuasion. A statement by the Military Governor of Eastern Nigeria early in 1966 reiterated what has been the official stand of successive Nigerian governments: 'In my first broadcast to the nation on my assumption of office.... I referred to the University Law which I said was in urgent need of review. You no doubt have noted by now that certain amendments have been made to the Law which had the effect of leaving things academic to academicians'. (14) He dispelled any fears that under a military government university professors and students would not be free to speak their minds and express their views.

The two cases considered emphasize the tremendous role of the university councils in the maintenance of academic freedom in Nigeria. The constitutions of these universities make it impossible for any external authority to discipline the actions of the staff and students of the universities unless they break the laws of the land. Also the university vice-chancellor or his aides cannot terminate the appointment of staff or send down students without seeking the approval of his council. The 1972 amendments to the laws of Ibadan and Lagos have not changed this. The calibre of members of these councils and their methods of appointment thus assume tremendous importance. If they are political appointees, they are more likely to become pawns in the hands of politicians who may want to interfere with academic freedom while appearing as its advocates.

Ashby's statement that academic freedom "will not become established in Africa without expatriate help" has not been borne out by the two cases. In the Ife case, only one non-Nigerian emerged as champion of academic freedom; all the other resignations came from Nigerians. Nobody, Nigerian or non-Nigerian, felt sufficiently aggrieved at Lindsay's termination to resign or even threaten resignation. Lindsay himself claimed that at the Senate meeting which discussed his suspension, the members who identifiably sided with the Vice-Chancellor were the Vice-Chancellor's colleagues from Michigan State University, implying that Nigerians rallied to the support of academic freedom while Americans betrayed it by supporting the Vice-Chancellor.

If academic freedom is to be safeguarded in Nigerian universities, it is necessary to ensure that everyone has the same general idea as to its meaning. The Ife Pro-Vice-Chancellor definitely had a different concept of academic freedom from the lecturers who feared the university was losing that freedom. Professor Lindsay probably conceived of himself as the defender of academic freedom when he unleashed his assault on every facet of the operations at Nsukka, including telling the University Council that it was incompetent to discharge the duties entrusted to it by the laws of the land. The University Council thought differently, hence it drew his attention to the 'universally accepted' meaning of academic freedom (not licence). Without such a clear definition, professors and administrators, university authorities and politicians may be acting at cross-purposes, each claiming to be upholding academic freedom.

It is heartening to note that there is no indication yet on the horizon of any threat to the freedom of scholarly investigation, regardless of where it may lead, or to the freedom of communicating the results of such investigation. The current arguments in the United States on the dangers to the freedom to publish the results of research inherent in the different categories of classified research which American universities are increasingly being required to carry out for the Central Intelligence Agency (CIA) are still remote from the Nigerian situation.

The Lindsay case illustrates the absolute necessity for outside organizations such as the International Association of University Professors to conduct more responsible investigations into reports they receive from their members before rushing to the press with hasty and often unfounded indictments.

Reference has already been made to the recent transfer of the power to appoint vice-chancellors from the council to heads of state or government. The Ife Pro-Vice-Chancellor's attempt to commit the university as an institution as well as the staff and students to the support of the government of the day, right or wrong, should serve as the danger sign. Many Nigerian vice-chancellors will act the same way, especially now that it is clear to whom they owe their appointment, and their loyalty.

REFERENCES

1 UNESCO, *The Development of Higher Education in Africa*, Paris, Unesco, 1963. 1.1: p. 12; 1.2: p. 17.

2 Ashby, Sir Eric, 'A contribution to the dialogue on African universities', *Universities Quarterly*, Vol. 20, No. 1 (December 1965), pp. 70–89. 2.1: p. 82; 2.2: p. 82.

3 Carr-Saunders, A.M., *New Universities Overseas*, London, George Allen & Unwin Ltd., 1961. 3.1: p. 199 (Quoting from Eni Njoku, 'The Relationship between University and Society in Nigeria', *The Scholar and Society*, No. 13, 1959, p. 83). 3.2: p. 200.

4 *Communication*, No. 45 (August 1965), pp.36–38.

5 Kirk, Russell, *Academic Freedom* An Essay in Definition, Chicago, Henry Regnery Company, 1955. 5.1: pp. 7–8; 5.2: p. 1; 5.3: p. 27; 5.4: p. 168.

6 MacIver, Robert M., *Academic Freedom in our Time*, New York, Columbia University Press, 1955. 6.1: p. 6; 6.2: p. 3; 6.3: p. 9.

7 Mountford, Sir James, *British Universities*, London, Oxford University Press, 1966. 7.1: p. 148.

8 Conant, James B., *Thomas Jefferson and the Development of American Public Education*, Berkeley and Los Angeles, University of California Press, 1962. 8.1: p. 29.

9 A Statement to a Special Congregation of Senior Staff of the University (of Ife) by the Pro-Vice-Chancellor, Dr. S.O. Biobaku on Thursday, 19 December, 1963 (mimeograph). 9.1: p. 1; 9.2: p. 2; 9.3: p. 3; 9.4: p. 4 9.5: p. 5; 9.6: p. 6; 9.7: p. 6.

10 *West Africa*, No. 2431, Saturday January 4, 1964 : p.19.

11 *West Africa*, No. 2437, Saturday February 15, 1964; p.187.

12 *West Africa*, No. 2438, Saturday February 22, 1964.

13 *University of Nigeria—Lindsay Correspondence* (Complete correspondence May 12, 1964 to March 2, 1965). No publisher indicated. Printed by City Printery Ltd., 2 Torrington Rd., Kingston, Jamaica, 1965. 13.1: pp. 1–2; 13.2: p. 2; 13.3: p. 3; 13.4: p. 5; 13.5: p. 4; 13.6: p. 6; 13.7: pp. 8–9; 13.8: p. 10.

14 An Address to the Faculties and Students of the University of Nigeria, Nsukka, delivered by His Excellency Lt. Colonel C. Odumegwu Ojukwu, Military Governor of the Eastern Provinces on April 23, 1966. (Mimeograph). p. 2.

15 Committee on Higher Education, *Higher Education;* report of the Committee appointed by the Prime Minister under the chairmanship of Lord Robbins, 1961–63, London, Her Majesty's Stationery Office, October 1963. 15.1: pp. 230–234.

16 Akintoye, S.A., *Ten Years of the University of Ife* 1962–1972, Ile Ife, University of Ife Press, 1973, pp. 15–20.

CHAPTER 10

CO-ORDINATION OF NIGERIAN UNIVERSITIES

The Commission on Post-School Certificate and Highter Education in Nigeria, it will be recalled, was emphatic in its recommendation that each Nigerian university should be autonomous. It also emphatically dissuaded the Nigerian government from attempting a federation of all the Nigerian universities into one university awarding the same degree, as in Wales and, sometime ago, in East Africa. Such a federation might result in imposing one single pattern on all Nigerian higher education, a situation the Commission considered undesirable, arguing that 'The hope for Nigerian higher education lies in its diversity'. (1.1)

On the other hand, a few pages later in its report, the Commission strongly recommended the establishment by the Federal Government of a National Universities Commission, on lines similar to the U.K. University Grants Commission, with the following functions:

(a) to secure money for the universities and distribute same to them;

(b) to co-ordinate (without interfering with) their activities;

(c) to provide cohesion for Nigerian higher education. (1.2)

In making this recommendation, the Commission was concerned that the limited funds available for higher education should be judiciously used.

The Federal Government accepted the recommendation, in the hope that it would preserve the overall national interest through the statutory establishment of the National Universities Commission, the Inter-Regional Manpower Board, and the All-Nigeria Academic Council. (2.1)

A National Manpower Board was thereafter established. Its main impact on the universities derived from the fact that it was the body that made manpower forecasts for the government, and the government passed the high-level manpower forecasts to the National Universities Commission, in the expectation that the forecasts would influence the admission of students to the universities. The National Universities Commission and the All-Nigeria

Academic Council will receive more detailed consideration because of their more direct impact on university administration and development.

In October 1962, the Federal Government established the National Universities Commission, with the following terms of reference:

(1) To inquire into (and advise the Government on) the financial needs both recurrent and capital of university education in Nigeria.

(2) To assist in consultation with the Universities and other bodies concerned in planning the balanced and co-ordinated development of the Universities in order to ensure that they are fully adequate to the national needs.

(3) To receive annually a block grant from the Federal Government and to allocate it to the Universities with such conditions attached as the Commission may think advisable.

(4) To act as an agency for channelling all external aid to the Universities throughout the Federation.

(5) To take into account, in advising the Federal Government, such grants as may be made to the Universities by Regional Governments, persons and institutions both at home and abroad.

(6) To collate, analyse and publish information relating to Universities finance and University education both in Nigeria and abroad.

(7) To make, either by itself or through committee, such other investigations relating to higher education as the Commission may consider necessary; and, for the purpose of such investigations, to have access to the records of universities seeking or receiving Federal grants.

(8) To make such other recommendations to the Federal Government or to universities relating to higher education as the Commission may consider to be in the national interest. (3.3)

A close study of these extensive terms of reference makes one ask, as did the Robbins Committee, whether it would be possible to secure the advantages of co-ordination while at the same time preserving the advantages of autonomy. Can a university which receives its grants from a body that is empowered to attach whatever conditions it considers advisable (and which conditions, presumably, the university must satisfy before or after receiving the grants) claim to be truly autonomous? One could go further and ask why such formal co-ordination is necessary. Does it imply that the universities would not themselves, acting individually or in voluntary association, be sufficiently responsive to national needs?

It has already been argued in the preceding pages that the doctrine of complete autonomy for state-supported universities has few if any adherents anywhere in the world, and that a developing country which relies very heavily on its few universities for its development cannot afford to subscribe to it. Apart from the fact that it provides all the funds needed by the universities, the government of a relatively poor and developing country has a grave responsibility to ensure a balanced educational development at all levels throughout the country.

Universities of the type built in Nigeria, Ghana and many other African countries are expensive propositions. A typical university campus is to all intents and purposes a city of its own, involving the construction not only of lecture rooms, offices, and laboratories but also of a network of roads, halls of residence for students, houses for different grades of staff (including 'villages' for the supporting staff), water supply (including, as at Nsukka, the sinking of bore holes for water), a health service, electrification, provision of primary schools for children of staff, stadiums, shopping centres, banks, vehicle maintenance workshops, petrol stations, etc. In addition to the infrastructure, a university requires a lot of money to establish and maintain a good library, laboratories and workshops, to recruit qualified staff in adequate numbers and to provide them with adequate research facilities. Even before the creation of states in Nigeria on May 27, 1967, the large regions which owned universities were already experiencing difficulties in providing them with adequate funds. With the creation of twelve states out of the four regions, it has become increasingly clear that only the Federal Military Government can stand the financial strain involved. The transfer of Nsukka to the Federal Military Government in April 1973 by the two state governments which owned it supports this contention. Ife and Zaria, until August 1975 owned by state governments, have also been taken over by the Federal Military Government. In the circumstances, it becomes imperative that the Federal Government must assume responsibility for co-ordinating university development in the country.

The areas for co-ordination should include the establishment of new universities and the programmes offered at such new universities. As will be discussed in greater detail later, the national interest has not always been the over riding factor leading to the establishment of new universities in Nigeria, regardless of public pronouncements to the contrary. The unco-ordinated duplication of facilities, particularly in expensive disciplines or disciplines for which qualified staff are hard to find, has had severe adverse effects on the quality of work in some universities. There have been instances of departments with one assistant or junior lecturer only who has taught the whole range of courses and presented students with honours degrees!

There is a definite trend towards co-ordination of university education in the few countries in which university education is not already an integral part of the national educational system under state control. Reference has already been made in the preceding pages to the argument by the Robbins Committee in the U.K. that independent determination of its affairs by each university was not likely to produce 'a pattern that is comprehensive and appropriate in relation to the needs of society and the demands of the national economy'. The Committee noted that co-ordination was imperative, and that the U.K. government should exercise some influence on such co-ordination.

Even in the United States, the trend towards co-ordination is clearly visible. A number of private universities and colleges, especially the smaller ones, are voluntarily coming together in one form of association or another, generally to share some common services and consequently reduce costs and thereby remain viable. Some adopt common admission standards so that any applicant offered admission to one of the member institutions automatically qualifies for admission to any of the other member institutions.

Attempts at co-ordination are much more pronounced in respect of the public or state-supported universities and colleges. An increasing number of states now establish supra governing boards to co-ordinate public higher education within the state. Francis Horn quotes a study by Martorana and Hollis which reported that in 1960 17 states had such 'more or less adequate permanent organizations for planning, programming, and co-ordinating public higher education'. (4.1) Six of the 17 states had single boards for governing and co-ordinating all public higher education in the state, eight had co-ordinating boards, each 'legally responsible for organizing, regulating, or otherwise bringing together the overall policies or functions (or both) in areas such as planning, budgeting, and programming', but which did not have authority to govern institutions. (4.2) Beside the 17 states, 26 others had two or more public institutions grouped under a single board for control or co-ordination. (4.2)

Inter-institutional co-ordination has also developed on a regional basis within the United States, providing greater co-ordination and control than the six regional accrediting associations and approved both by the U.S. Congress and by the legislatures of the participating states. The three regional bodies are the Southern Regional Education Board (serving 16 Southern States), the Western Interstate Commission for Higher Education (serving 13 states, including Hawaii and Alaska), and the New England Board of Higher Education (serving the six Northern States). Horn quotes Martorana and Hollis as declaring that 'the period has passed when a college can be an island into itself'. (4.3)

With six universities in Nigeria, four more on the drawing boards, and many more developing under false names, there is clearly some need for co-ordination of university education in the country. The effectiveness of the National Universities Commission (N.U.C.) as the machinery for effecting this co-ordination will now be examined.

THE NATIONAL UNIVERSITIES COMMISSION
The initial, (i.e. 1962) terms of reference of the N.U.C. have already been quoted. The Commission initially comprised a chairman, a full-time Secretary, an honorary adviser (Sir Eric Ashby), and ten other members. In its first report issued in 1963 after the members had visited all five universities and had at least a feel of the magnitude of their assignment, the Commission described its function as that of 'stimulation, encouragement, and co-ordination'. (3.2) That was a judicious choice of vocabulary for a commission which was bound to run against serious counter currents.

The N.U.C. needed some years to find its bearings, and for the universities to adjust to its encroachment upon the inner city. However, it was not long before its weaknesses became evident.

The first of these is perhaps the most important because it impinges on what is undoubtedly the major reason for the establishment of the commission—the desire to ensure a judicious use of the scarce funds available for higher education. The commission has been unable to check expensive and unnecessary duplication of facilities in the different universities, and it appears to lack the full power to do so.

This shortcoming was most evident in respect of the three universities established by the erstwhile regional governments—Nsukka, Ife and Zaria. In each of these universities, the N.U.C. could exercise effective financial control only over the portion of the costs provided by the Federal Government. Prior to the creation of the 12 States in 1967, this did not exceed 50% of both capital and recurrent costs; in two cases (Nsukka and Ife) it covered only 30% of capital costs and 50% of recurrent costs. In the circumstances, a regional university could persuade the regional government financing it to provide it with funds to introduce programmes which were not approved by the N.U.C. All that the N.U.C. could do in this regard was, as stipulated in its terms of reference (No. 5), to take such grants by regional governments 'into account' in advising the Federal Government, whatever that meant.

The Commission was probably aware of this major handicap, hence it recommended greater co-operation between the Federal and Regional governments in the consideration of its recommendations on university development, if the Commission was to exercise 'some measure of centralized control of expenditure of public funds from whatever source'. (3·3) Unfortunately this important recommendation which should have been treated separately was mixed up with the plea for the creation of the Commission as a statutory body. The report did not give any justification for the plea other than merely citing the countries where such action had been taken: 'Without going into the merits of such an Act, we wish to mention the precedents for similar bodies established by Acts of Parliament in Australia and India'. (3·3) The Federal Government of the day rejected the plea. Although the recommendation about co-operation between the Federal and Regional governments formed part of the plea, the Federal Government reaction made no reference to that recommendation.

As mentioned earlier, the Federal Government also rejected the N.U.C. recommendation that the Federal Government should be empowered to nominate representatives on the governing council of each regional university 'In view of the heavy financial responsibility for University development which we are asking the Federal

Government to take on'. (3·3) In rejecting this recommendation, the Federal Government in my view rejected an opportunity for effective partnership with the regional universities and for effective co-ordination. It was not until after the end of the civil war that the Federal Military Government appointed representatives on the governing councils of all Nigerian universities.

The N.U.C. recommendation that a National Universities Fund should be created, into which all grants and subventions to the universities should be paid (3.4) and which would be managed by it would be effective only if it receives the full co-operation of the various state governments which own universities as well as foreign donor agencies.

Another major problem faced by the N.U.C. was that, as a Federal establishment, its successes and failures and its very existence were heavily dependent on the continued existence of a strong Federal Government. Prior to the January 15, 1966 military takeover of the Nigerian government, higher education was on the concurrent legislative list, which meant that both the Federal and the Regional governments had the power to operate universities. The effect of this dual responsibility on national co-ordination of university education has just been discussed. The military government which came into power in January 1966 moved towards unitary government for the whole country and consequently abolished the regions as previously established. The Supreme Commander charged the Committee of Vice-Chancellors to produce a blue print on a national system of higher education. Such a system would undoubtedly have obliterated many of the shortcomings sketched above and considerably strengthened the arms of the N.U.C. Unfortunately the blue print had not been finalized before tragedy struck Nigeria for the second time in seven months. A rising within a section of the army overthrew the Supreme Commander and, with him, the plans for unitary government.

The sad events that followed the July 29 (1966) coup sent many Nigerians packing to their regions of origin. When later it was decided that Nigeria should continue as a political entity, the regional set up which had been abolished some months previously was again resuscitated. Eastern Nigeria proclaimed itself the 'Republic of Biafra' on May 30, 1967, the University of Nigeria, Nsukka subsequently becoming the 'University of Biafra', naturally falling outside the authority of the N.U.C. The civil war raged from July

1967 to January 1970, ending with Nigeria reunited, as one nation. Nsukka again became the University of Nigeria, coming under the authority of the N.U.C. more than ever before as the Regional Government which established it had been split into three States, one of which (the Rivers State) would have nothing to do with the university while the other two were so impoverished by the civil war that they could ill afford the funds (estimated at ₦11 million) for the reconstruction of the war ravaged university.

Without wishing to sound like a prophet of doom, one is constrained to make the point that the sad events of 1966 and their aftermath have made many Nigerians recognize that there is no place like home, home in this context being not the country but one's own region or state of origin. These events heightened distrust among people of different ethnic groups, culminating in mass repatriation of families to their home regions. Among the persons who moved were university professors and students who considered their lives and/or careers threatened in regions other than their own. Those whose regions had established regional universities thanked their stars and commended the founding fathers for their foresight. The difficulty of resettling some of the displaced professors and students because their disciplines did not exist in their 'home' universities led to the addition of such 'missing' disciplines to those universities, regardless of what the N.U.C. might have recommended. Nsukka acquired the faculty of medicine and departments such as pharmacy, microbiology and biochemistry that way; so did Lagos add a department of mass communication, to cater for students of journalism who left Nsukka, then the only Nigerian university offering that subject.

Although the war is long over and the Federal Military Government is making efforts to foster the spirit of oneness among Nigerians, the recent post-war rush to establish colleges of arts and science, basic studies, technology, science and technology, management and technology, or call it what you will, in the various states shows that the basic distrust remains. Even states which have very few lower schools and so cannot complain that their qualified students cannot be absorbed by the existing universities have gone ahead to establish these colleges.

One example is enough to illustrate the point. Many university teachers of South-Eastern State origin who had identified themselves with Nigeria (rather than with 'Biafra') during the civil war and so had remained in Ibadan, Lagos and Ife universities during the war, would not accept appointments at the University of Nigeria, Nsukka after the end of the war, even though their home State became a joint proprietor of the university. They applied pressure on their State Government to demand the establishment of a campus in their State. Nsukka was accordingly directed to open a new campus on a site to be chosen by the Government of South-Eastern State. In fact the original expectation was that Nsukka should uproot some of its existing faculties and transfer them to the new campus, a move that did not succeed because the East Central State authorities soon recognized that any faculties removed from Nsukka would ultimately be a loss to the State, as one did not need prophetic vision to foresee that the new campus would assert its independence at the earliest opportunity. With the opening of the new campus in Calabar in 1973, the South-Eastern State university staff who would not go to Nsukka have joined the staff of the Calabar campus of the same university. Many staff members from the State who had been at Nsukka all along have also moved over to Calabar. Until the new campus was opened, the 'interests' of the South-Eastern State were secured at Nsukka by the agreement reached between the governments of the two States to share the major administrative positions at the university—to the exclusion of Nigerians from other states, contrary to the provisions of the university law.

No matter what the publicised objectives of the state colleges of arts and science, etc., one thing is certain. Nigerian academicians want 'safe seats' in their home states, where competition for vice-chancellorship, deanship, registrarship or professorship will be much more restricted and therefore favourable to them, and perhaps even more important where they can seek refuge should the Federal structure crack again or the Federal universities (which are free-for-all) prove too competitive or uncomfortable for them. Lagos lost practically all its non-Yoruba academic and senior administrative staff following its 1965 crisis. Ibadan and Ahmadu Bello lost practically all their Igbo staff in 1966 while Nsukka lost its Yoruba and other non-Igbo staff. Each new college opened has led to a further drain from the existing institutions, particularly of staff from the state in which the college is located teaching in universities outside that state. The more the university staff and students gravitate to their state colleges, campus or universities, the more each state strives to assert its ownership of these institutions and to resist Federal control, and the more impotent the N.U.C. becomes as a national co-ordinating body.

The work of the N.U.C. might have been made easier if the announcement made by the Federal Military Government in 1972 assuming responsibility for the establishment of all new universities in Nigeria had been more embracing It did not apply to existing universities established by the erstwhile regional or state governments, except the states concerned opted to transfer their universities to the Federal Government. Neither did it embrace the colleges of arts and science, etc. We therefore have the interesting situation in which the governments of East Central State and South Eastern State request the Federal Military Government to take over Nsukka, on the grounds that they cannot jointly finance it, while each of them promptly proceeds to establish its own colleges under different names. As the chairman of the governing council of one of these new colleges remarked, the decision to hand over Nsukka to the Federal Military Government and establish a new college within the state is a shrewd one: it leaves the state with two institutions of higher learning instead of one!

At its inception, the Mid-West Institute of Technology proclaimed that it was established to complement rather than duplicate the work of the universities by providing the country with technical manpower of the type not provided by any Nigerian university, but, at the opportune moment, it threw off the mask and proclaimed itself the University of Benin, accepting students for many courses already available in other Nigerian universities. Judging from this example, there is little doubt of the direction in which most of the state colleges of arts and science, etc. are moving. The architects of these colleges will tell you in confidence that their declared objectives are different from their undeclared but real objectives, which is to develop into a full-scale university at the opportune moment. Bearing in mind that few, if any, states in Nigeria can add the financing of full-scale universities to their other heavy financial commitments, it appears probable that each will, as Benin did, present the Federal Government with a fait accompli. By that time the opportunity to co-ordinate their development nationally will have been lost.

Although the Federal Military Government which came into power with the coup of July 29, 1975 has now taken over all Nigerian universities, the effectiveness of the N. U. C. will still remain impaired if these various state-owned colleges or institutes remain outside its sphere of authority. These institutions—including the advanced teacher training colleges or colleges of education as most of them now answer—constitute part of higher education. It is interesting that the National Union of Nigerian Students has been more progressive in its outlook than the government, by according its membership to students of these institutions along with university students. The terms of reference of the N.U.C. should be modified to embrace all higher education. Alternatively another body should be set up by the Federal Government to co-ordinate the development of these colleges.

A comment on the role of the N.U.C. in the formulation, guidance or co-ordination of academic policy. The declaration by the Federal Government in 1961 of its intention to establish an All-Nigeria Academic Council, at the same time that it declared its intention to establish the National Universities Commission, would suggest that it was not intended that the N.U.C. should concern itself with academic matters (except in so far as they had financial implications). However since making the declaration in 1961, the All-Nigeria Academic Council has not been established. The terms of reference of the N.U.C. made no specific reference to academic matters, but at least three of these terms of reference (nos. 2, 7, 8) are so vaguely worded that they could be interpreted to justify any attempts on the part of the N.U.C. to get involved with academic matters (including details of the curricula) within the universities. The 1963 N.U.C. report showed such involvement, and revealed the tremendous dangers of allowing such involvement to continue.

Whatever may have been the qualifications of the pioneer members of the N.U.C. for handling financial problems, one can say without being offensive that most of these men were not qualified to give progressive leadership to the universities in respect of academic matters; hardly any of them had served in any university, and hardly any served in any capacity that brought him in touch with current developments in university education. For comparative purposes, the U.K. University Grants Committee at the time had a full-time Chairman and eighteen other members, ten of whom were actively employed in the universities, two were connected with other forms of education, one came from a research establishment, and three from industry. (5.1) It was therefore appropriate that the commission should concentrate its efforts on the more obvious aspects of its terms of reference, leaving academic matters for more appropriately qualified persons or groups.

As has already been said, the success or failure of the N.U.C. depends, among other things, on the continued existence of a strong Federal Government in Nigeria. Post-war Nigeria currently enjoys such a strong Federal Government, and some of the important recommendations rejected by the Federal Government in 1963 have now been implemented.

One such recommendation is the establishment of the N.U.C. into a statutory corporation: it had hitherto been a sub-division of the cabinet office. 'Decree No. 1: National Universities Commission Decree 1974' established the N.U.C. as a 'body corporate with perpetual succession and a common seal', with effect from 15th January, 1974. The new Commission was not, however, formally inaugurated until mid-1975.

The 'statutory' N.U.C. differs from its predecessor in some other important respects. It now reports to the Head of the Federal Military Government through the Federal Commissioner for Education rather than direct to the Head of the Federal Military Government. According to Section 4 Sub-section (2) of the Decree, 'The Commissioner may give the Commission directives of a general character or relating generally to particular matters with regard to the exercise by the Commission of its functions under this Decree, and it shall be the duty of the Commission to comply with such directives.' One advantage in this change is the opportunity it presents to relate university education to the rest of the educational system.

Another major difference is that the new N.U.C. has an Executive Secretary, appointed by the Head of the Federal Government, who, according to Section 5 Sub-section (2) of the Decree 'shall be the chief executive officer of the Commission and shall be responsible for the execution of the policy of the Commission and the day to day running of the affairs of the Commission.' He is a non-voting member of the Commission, and can be removed from office only by the Head of the Federal Government. One hopes that this development will provide a dynamic secretariat for the N.U.C., something it has lacked since its first secretary received a ministerial appointment during the civil war. The secretariat, in the intervening period, had become a transit camp for high ranking civil servants with little experience of and little interest in higher education, while the government made up its mind about their ultimate reassignment.

Specific provision has now been made in the membership for seven (out of a total of 19) members to be appointed by the Head of the Federal Military Government from Nigerian universities, representing the main disciplines available in the universities. This provision should enrich the Commission.

Practically all the functions of the 1962 N.U.C. are embodied in the 1974 N.U.C. Decree. But the 1974 Decree has some important additions. The N.U.C. is now to advise on the creation of new universities and other degree-granting institutions in Nigeria. Section 4 Sub-section (1) (b) is worth quoting in full:

> to prepare, after consultation with all the State Governments, the universities, the National Manpower Board and such other bodies as it considers appropriate, periodic master plans for the balanced and co-ordinated development of universities, in Nigeria and such plans shall include—
>
> (i) the general programmes to be pursued by the universities in order to ensure that they are fully adequate to national needs and objectives,
>
> (ii) recommendations for the establishment and location of new universities as and when considered necessary, and
>
> (iii) recommendations for the establishment of new faculties or post-graduate institutions in existing universities or the approval or disapproval of proposals to establish such faculties or institutions.

Compared with the equivalent 1962 term of reference which merely empowered the N.U.C. 'To assist in consultation with the universities and other bodies concerned in planning the balanced and co-ordinated development of the universities in order to ensure that they are fully adequate to the national needs', the new N.U.C. is much better placed to achieve co-ordinated and balanced university development in Nigeria.

Whether or not this will be achieved is yet to be seen. Provided the trend towards a strong Federal Government continues—a Federal Government increasingly assuming overall responsibility for national educational development—the N.U.C. would appear to be in for a new lease of life. The position would, however, change drastically should Nigeria revert to a relatively weak Federal Government.

Moreover, much depends on how seriously the government and the universities take the N.U.C. The Commission has power to *prepare* periodic master plans, not to *enforce* them. Excellent master plans have been known to have been shelved away in government archives or to be mutilated beyond recognition by the time 'other factors' have been taken into consideration. It is not clear why the 1974 Decree stipulates in Section 4 Sub-section (1) (f) that the N.U.C. is to allocate Federal Government grants to the universities 'in accordance with such formula as may be laid down by the Federal Executive Council', a stipulation absent from the 1962 provisions.

THE ALL-NIGERIA ACADEMIC COUNCIL

As has been stated, the Federal Government declared as far back as 1961 its intention to establish an All-Nigeria Academic Council, with representation from the different Nigerian universities, to ensure among other things the maintenance of high academic standards among the universities. For some unpublicised reasons, the Federal Government has failed to act on this declaration of intent, even though the two other bodies announced at the same time have long since been established. One Nigerian university vice-chancellor once remarked that the proposal had been overtaken by the establishment of the Committee of Vice-Chancellors. In his view, the Committee of Vice-Chancellors has assumed the functions which would have necessitated the creation of the All-Nigeria Academic Council.

THE COMMITTEE OF VICE-CHANCELLORS OF NIGERIAN UNIVERSITIES

The Committee of Vice-Chancellors of Nigerian Universities was modelled after the U.K. Committee of Vice-Chancellors and Principals, and received an initial grant for its establishment from the Carnegie Corporation of New York. It is an informal body which has no authority to force its decisions or recommendations on any university nor to speak officially on behalf of Nigerian university education. Its decisions invariably take the form of recommendations which may or may not be accepted by the appropriate administrative machineries of the respective institutions. By its very nature, however, it is without doubt an influential body which has established working relations with the National Universities Commission and has a paid full-time secretary. Its pronouncements on Nigerian university matters carry understandable weight with the public.

The Committee has, as the need arose, established some sub-committees, each presided over by a vice-chancellor but having members nominated by the different institutions (generally by their vice-chancellors), to do the spade work and transmit its recommendations to the Committee for consideration. The senior staff superannuation scheme for Nigerian universities resulted from the work of one of the sub-committees. The scheme received clearance from the governing councils of the participating universities and also from the Federal Government prior to its implementation.

Another sub-committee was charged with responsibility for university entrance requirements and scholarships. One of its major assignments was to consider the advisability and formulate the procedures for centralising applications for admission to the universities. Its work on scholarships developed into a study conducted by the Ford Foundation in July 1964 of 'the need for and feasibility of establishing a central student loan fund in Nigeria'. A series of consultations involving representatives of the Governments, the universities and the Ford Foundation (and other possible benefactors) followed the presentation of the report of the study.

Resulting from the work of its sub-committee on entrance requirements and scholarships, the Committee initiated action on the study of the sixth-form as a qualification for university entrance. Nothing tangible appears to have emerged from the study. In 1974, the Committee invited two overseas experts to study the problem of establishing a matriculation examination for admission to Nigerian universities, ostensibly to reduce its dependence on examinations conducted by the West African Examinations Council.

Other areas of concern which have come within the ambit of the Committee of Vice-Chancellors are: standardization of the university calendar, increase in the number of class weeks, standardization of university fees, conditions of service for staff, costs of student services, national service by students, and the problem of attracting Nigerian trained personnel working in the U.S.A.

The Committee of Vice-Chancellors has done some constructive work and helped to foster a spirit of cooperation and co-existence rather than that of cut-throat rivalry among the universities. Moreover it has provided an invaluable platform for the heads of the universities, and also for the members of their sub-committees and working parties, to exchange ideas and share experiences on matters of common concern to the universities. Above all, it provides an opportunity for a vice-chancellor to relax in the midst of his equals, which is an important consideration for the vice-chancellor who finds that his position prevents him from relaxing fully among members of staff of his own university.

Regardless of this acknowledgement, the Committee cannot be an adequate substitute for a National Academic Council. As at present constituted, it is exactly what its name suggests—a committee of vice-chancellors. The members attach tremendous importance to the exclusive nature of the club. A ridiculous instance of the Committee's pre-occupation with the sanctity of its membership occured in 1970. For the whole of 1970 Nsukka could not participate in the work of the Committee because its first post-war interim executive head did not bear the designation of vice-chancellor. He had another designation, but was recognized as head of the university *ad interim* by Nigerian and foreign governments, the foundations, and other organizations. He received an invitation to and attended the Conference of Overseas Vice-Chancellors and Principals held in Ottawa, Canada in September 1970, and another invitation for talks with the Inter-University Council in London. The fact that Nsukka was passing through its most difficult period and had in fact sought assistance from other Nigerian universities with its post-war rehabilitation programme (including placing library and laboratory facilities at the disposal of Nsukka students and staff during the vacations) carried little significance. Until the head of Nsukka carried the designation of vice-chancellor, Nsukka had no place on the Committee of Vice-Chancellors. The Committee even went to the incredible extent of cancelling a meeting it had scheduled for Nsukka until someone had been named vice-chancellor. The result was that while the President of Ford Foundation of America, Government functionaries, members of the diplomatic corps, and others visited Nsukka to assess the rehabilitation problem, no vice-chancellor of a Nigerian university came to Nsukka throughout 1970.

Because of its rotating chairmanship, and the turn-over in vice-chancellors, the Committee requires a resourceful and dynamic secretariat and a number of standing committees whose members and chairmen need not be vice-chancellors, especially bearing in mind how overworked each vice-chancellor is. Its membership is small—currently six—and this places a great deal of importance on the personal relationships among the vice-chancellors. Any hardening of the lines could have adverse effects on the effectiveness of the group.

It is hoped that the Committee will outgrow its craze for inviting 'experts' from Europe and America to study practically every problem facing Nigerian universities. The vice-chancellors must have little regard for the pool of talent within Nigeria (inside and outside the campuses) if they find it necessary to recruit overseas experts to advise the Nigerian universities on such problems as halls of residence administration and problems of university admissions. Some of these experts, if they were on the staff of Nigerian universities, would not have been considered qualified or competent for the same assignments !

OTHER COMMITTEES

Following the lead given by the vice-chancellors, other informal inter-university committees have sprung up, for example the Committee of Registrars of Nigerian universities and the Committee of Chief Engineers. The general objective of each committee is to harmonise policies and practices among the universities, and to share experiences and ideas. These are welcome developments.

REFERENCES

1 *Investment in Education*, Report of the Commission on Post-School Certificate and Higher Education in Nigeria, Lagos, Federal Ministry of Education, Nigeria, 1960. 1.1 : p. 25; 1.2 : p. 33.

2 Federation of Nigeria, *Educational Development* 1961–70, Lagos, Sessional Paper No. 3 of 1961. 2.1 : p. 8.

3 Federal Republic of Nigeria, *University Development in Nigeria:* Report of the National Universities Commission, Lagos, Federal Ministry of Information, 1963. 3.1 : pp. 1–2; 3.2 : p. 33; 3.3 : p. 40; 3.4 : p. 42.

4 Horn, Francis H., 'The Organization of Colleges and Universities', in *Administrators in Higher Education:* Their Functions and Co-ordination, New York, Harper & Brothers, Publishers, 1962, Chapter 4. 4.1 : p. 49; 4.2 : p. 50; 4.3 : p. 51.

5 Committee on Higher Education, *Higher Education*, Appendix Four: Administrative, Financial and Economic Aspects of Higher Education, London, Her Majesty's Stationery Office. 5.1 : p. 5.

Other References

Committee of Vice-Chancellors of Nigerian Universities, *Sessional Report* 1969/70 & 1970/71 (mimeograph).

CHAPTER 11

THE BALANCE SHEET

This book began with an affirmation that the establishment of the indigenous Nigerian or African university (as distinct from the American or European university) is both necessary and practicable. It is appropriate to ask, in this final chapter, what success if any has so far been achieved.

Let us consider the favourable side first. The 'ivory tower' concept of the university has generally been demolished. It is now generally accepted that university courses and research activities should be relevant and geared to national needs. It is not unusual to find the universities making special efforts to publicise their efforts to meet national requirements. The contents of courses have been modified, wherever possible, to include the study of local problems, history, flora and fauna. As a result, a typical degree programme from a Nigerian university, particularly in the arts, humanities, social sciences and medicine, includes many more courses pertinent to the Nigerian and African environment than would a comparable degree programme from America or Europe.

In addition to reviewing the contents of courses, Nigerian universities have established institutes and departments to tackle specific problems of their communities. The institutes of education, economic development, African studies, and child health are some examples. Continuing education or extra-mural programmes at some of the universities are among deliberate efforts to identify the university with the problems of society. Research projects among university staff have invariably swung away from excessive fundamental research to research related to local problems. Even engineering faculties do not wish to be left out. If wars can be said to have good effects, the Nigerian civil war opened the eyes of university people, particularly on the 'Biafran' side, to the many ways in which even the so-called 'useless disciplines' could be made useful in solving the problems of society.

The establishment of new departments or faculties within the universities is now determined largely by local needs. It is for that reason that the teaching of classics and the dead languages of Latin and Greek has not spread beyond Ibadan.

Commendable efforts have been made by Nigerian universities to promote indigenous culture. The universities of Ibadan and Ife deserve special mention. Exhibitions of traditional arts and crafts, support of traditional drama troupes, naming of campus streets after indigenous historical personalities and landmarks, and the encouragement of student cultural societies are among the methods adopted to promote indigenous culture. Lagos attempted to design academic costumes to reflect traditional dress styles, though not with as much success as they did with the design of the ceremonial mace.

In terms of personnel, the ratio of indigenous to expatriate staff has improved tremendously in recent years. At the time of writing, all Nigerian universities had Nigerian vice-chancellors. Most policy-making positions were also held by Nigerians, except possibly at Ahmadu Bello University which is likely to retain large numbers of expatriate staff in key positions, not necessarily because there are no suitable Nigerians to fill them but probably because no suitable Nigerians from the Northern States are as yet available. The recent craze to establish colleges of arts and science or science and technology or basic studies in each state has led to a drain of qualified personnel from the universities to these colleges. Nevertheless it is correct to say that the management of Nigerian universities is more firmly in Nigerian hands now than ever before. This creates a more favourable atmosphere for the establishment of truly indigenous universities.

Notwithstanding the foregoing, and some other achievements which may have been omitted, it would not be accurate to say that the Nigerian university has emerged. One would agree with Dr. Okafor when he observed towards the end of his book that 'It will be some time before one can speak or write of a university which is peculiarly Nigerian'. (1·1) No university in Nigeria has to date developed undergraduate curricula specifically tailored for the Nigerian society. Internationally acclaimed undergraduate programmes do exist in abundance in the universities, but they resemble the humorous attempt to produce an ideal bride for the Prince of Wales by assembling a pretty nose from here, a good figure from there and a lovely pair of eyes from yet another source.

What has been said of universities in Nigeria is also applicable to universities in many other African countries. If anything, the situation is worse in some of them, including Ghana and Sierra Leone. This is disappointing when it is remembered that many of these universities were established after the attainment of political independence by the countries concerned. What are the reasons for this state of affairs?

The first reason is that many African educationists have great difficulty in breaking away from their past. Whereas most vice-chancellors of Nigerian universities can, with minimum preparation, deliver learned lectures on mediaeval universities, few of them are conversant with modern trends in higher education. (It was not accidental or through ignorance that the chapter on historical review omitted any attempt to trace the origins of Nigerian universities to the mediaeval universities in Bologna and Paris!)

In the introduction to his *Universities: British, Indian, African*, Ashby repeated a point that has featured in one form or another in his previous writings on the African university:

> On one hand there is no doubt that Africans avidly accept all the western education they can get, and on the whole prefer it as little altered as possible from the patterns of education to be found in Europe. (One reason for this is that the least adapted patterns of higher education lead to the most prestigious posts). (2.1)

Later on in the book (2.2) while assessing the virtues and defects of the Commission on Post-School Certificate and Higher Education in Nigeria, Ashby quoted an extract from Hanson's *Imagination and Hallucination in African Education* in which Hanson drew attention to the reluctance on the part of African educators to modify educational programmes inherited from their former colonial masters. I shall quote Hanson a little more extensively than Ashby, in order to include a few other comments which I consider relevant to my purpose:

> It is understandable why the European and American experts who still play an influential role in education in most African nations should cherish the educational systems by which they themselves were nourished. What is not as clearly recognized by those who have been anticipating an essential change in education following independence is that the first generation of Africans who have taken the place of the colonial authorities

in most nations face equal, or even greater, intellectual and emotional difficulties in breaking with the past. They are frequently as conservative concerning the educational status quo as are the most traditional of the 'colonialists.'. . . . Most African educators are deeply concerned lest modified programmes be viewed as being of lower stature or less value than their original European counterparts, lest they be viewed as 'watered down'. The surest way to avoid any such implications (and to assure that African certificates maintain the international gold standard of education) is to pay lip service to adaptation, or make token modifications, but to adhere essentially to patterns, syllabi, and examinations which vary little, if at all, from inherited European models. Consequently, in most nations little or no fundamental program innovation has appeared in academic programs since Independence. As one African scholar and educator complained to me, 'The few innovations which have been proposed since Independence have been suggested by the French, not the Africans'. (3·1)

In an earlier section, an attempt was made to explain why the Nigerian staff and students at Ibadan were such ardent supporters of London standards. A Nigerianization officer was once asked during a recruitment visit to Ibadan why the Nigerian Federal Government attached such indefensible importance to honours degrees for appointments to the administrative service. He replied by recalling a discussion at the Legislative Council several years before Nigeria attained independence, when some members expressed dissatisfaction with the snail's-pace rate at which Africans were being promoted to senior administrative positions, compared with the number of young inexperienced administrators being imported from Britain. The explanation given was that each of those British officers held an honours degree, and that Africans aspiring to similar positions must obtain similar qualifications if the standards of the service were to be maintained. So, according to the Nigerianization officer, it was ruled that a 1st or 2nd class honours degree must be a requirement for appointment to a senior administrative post and so it has remained. To alter it in any way would be considered an unfortunate compromise with world standards.

It is regrettable that this attitude still persists, even after a decade of political sovereignty. In some instances it has been carried to ridiculous extents as in post-war Nsukka. Reference has been made in an earlier chapter to the commendable efforts made at Nsukka in 1970 to involve academic and senior administrative staff, students and alumni in a comprehensive re-appraisal of the university, an exercise which, if properly carried out, might have transformed the University of Nigeria into a Nigerian university in the true sense of the word. However this promising trend was shifted by the appointment of a new vice-chancellor in 1971. His intent was to model Nsukka after Oxford University. The trappings of the old English universities, which Nsukka had firmly resisted right from the start, were promptly introduced as innovations aimed at raising the stature of the university and making it toe the line. Among these were an annual matriculation ceremony, the requirement that undergraduates must wear academic gowns at matriculation, to see the vice-chancellor, at examinations. Other innovations lined up or already introduced included the inauguration of university sermons and choir scholarships. Nsukka which marked a new era in university development in Nigeria immediately took a roundabout turn! Contrary to the philosophy of seeking to evolve a unique pattern of education for Nigeria, which the university still affirms in its annual calendar, Nsukka under Prof. Kodilinye appears to be aiming at becoming Oxford University located at Nsukka.

A second reason for the non-emergence of the Nigerian university has been the excessive reliance on advice from Europe and America. With the notable exception of Ife, the other Nigerian universities have been established on the recommendations of foreign or international commissions. T.H. Silcock's observations on foreign commissions on university education are worth repeating here:

> Nor have visiting professors and foreign commissions of inquiry into university problems helped much in applying basic academic principles. The Carr-Saunders Commission Report for Malaya recommended a model derived, like that in the earlier Asquith Commission Report on Higher Education in the Colonies, from a British provincial university. The Darwin Report on universities in Thailand nominally takes other models into account, but actually is based largely on British models. The Allen Report on Universities in Indonesia—apart from indulging in fashionable criticism of the Dutch university system—appears to judge universities of Indonesia largely by conformity to an American model. . . . . Nevertheless, it is fair to say that nowhere has an attempt yet

been made to base the system on basic values of university life, or on a comparative study of universities elsewhere. (4.1)

The analysis of the curricula at Ibadan, Nsukka and Lagos illustrates that Silcock's observations which refer specifically to Southeast Asia could be extended to Nigeria. One interesting discovery I made on reading Silcock's book was that a handful of experts on overseas education seemed to have split most of these commissions among them, especially the commissions in Africa. Sir Alexander Carr-Saunders, cited by Silcock as Chairman of the commission on the University of Malaya, was a member of the Asquith Commission, Chairman of the Commission on Higher Education for Africans in Central Africa, and Chairman of the Inter-University Council group on the University of Northern Nigeria (now Ahmadu Bello University). He, the late Sir John Lockwood and Sir Eric Ashby seem to have shared most of the commissions on higher education in English-speaking East, West and Central Africa. Little surprise if the different countries in which they exercised their influence developed similar university patterns!

At the time Ibadan was founded, there was an excuse for such commissions. Carr-Saunders supplied the excuse in his *New Universities Overseas:* 'University schemes of study are always in course of modification in the light of experience. When the new colleges were founded local conditions were little known and there was no accumulation of experience'. (5.1) He went on later to state: 'There is now the experience of some ten years upon which to draw'. (5.1) The dependence of the undergraduate curricula of all Nigerian universities on foreign university models in 1973 (twenty-five years after Ibadan was founded) makes one wonder whether the Nigerian universities have made much use of the years of experience which should provide the basis for planning or modifying their programmes. Many of the persons who served on these commissions received no special training in university development. There would therefore appear to be no reason why Nigerian vice-chancellors and professors should look to them for advice on the development of the Nigerian university.

The overseas experts on African higher education have not always made things easy for the African educationist. Like his contemporary in politics, the African educationist has had his training and served his apprenticeship under a system which was not designed to grapple with the problems which now confront him. He therefore had no tradition of a truly indigenous university to fall back on. If he must fashion a pattern of higher education for his environment, he must have room to think, he must have the freedom to experiment and to evaluate the results of his experiment. Unfortunately, his critics overseas, who sometimes say he lacks imagination and originality, who accuse him of running or establishing universities which are no more than carbon copies of western universities, are, in different contexts, constantly drawing his attention to the supranational nature of the university community and making him sound ridiculous or unneccessarily emotional when he talks about the Nigerian or the African university.

Evidence abounds to show that some influential overseas experts who have ostensibly been helping Nigerians to evolve truly Nigerian universities geared to the needs of Nigeria, and who blame African educators for lack of originality and imagination, do not, in their heart of hearts, believe that there can be anything called the Nigerian or the African university. Many of them are much more interested in propagating their own concepts of university education than in helping to evolve the new university systems which they often proclaim they are advocating. Nsukka is uncritically accepted in many American academic circles, not because of the extent of its originality but because it is the closest approach to the American university in Nigeria, a country where American education had been deprecated under the British colonial government. The success of Nsukka is counted a success for the American educational system, with tremendous potentialities for further inroads into territories that once were undisputedly a British monopoly. This explains the negative response of some American experts on African education when the Nsukka vice-chancellorship fell to a Nigerian in mid-1966. The fact that the Nigerian was British educated weighed more heavily on the minds of these experts than the fact that the Nigerian was one of Africa's outstanding scholars who had held a vice-chancellorship at another university and was qualified to have been appointed vice-chancellor at Nsukka as far back as 1960 when the new university was opened. In many British university circles, on the other hand, Nsukka was uncritically dismissed for being an American-type university, while Ibadan, which has not displayed tremendous imagination in its curriculum development, is uncritically acclaimed as the beacon of hope for Nigerian higher education.

I am not attempting to exonerate the Nigerian or African educator from blame by shifting the blame to others. I am only trying to illustrate some of the problems which contribute to his dilemma. Within his home setting he faces the sharp criticism of fellow Nigerians who have little sympathy for any innovation which means a major departure from the university systems they have come to accept, respect, or even venerate. Abroad, he faces experts on African education who blame him for lack of the imagination and the courage required to build a new university in Africa but who would rather see him transplant or adapt their own foreign university systems or their own concepts of what the African university ought to be.

The decision by the Nigerian governments as from 1960 to break free from the university college special relationship with London University pattern of development was a deliberate attempt to create room for 'the experiment, the innovation and the adaptation to local needs which Nigerian universities must have'. (3·1) If this hope is to be achieved, the Nigerian university must be less preoccupied with foreign models. There is unquestionable validity in the following conclusion reached at the 23rd Educational Conference sponsored by the American Council on Education in New York on October 30–31, 1958: 'There is no such thing as a single best pattern of education and never will be, but by constant experimentation we may get closer to an ideal'.

This is not to say that the Nigerian university should build a cocoon around itself. The Nigerian university can learn from university developments in other parts of the world, if only to avoid avoidable errors. My main emphasis is that it must not be primarily preoccupied with university developments in other parts of the world, as has been the practice. As a university, it should no longer be satisfied with playing the role of an extension agency — trying out experiments on university education developed by universities elsewhere. It should recognize that it is in a much better position than these overseas universities to develop experiments in Nigerian university education, and face its responsibilities with courage and confidence. Rather than pride itself for being a facsimile of the leading university in the world (if any university can be so designated) it should derive its pride from the fact that it has developed the best university education for Nigeria. The university world is so heterogeneous that it would have no basis for rejecting a new kind of university.

When Ashby, in a passage quoted in an earlier section, asked why Ibadan in drawing up its post-1962 curricula did not familiarise itself with developments in the newest English universities, I wondered why Ibadan, established in 1948, should wait for Sussex, established in the 1960s, to provide it with guidelines for curriculum development. If Sussex, a brand new university, could do it, why not Ibadan? Was it that the professors at Ibadan were devoid of ideas or that they were afraid of the consequences of being different?

NEED FOR RESEARCH INTO NIGERIAN HIGHER EDUCATION

If the Nigerian university is to emerge, universities in Nigeria must engage actively in research into the problems of Nigerian higher education. Such research could cover such issues as the different facets of the undergraduate curriculum, the most effective predictors of success at the university, university teaching methods, state-university relationships, etc. Results of such studies would provide a more reliable basis for many of the decisions which would influence the course of university development in Nigeria. One hopes that they would, in addition, compel many educators to question some of the assumptions on which decisions had previously been based. Two possible approaches to the organization of such research are described below.

The first approach is within the university itself. Every Nigerian university now has a faculty of education. As these faculties develop postgraduate studies, it would be very helpful if at least one or two of them could include facilities for postgraduate studies in higher education. This should lead to the availability of academic staff whose research interests would be primarily in the field of higher education. It would also lead to a flow of theses or dissertations on problems of Nigerian higher education, as well as providing educational programmes for persons seeking careers in university teaching or administration.

Also within the university, the academic and administrative staff could be encouraged to develop research interests in the problems of higher education. Each university registry annually compiles files of data on staff and students. Quite often these data serve no purpose except for the preparation of the annual report of the university, or for answering an occasional question at the legislature;

and yet these data could without much difficulty serve as useful research data. No Nigerian university can compare with certainty the performances of students entering the university with the different entry qualifications or of students with previous secondary school education and those without, even though each registry keeps annual records on every student. Most Nigerian university administrators do not, in any case, see that their work has research possibilities, while most of the academic staff have not considered Nigerian higher education as fertile ground for research topics, except perhaps for the professors of education. The stimulation of interest can come in many forms, including the organization of university-wide seminars on the problems of higher education. The field has attractions for the sociologist, the economist, the psychologist, the historian or the political scientist if only he could be made aware of these research possibilities.

The second major approach is at the national level. There is at present no broad-based inter-university or national forum for discussing the problems of higher education, and yet there are many issues which have implications for Nigerian higher education as a whole. There is need for a forum which could influence the development of higher education throughout the country, and help to formulate guidelines for the individual universities. Such a forum could also speak for Nigerian higher education whenever the occasion arises.

The functions of both the National Universities Commission and the Committee of Vice-Chancellors have already been considered in an earlier section. Both bodies have their own roles in the development of Nigerian higher education, but neither is a substitute for the forum I have in mind. The major responsibility of the N.U.C. is to allocate Federal Government funds to the universities, and its members are chosen with this factor in mind. Even now that the Commission includes university people in its membership, it can neither speak for Nigerian higher education nor can it be expected to provide academic guidelines for the universities. The Committee of Vice-Chancellors has provided some leadership, but it is essentially a vice-chancellors' "club", and therefore not the appropriate national forum.

The Nigerian Association of University Teachers covers all the Nigerian universities. It is, however, to all intents and purposes, a trade union whose primary concern is naturally the improvement of the working conditions of its members. University administrators cannot join the association unless they also hold teaching appointments; the academicians are probably afraid of contamination!

The three bodies named above confine their activities, interests and spheres of influence to universities. None of them draws in the other branches of Nigerian higher education—notably the advanced teacher training colleges, the post-secondary colleges of technology, and the new colleges of arts and science, science and technology, etc. I consider it in the interest of Nigerian higher education as a whole to draw these and other recognised branches of higher education under the same umbrella with the universities.

I strongly recommend the establishment of a *Nigerian Association for Higher Education* as the body to provide this national umbrella and forum. This would be a registered, non-governmental, self-governing, professional organization whose broad objective would be the advancement of Nigerian higher education. It would have no powers to dictate to any higher educational institution, but it could help these institutions in any way possible to achieve their various educational objectives.

Its membership would be on an individual rather than institutional basis, open to the academic as well as senior administrative staff of the different institutions; membership could also be extended to persons not employed by the universities but whose work is closely related to higher education, including members of university councils and the National Universities Commission.

The general functions of the Association would include the sponsorship of studies of different facets of higher education, by individuals, committees or commissions appointed by the Association from among its members. The sponsorship would also include the publication of the findings of the different studies. The annual conferences of the Association would provide an excellent opportunity for public interaction on the major issues in Nigerian higher education, in an atmosphere bringing together vice-chancellors, professors, assistant lecturers, administrators, members of University councils, representatives of the government, industry and business. It is hoped that each annual conference would be developed around some major issue(s) or problem(s) in Nigerian higher education (including the different areas of higher education), in the attempt to find solutions to such problems or issues.

The Association would publish a journal devoted entirely to the problems of higher education, to provide a venue for disseminating the results of the various research projects which, it is hoped, would be going on at the different institutions as soon as the impetus has been provided.

The Association need not eliminate the Committee of Vice-Chancellors (which functions on institutional bases) nor the Association of University Teachers. It could establish working relationships with these and similar bodies concerned with higher education. The association should, however, be the number one speaker for Nigerian higher education as a whole.

A poll conducted in 1970/71 by a group of enthusiasts indicated that a large number of Nigerian university teachers and administrators were anxious to join and support a Nigerian Association for Higher Education if established.

REFERENCES

1   Okafor, Nduka. *The Development of Universities in Nigeria*, London, Longman, 1971. 1.1 : p.194

2   Ashby, Eric (in association with Mary Anderson), *Universities: British, Indian and African.* A Study in the Ecology of Higher Education, Cambridge, Massachusetts, Harvard University Press, 1966. 2.1: p. xii; 2.2: p. 275.

3   Hanson, John W., *Imagination and Hallucination in African Education*, East Lansing, Michigan, Michigan State University (no publication date). 3.1: p. 13.

4   Silcock, T.H., *Southeast Asian University*, A Comparative Account of Some Development Problems, Durham, North Carolina, Duke University Press, 1964. 4.1: p. 9

5   Carr-Saunders, A.M., *New Universities Overseas*, London, George Allen & Unwin Ltd., 1961. 5.1: pp. 221–222.

6   *Investment in Education*, Report of the Commission on Post-School Certificate and Higher Education in Nigeria, Lagos, Federal Ministry of Education, Nigeria, 1960. 6.1: p. 26.

7   Saunders, J.T. & Dowuona, M. (eds.), *The West African Intellectual Community*, Papers and discussions of an International Seminar on Inter-University Co-operation in West Africa, held in Freetown, Sierra Leone, 11–16 December, 1961. Ibadan. Ibadan University Press, 1962. 7.1: p. 103; 7.2: p. 104.